Pearson Edexcel GCSE (9–1)

Drama

Second Edition

Revision Guide

Series Consultant: Harry Smith

Authors: William Reed and John Johnson

Also available to support your revision:

Revise GCSE Study Skills Guide   9781292318875

The **Revise GCSE Study Skills Guide** is full of tried-and-trusted hints and tips for how to learn more effectively. It gives you techniques to help you achieve your best – throughout your GCSE studies and beyond!

Revise GCSE Revision Planner   9781292318868

The **Revise GCSE Revision Planner** helps you to plan and organise your time, step-by-step, throughout your GCSE revision. Use this book and wall chart to mastermind your revision.

> **For the full range of Pearson revision titles across KS2, 11+, KS3, GCSE, Functional Skills, AS/A Level and BTEC visit:**
> www.pearsonschools.co.uk/revise

Contents

. . . .

A small bit of small print

Pearson Edexcel publishes Sample Assessment Material and the Specification on its website. This is the official content and this book should be used in conjunction with it. The questions in *Now try this* have been written to help you practise every topic in the book. Remember: the real exam questions may not look like this.

All extracts from performance texts are taken from the editions prescribed in the specification.

Key roles in the theatre

In the written exam for Component 3 (Theatre Makers in Practice) of your GCSE Drama course, you will need to consider how theatre is made from three different perspectives: performer, director and designer. Each role brings different elements to life which, when combined, can produce a powerful and entertaining production.

Performer

Often referred to as actors, performers use a range of **physical and vocal skills** to convey narrative and plot to an audience. Performers make decisions about how a character might be interpreted and then shown on stage. They then use **facial expression, body language, proxemics** and **voice** to bring their ideas to life for an audience. See pages 5–25 for more on the role of the performer.

The pensive look into the middle distance indicates this performer wants his character to show a moment of thoughtful contemplation.

The director is at the centre of all matters relating to the production.

Director

The director has overall creative control of the piece and brings together all of the different dramatic elements. A director will consider what approach to the text the production will take and will also take control of the overall **vision**. It is the role of the director to make decisions about the **style** and **genre** of the production and to work alongside performers and designers to create a **consistent** and creative production. There is more on the role of the director on pages 26–40.

Designer

Designers tend to specialise in specific aspects of the production. They will have experience in different elements of design, such as **lighting, sound, costume** or **set design**. They work closely with the director to ensure the overall concept of the production is consistent, as well as providing creative solutions to different problems. Each design skill is vital in helping to communicate ideas to the audience, using components such as colours and materials to convey different ideas. You can find out more about the role of the designer on pages 41–67.

Designers work as a team to enhance the visual and audio experience for an audience.

Now try this

Think about a live performance you have seen recently. Explain how each of these different roles had an effect on and enhanced the production.

Try to think of specific moments that stood out. Was it an acting performance, design effect or directorial concept?

1

The audience

The **audience** is essential to a performance. In the exam you need to show you have considered how the audience will be central to your ideas.

The relationship between performers and audience

The audience must be at the heart of all productions. A performer, director or designer will always consider the effect they want to have on the audience when making their decisions about, for example, **characterisation**, **style** or **costume**. Every moment in a production must **communicate** the **purpose**, **message** and ideas to whoever is watching.

By making careful choices – for example, about where a performer is positioned, the speed with which the lighting changes, the use of symbolic props, costume or set, or a specific type of sound effect – it is possible to control how an audience **reacts** or what it **understands**. You can find out more about managing the audience on page 32.

Considering the audience

When it comes to the audience, there are many things to consider. For example:

- **Director**: Where will the audience members be positioned and how will this affect their perspective on the performance?
- **Performer**: What do I want the audience to feel about the character I am playing?
- **Designer**: What messages will my design ideas give to the audience about specific moments in the play, and how will those ideas enhance the events or emotions of the scene?

A director needs to think about the impact each moment of the production will have on the audience, as well as how those moments will all work together to help the audience understand both the plot and the style of the production.

Turn to page 30 for a reminder about consistency of style and communication with the audience. Turn to page 32 for more on how the audience will be central to the ideas you have as a director.

Target audience

It is important to identify the target audience for a production. Being clear about who a production is aimed at helps to inform the more detailed decisions about how the piece will be presented.

For example, if the target audience is young people aged between 14 and 25 years, they are likely to have different expectations about a live performance than a middle-class, middle-aged audience. In turn, this may affect production choices, such as the type of music or technology used, or the volume levels of sound effects.

Selecting a target audience

Decisions about the target audience can be affected by the following factors:

- **Content and material** – The overall narrative of the piece may interest one particular demographic (group of people) more than another.
- **Language** – Swearing may be unacceptable or offensive to some, while technical or very specific vocabulary might appeal to some more than others.
- **Themes/issues** – Different sections of society may be attracted to different themes or issues. Is there anything in the play that indicates who might take an interest?

Consider whether there is a way to reimagine a piece to appeal to a specific demographic.

Now try this

Select a target audience for your performance text. Explain why you have chosen this particular demographic and outline some of the key features of the piece that you feel will appeal to that audience.

While you may have a specific target audience in mind, remember that the production should be accessible to as many different people as possible.

Theatrical concepts

When answering exam questions, you will need to demonstrate your understanding of a wide range of theatrical ideas and concepts. Becoming familiar with and understanding these concepts will help you achieve consistency in your answers and will provide a solid foundation from which to develop your ideas.

Genre – The type or category of play as it was written, such as comedy, historical drama or political satire. See page 28 for more about genre.

The twin masks of Comedy and Tragedy date back to Ancient Greek theatre.

Style and form – The way in which a piece of theatre is performed. For example, Frantic Assembly's physical and modern interpretation of *Othello* is very different to a more traditional approach to the play. Turn to page 28 for more about style.

Physical theatre puts the body and movement at the heart of the production.

Social, historical and social context – Understanding when a play was written and under what circumstances – the context – can provide a huge amount of information about the intentions of the piece. For more about contexts, turn to page 34.

For example, by understanding the political climate in 1950s America and McCarthyism, we can draw strong parallels between those events and the events of Arthur Miller's *The Crucible*, revealing a powerful subtext to the work.

THE ACCUSED

Spatial positioning – This may be between performers, the audience and the set, and is sometimes called **proxemics**. The distance between characters can be a very clear indication of the relationship between them. Equally, having performers and audience sharing the same space can help bring the audience right into the performance. Turn to page 39 for more about spatial positioning.

Spatial positioning helps to shape a production and communicate its message.

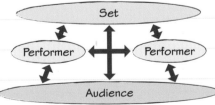

Structure – The way in which the play is constructed. This will include the building of tension, climax and anti-climax. It may also refer to how many acts or scenes make up the play.

| Act 1: Exposition – building tension | → | Act 2: Rising action – climax | → | Act 3: Building tension – climax | → | Act 4: Rising action – resolution |

A top-level overview of the structure of *The Crucible*.

Stage directions – These are very much part of the play; they give instructions as to what the playwright wants the performer to do physically. They may also indicate a wide range of other important information, such as the time or location of a scene, costume requirements, notes on characterisation or how a line should be said. They should always be considered very carefully.

Exit, pursued by a bear

A famous stage direction from Act 3, Scene 3 of Shakespeare's *The Winter's Tale*.

Types of staging – This describes the different performance spaces available for a theatrical production. Different types of space position the audience in different ways, leading to different audience experiences. You can revise different types of staging on page 29.

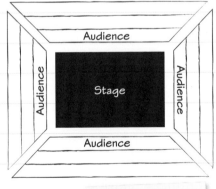

Theatre-in-the-round

Concepts

Now try this

Outline an overall vision for a production of your performance text.

Think about the concepts on this page and the decisions you will make about them in relation to your performance text. How will they help to shape your overall concept?

Conventions and terminology

In the exam you will need to consider how – as a performer, director and designer – you can create impact and meaning for an audience. Theatre conventions are techniques for communicating ideas to those watching a production. When you write about your ideas in the exam, it is important to demonstrate your understanding by using the correct technical vocabulary whenever you can.

Theatre conventions

As theatre has evolved, different conventions have developed and have often merged together to create a new approach to communicating with an audience. While it is impossible to list all of the contemporary (current) ways in which performers, directors and designers communicate their ideas, some of these techniques include:

- ☑ direct address to the audience
- ☑ symbolic costume and set
- ☑ multimedia (such as music and projection)
- ☑ multi-role (where a performer plays more than one character).

The set for the 2011 National Theatre production of *Frankenstein* combined strong, symbolic elements, such as an array of light bulbs to represent the electricity used to bring the Creature to life.

The importance of technical vocabulary

In the exam you need to use **appropriate technical vocabulary and drama terminology** whenever you can. This will help you to:

- 👍 demonstrate your knowledge and understanding of the subject
- 👍 show your understanding of the different roles in theatre
- 👍 express your ideas and communicate your intentions clearly
- 👍 write strong answers.

In this Revision Guide, key drama vocabulary and terminology is often given in **bold**. If you are unsure what a term means, take a moment to find out. Make sure you are ready to use the terms in the exam!

How much of this technical vocabulary do you know? How many other terms can you think of?

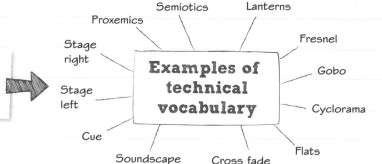

Examples of technical vocabulary

Semiotics · Lanterns · Proxemics · Fresnel · Stage right · Gobo · Stage left · Cyclorama · Cue · Flats · Soundscape · Cross fade

Now try this

Look at the examples of technical terms in the spider diagram above. Decide which role – performer, director or designer – each term belongs to. Then write a definition for each term.

Beware: some of the terms belong to more than one role! Think carefully about the situations in which each term might be used.

The performer

A **performer** is an actor, musician, dancer or anyone who is involved in entertaining the audience. It is the performer's task to tell the story of the play, to learn and deliver the text and to portray the characters and intentions of the playwright.

Performance skills – The performer uses various skills to communicate with the audience, including **voice, movement, characterisation** and **use of space**.

Developing the performance – A strong performer works continuously on developing their performance. This starts in rehearsals but continues as the live performance work progresses and the performer develops a closer understanding of the play, the playwright's intentions and the director's vision.

Engaging the audience – Perhaps the most important aspect of being a performer is the relationship with a live theatre audience. This **communication** makes live theatre unique.

The role of the performer

Communicating character – Performing often requires the interpretation of a particular character, and this can be vital in helping to tell the story of the piece.

Working with others – Performers rarely work on their own and even solo shows include a design team or director – so working with others or as part of an **ensemble** is a key aspect of performance.

Working with the text – Performers may have to consider an actual text, working with the language of a play and considering the playwright's intentions. The 'text' might also be a stimulus such as a poem, a quotation or an image, particularly in devised theatre. The performer must explore and understand the text in as much depth as possible.

Conveying the interpretation, style and purpose – Directors (and designers) often have a strong **vision** for how they want to interpret a play: they will have selected a **style** and have a clear sense of **purpose** and **message**. A performer needs to understand what the director is trying to say and consider how they can help to communicate this vision to the audience.

The early stages of rehearsal

In the early stages of a production, the performer will work closely with the text (or stimulus if working on a devised piece). A performer will try to understand the text by finding out as much information as possible about the **character** they are playing and the world of the play. This knowledge can be gained from the whole text, including **stage directions** and notes from the playwright.

For example in the opening scene of *An Inspector Calls*, playwright J.B. Priestley uses extensive stage directions to help describe the scene and to help the performers understand and interpret the characters.

In this example of a possible opening stage direction, the performer is given a great deal of information in this opening stage direction. They are told about the age and physical appearance of the character as well as his personality and way of speaking. This information will help the performer to understand and develop the role.

MARK CORNELL [*is a slight, wiry and highly energetic man in his late thirties. His polite, 'public schoolboy' demeanour and his refined tones contrast with his casual, even scruffy, appearance.*]

Now try this

When a performer approaches a play, what questions will they need to ask in order to develop their character fully? List the questions to ask in the early stages of a production.

Think about points that relate specifically to the character, such as their age, as well as their relationships with others and position within the world of the play.

Tone and intonation

Controlled use of the **voice** is one of the key skills a performer has at their disposal. Choices about the way a line is spoken will have a significant impact on its **meaning**, as well as the **communication** between performers and the **audience**.

The importance of voice

Voice can convey:

- ✓ emotions
- ✓ relationships
- ✓ intentions
- ✓ subtext.

Carefully combining different vocal elements is vital for a successful performance.

The voice can be a powerful way of communicating the **subtext** – that is, the meaning underneath the surface of the text. Performers can use various **vocal techniques** to convey the subtext.

For example, consider the performer playing Viola/Cesario in Act 2, Scene 4 of Shakespeare's *Twelfth Night*. In this scene, Viola is in her disguise as Cesario. She is talking to Orsino, Duke of Illyria, with whom she is in love, and who does not know that Cesario is really Viola – a woman.

Orsino asks Cesario about the object of his affections: 'What kind of woman is't?'

Viola/Cesario, unable to reveal openly that it is no woman but rather Orsino that she loves, replies: 'Of your complexion'.

A performer delivering Viola/Cesario's line here will draw on a range of vocal techniques to communicate the subtext of Viola's love for Orsino to the audience.

Tone – This describes how the lines are said to convey meaning. For example, a sarcastic tone might mean that while a character says he is pleased to see someone, in fact he is not.

Vocal skills and the impact of voice

Intonation – This describes the rise and fall of the voice to help provide variation and interest. For example, varying intonation will make speech more natural, and help to communicate meaning and keep the audience engaged.

Using tone

Tone is not about what is said but **how** it is said. It is vital for showing meaning and emotion, providing the **context** for each of the words.

For example, during Act 2 of *An Inspector Calls*, Mrs Birling becomes very angry with Inspector Goole. However, as she realises she is partly responsible for Eva's death, she becomes distressed. A clipped, haughty tone when speaking to the inspector would emphasise an attempt to gain the higher status. This could be contrasted with an anxious, upset tone, highlighting her realisation of the terrible consequences of her actions.

Using intonation

Intonation is about the performer making their voice sound interesting and engaging. It is particularly important when delivering long speeches.

For example, in *Twelfth Night*, Duke Orsino opens the play with a speech about his love for Olivia. He speaks the famous line, 'If music be the food of love, play on'. The performer playing this role might start with a soft intonation, rising on the key words 'food of love' and building to a forceful and commanding use of voice to urge the musicians to play.

Now try this

Choose **one** scene and **one** character from your performance text. Explain how, as a performer, you would use tone to communicate your character's intentions and the meaning of the text at this point.

Give reasons for your ideas and remember to use quotations from the text to support your answer.

Pause and pitch

The **way** in which words are spoken can have a particular impact on the audience and can affect the audience's experience when watching a performance.

Using voice to communicate character

Voice can be very important when developing and communicating a character. Voice can convey a character's:

- age
- background
- emotional state
- status.

Understanding use of voice can help a performer to find a way to convey their character to an audience.

The term **emotional state** describes how a character is feeling at a particular moment in the play. A performer can use vocal skills to portray a character's emotions.

For example, in Act 1, Scene 2 of *DNA*, Leah speaks to Phil. In this **monologue**, Leah's anxiety and sense of frustration builds as Phil fails to respond to her questions. As the scene progresses, Leah's emotional state becomes more intense. A performer might use a high **pitch** to demonstrate this.

Pause – Starting and stopping to emphasise a point or provide contrast and variation. For example, a pause in the middle of a sentence might convey nerves about admitting a crime.

Vocal skills and the impact of voice

Pitch – How high or low the voice is. For example, a low pitch might indicate a solemn secret being shared, while a high pitch might convey joy.

Using pauses

Pauses can add **tension** to a scene and can give **emphasis** to a word or phrase.

For example, in Act 1, Scene 1 of *Government Inspector*, the Mayor of the town gathers many of the important townspeople in a room at his home. He then delivers the unpleasant news that the town is to be visited by a government inspector. The performer playing the Mayor might use pause in his delivery of the news to the anxious town officials to add gravitas (seriousness) to the scene.

Using pitch

The use of **pitch** can add an extra level of drama to the delivery of a text. Performers who keep pitch on the same level may fail to engage with the audience.

For example, in Act 3 of *The Crucible*, Abigail and the other girls begin to scream that Mary Warren is sending spirits to harm them. The performers playing the characters of Abigail and the other girls need to make use of a high pitch in order to be able to convince the court and the audience of their hysteria. A low pitch would be inappropriate in capturing the emotion of the scene.

Now try this

Choose **one** scene and **one** character from your performance text. Explain how, as a performer, you would use pause and pitch to express the scene successfully. Give clear reasons for each idea.

Remember to look carefully at the **context** of the scene, as this will help you to understand how pause and pitch can be used most effectively.

Clarity and pace

A performer must make sure that they deliver the text in a way that makes sense to the audience. Using **clarity** and **pace** effectively is an important way of communicating character and meaning.

Creating character and manipulating meaning

A performer can use the clarity and pace of their vocal delivery to bring their character to life for an audience.

- Each word and each line in a text can be delivered differently, depending on what a performer wants to show about the character or their situation. For example, is the character young, old, ill, enthusiastic, tired, embarrassed, angry, in a hurry? Using the right pace can help to make this clear.

- A skilful performer might vary their approach to clarity too. For example, mumbled speech, like a fast pace, might suggest annoyance.

Try this for yourself. Pick a line in your performance text and try delivering it at different speeds and with varying degrees of clarity. How does this change the way the character comes across?

In the exam

In Section A (Bringing texts to life) of the exam, you will need to consider the different **elements** of vocal delivery and how you would use this skill in a production of your performance text. Understanding the **effect** of each vocal element will help you to **apply** these skills to your answers on the production of your performance text.

 Links For more about Section A of the exam, turn to pages 84–102.

Clarity – This is making sure the audience can hear the words and that their intended meaning is clear. For example, even if a character is scared and cowering, the voice must be clear and the audience able to hear and understand it.

Vocal skills and the impact of voice

Pace – This refers to the rhythm and speed with which words are spoken. For example, a fast pace might indicate excitement, while a slower pace might suggest sadness.

Using clarity

For a role to be successful, a performer must be **understood**. **Clear diction** is therefore important, but so is **clarity of intention and emotion**. A performer might, for example, deliberately avoid clarity to suggest confusion, drunkenness or injury.

For example, when Adam appears towards the end of Act 3 in *DNA*, he is confused and frightened after his experience. A performer could portray this by stammering and muttering some of the words. While this may reduce some vocal clarity, the emotions expressed will be very clear to the audience.

Using pace

Stanislavski called pace the **tempo-rhythm** of the character.

The pace used by a performer can paint a vivid picture for the audience of the type of character they are playing, as well as helping to highlight the **meaning** of each word spoken.

For example, near the end of *100*, the Guide begs Alex to choose a suitable memory before time runs out and leaves Alex in the void forever. The performer playing the Guide might use a fast pace to show the urgency of the task and the fear that he is feeling on Alex's behalf.

Now try this

Choose **one** scene and **one** character from your performance text. Explain how, as a performer, you would use pace and clarity to express your character's intentions. Give clear reasons for each idea.

Start by identifying the intentions of the character in the scene. Then work out how you could convey those intentions.

Accent and inflection

Accent is more relevant to some performance texts than others, though it is always an **aspect of voice** a performer needs to consider. The use of **inflection** can also change the way a voice sounds to the audience.

Using accent and inflection

When a production involves multi-role, a performer may need to play more than one character. This might involve very different personalities, backgrounds, ages and even genders - and the performer will need to use their voice in very versatile ways. For example, in the 2013 production of Robert and David Goodale's comedy *Perfect Nonsense*, Matthew Macfadyen (here on the left) played the stiff man servant Jeeves opposite Stephen Mangan's excitable Wooster. But Macfadyen also played a number of other roles, including a woman, making use of accent and inflection to provide distinctive characterisation.

Accent – This is used to indicate where a character is from, specifically which country or region. It may also help distinguish class and status.

> **Vocal skills and the impact of voice**

Inflection – This refers to the ups and downs of spoken language. For example, inflection can go higher at the end of a sentence to make the outcome sound as though it is a question. This is known as 'upward inflection'.

Using accent

Accent is very important in helping to show a character's background. A performer's accent can help to convey a great deal about their role.

For example, the performers playing the roles of Mrs Birling and Edna in *An Inspector Calls* will make use of accent to convey their characters' background and status to the audience. J.B. Priestley describes Mrs Birling as socially superior to Mr Birling, which tells the performer that she should be upper class in the way that she speaks (and acts). Edna is described by Priestley as the Birlings' maid, and is likely to be of lower status than the other characters. The performer playing the character of Edna should use an accent that portrays this difference to the audience.

Using inflection

The use of inflection can alter the way a line is delivered and understood. A performer must therefore pay close attention to their use of inflection when speaking.

For example, in Act 3, Scene 4 of *Twelfth Night*, Malvolio is fooled into wearing cross-gartered yellow stockings. He enters onto the stage moving towards Olivia, as he believes she is in love with him. Olivia is taken aback by Malvolio's strange behaviour and asks, 'Wilt thou go to bed, Malvolio?' The way in which this line is delivered can indicate how Olivia feels towards Malvolio, such as whether she is scared of him, feels anxious by the way he is acting, or is simply bemused by it. In this way, inflection can be used to alter the meaning of the question.

Now try this

Choose **one** character from your performance text and explain how **accent** is important to the vocal delivery of that character. Explain clearly why this element of voice is important.

 Remember that accent can be used to distinguish status or class.

Emphasis and volume

Putting **stress** or **emphasis** on certain words affects how dialogue is **communicated**, as does how **loudly** or **quietly** lines are delivered in performance.

A performer's use of volume

Consider a performer's use of vocals to portray character in performance. By varying volume and emphasis when speaking lines, a performer can better show their character's intentions.

For example, the character of Danforth in Arthur Miller's *The Crucible* might use volume to show that he is the leading judge in the court of the Salem witch trials, suggesting his authority and high status – it is paramount that his voice can be heard. When dealing with Proctor's accusations regarding Abigail's lying, the performer could also make use of a loud voice and emphasis on the text to show Danforth's authority in dealing with the serious nature of Proctor's claims.

When deciding on how to use vocal skills as a performer, consider the level of **projection** required when delivering your character's lines.

As another example, consider the first time we meet Eric Birling in *An Inspector Calls*; the performer playing him might use louder vocals to show he is comfortable with his surroundings, enjoying himself at the meal. Eric's use of voice may alter later on, however, when the Inspector reveals the truths behind the death of Eva Smith. At this point in the play, Eric's voice may become quiet, to show his shame and sadness at what has happened.

Stress/emphasis – This is used to place greater importance on specifically chosen words, or to highlight the meaning behind those words. For example, in 'I'm leaving', placing stress on 'I'm' makes it clear who is leaving, whereas stressing 'leaving' puts the emphasis on the action.

> **Vocal skills and the impact of voice**

Volume – This refers to how loud or quiet the voice is. For example, a shout might convey aggression while a whisper might suggest secrecy or fear.

Using emphasis when delivering text

Putting stress or emphasis on particular words can completely change a sentence. Performing Hamlet's 'To be, or not to be' speech, for example, and putting emphasis on 'To be' or 'not', will change how Hamlet's state of mind is portrayed.

For example, in *Twelfth Night*, when Olivia meets Viola for the first time in Act 1, Scene 5, she is fascinated by the way Viola (dressed as the boy messenger Cesario) speaks to her. This intrigue could be emphasised by the performer playing Olivia by putting stress on the line 'Unless, perchance, *you* come to me again'. Putting the stress on 'you' allows the performer to communicate to the audience that Olivia is interested in seeing Cesario again, and to suggest that this could be a blossoming relationship.

Considering volume with voice

It is important to be loud enough in performance, as a modern audience expects to be able to hear each word clearly. As outlined above, volume can also alter the meaning in delivery of the text.

For example, **amplification** is important in the opening of *1984*. At this point the audience can hear a voice but cannot see the performer speaking the lines. If this opening is spoken quietly, the text might come across as sinister or give a sense of mystery. If the performer amplifies their voice, making it very loud, the language may sound angry or aggressive, creating a sense of danger or anticipation. This is just one example of how volume in the use of vocal skills can affect a scene.

Now try this

Find **one** moment from your performance text where a character or characters might make use of volume or emphasis. Explain your answer.

Your reasons may depend on a change of intention or atmosphere, for example.

Diction and nuance

Making every spoken word clear is very important, as is the use of **nuance** to add **subtlety** to a performance.

Using diction

A performer's voice can convey a character's thoughts and feelings to the audience. Their use of voice can also allow the character's **intentions** to be more accurately conveyed, which is essential when staging the relationships within a play.

In your performance text, to what extent are diction, and how a performer speaks a line, important in terms of how a character's feelings or intentions are conveyed to the audience?

The **diction** in the voice (pronouncing each spoken word clearly) allows a performer to be more **responsive** on stage.

For example, in Act 1, Scene 4 of *Blue Stockings*, the character of Tess responds to a lecture by Dr Maudsley, in which he gives an opinion that annoys her. In her response – 'I am not agitated because I am a woman!' – the performer playing Tess would need to use effective diction to convey Tess's disgust and disagreement.

Diction – This is **pronouncing** each spoken word clearly. It is important for performers to **articulate** what they are saying so that the audience can understand what is happening on stage. This is sometimes known as how a performer **enunciates** their words.

Vocal skills and the impact of voice

Nuance – This describes the small differences in sound that can alter how a line is spoken to change the meaning or feeling in the text. The use of nuance in vocal skills is often very subtle. Nuance has similarities to how a performer uses intonation and tone. For more on a performer's use of intonation and tone, turn to page 6.

Where nuance is important

Nuance adds subtlety to a play and can allow the performers to convey a character's true thoughts or feelings to the audience.

For example, in *Twelfth Night*, the tension between Viola (as Cesario) and Duke Orsino becomes greater as the play progresses. At the play's height, in Act 2, Scene 4, the two characters talk about being in love. The performer playing Viola may use nuance in the way she says the line, 'As it might be, perhaps, were I a woman....' Here, a slight difference in **sound** would suggest her true feelings towards the Duke, while at the same time being careful not to overtly announce her love.

Considering diction

Speaking with a clear voice that can be heard by all of the audience is important. Diction becomes even more essential in certain key moments.

For example, towards the end of the play *Blue Stockings*, in Act 2, Scene 11, when Mrs Welsh enters the scene, she is determined to find out the outcome of the vote. She asks, 'Mr Peck. Is there any news?' The use of diction here is vital, as there must be **clarity** in the way that the line is delivered and the question asked, to show how important the outcome of the vote is to Mrs Welsh in particular.

Now try this

Choose **one** key moment from your performance text and explain why nuance and diction would be important to the delivery of the text at this point. State your reasons for each idea clearly.

Compiling a list of key moments is a great way of revising your overall knowledge and understanding of your performance text.

Facial expression and body language

A performer's use of **physical skills** is central to how they **interpret** and **convey** the message of the text. So it is vital to consider how **facial expression** and **body language** might be used to communicate with the audience.

A performer's use of facial expression

Facial expression is a powerful way of communicating with the audience. Humans are capable of making 10 000 unique facial expressions with just 43 muscles in the face.

Facial expressions can be grouped into seven basic emotions:

- fear
- sadness
- happiness
- anger
- contempt
- disgust
- surprise.

A performer's facial expression can convey a great deal of information about how their performance character is feeling. Here, the wide-eyed expression, combined with the gesture in the performer's hands, clearly suggests fear.

Facial expression – A performer's facial expression can reveal a character's innermost feelings or thoughts, as well as showing their response to what is happening on stage or to other characters.

The use of movement and physical skills

Body language – This is the way a performer communicates **non-verbally**. Performers can use their body in a wide variety of ways to convey emotional responses. Body language can provide an incredibly powerful and instant way of transmitting information and connecting with the audience. See pages 13–15 for more on different aspects of body language, such as stance and gesture.

Where body language might be used

Body language might be used to communicate a message non-verbally to an audience – this might be **subtle** or **overt**.

For example, consider the role of Dr Maudsley in the opening of *Blue Stockings*. Maudsley is stubbornly against the idea of degrees for women. A performer approaching this role may make use of crossed arms and an upright posture, leaning his head forward slightly and perhaps shaking his fist or pointing in an aggressive way. This overt use of body language would highlight Dr Maudsley's stubborn feelings and immovable opinion.

Where facial expression might be used

Facial expression can be used to add another **layer** to the performance, helping to underline what is being said or suggesting an alternative meaning or **subtext**.

For example, in Act 5, Scene 1 of *Twelfth Night*, when Sebastian and Viola appear on stage together for the first time, the surprised, confused and shocked responses of the other characters can be shown by their facial expressions. For example, when Duke Orsino says 'One face, one voice, one habit, and two persons', the performer playing the character can add to the confusion and the comic style of the piece through the use of facial expression.

Now try this

Find **one** moment from your performance text where a character could use facial expression and body language to communicate (overtly or in a subtle way) how they are feeling to the audience or other characters on stage. Explain your answer.

Always consider how the character's use of body language and facial expression conveys how they are feeling at that particular moment, for example, when responding to other characters on stage.

Gesture and proxemics

A performer's use of **physical skills**, including **gesture** and **proxemics**, is central to how they **interpret** and **convey** the message of the text and communicate with the audience.

A performer's use of gesture

Gestures:

👍 can help to sum up how a character feels at any given moment in the production. A character shaking a fist, for example, may convey a great deal to the audience without the need for words

👍 can be **socially, culturally or historically** significant. It is important to be aware of this when approaching your performance text.

> For example, *The Crucible* is set in a **puritanical society** in which people follow strict religious rules. Therefore a character not showing proper respect to God, such as by turning their back on a priest or court official, would be seen as suspicious and bordering on criminality.

A performer's use of proxemics

Proxemics describes the use of space on stage.

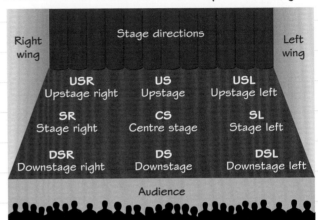

> Using a stage diagram and **drama terminology** can help you to describe where performers are positioned on stage.

Gesture – A gesture is a way of expressing a character's thoughts or emotions and often works together with **body language**. Gestures can reflect an **action** and can be an **instant** way of communicating.

The use of movement and physical skills

Proxemics – This describes how performers use stage space. The use of space can communicate **relationships** between performers and/or between performers and audience members.

Using gesture for effect

Performers can use gestures as an action to communicate a moment with a text.

> For example, in *Blue Stockings*, when Mr Peck enters with the news that the vote went against the female undergraduates, denying them the right to graduate, he takes his hat off and pauses. Mr Peck's use of gesture and his obvious difficulty with breaking the news **foreshadows** the women's disappointment that the vote was lost. The performer playing Mr Peck can make this moment significant through the use of considered gesture.

The use of proxemics in performance

Proxemics can be used in particular to convey a relationship to the audience. In certain plays a playwright will suggest how they can be used to communicate a situation.

> For example, in *An Inspector Calls*, during the early part of Act 1, the Inspector shows a photograph of Eva Smith to Mr Birling. As Eric and Gerald try to see the photograph, the stage directions describe how the Inspector positions himself between those characters and the photograph. The use of space is significant here, adding a sense of mystery and tension, as Eric and Gerald are prevented from looking at the photo.

Now try this

In your performance text find and explain:

(a) one key moment where the use of gesture is significant and

(b) one key moment where proxemics is important in the staging of the scene.

> A playwright may help you by suggesting the use of gesture or space. At other times you may identify a moment in your performance text where gesture or space could be used for effect, though this might not necessarily be marked in the script.

13

Stance and stillness

Stillness and a character's **stance** are two of the ways in which a performer's body language can be used to communicate with the audience.

A performer's use of stance

Stance can also be described as **posture**. A performer's use of stance can reveal the following about a character:

- Status
- Gender
- Profession
- Age
- Emotional state
- Physical well-being.

For example, at the end of *DNA*, we learn that the character of Adam has endured great suffering, which has affected him physically, emotionally and mentally. To convey this, a performer might show the character of Adam with a bent-over posture and a stance that hints at his disturbed **state of mind**. The performer might hold his body in a tense and rigid way to show how vulnerable he feels at this moment in the play.

A 'hands on hips' posture such as this clearly shows this character's serious state, as well as suiting his uniform/profession.

Stance – This describes the way a person stands or the **pose** they adopt. A person's stance is affected by their emotional, environmental and physical experiences. For example, if a person is upset, tired and cold they may look down with arms crossed and held close to the body, and knees slightly bent. This is a non-verbal way in which a performer can communicate their character's situation to the audience.

The use of movement and physical skills

Stillness – This describes a person's lack of movement. A performer may keep still on purpose, for example to convey a character's caution or lack of control over their physical response. For example, a character may stand rooted to the spot because they are afraid or in shock.

The use of stance to convey character

Stance or posture might be used to communicate a character to an audience.

For example, the performer playing the role of Ketu's brother in *100* 'stands watching' and is described as 'intimidating'. As he is only on stage for a few moments and does not speak, it will be vital that the performer playing the brother uses stance effectively – to show the character's intimidating intentions, as well as his dismissive and angry feelings towards Ketu's theories.

Use of stillness in performance

A performer may choose to use stillness as a way of conveying a particular **response**.

For example, in *Blue Stockings*, the character of Dr Maudsley is well respected by the students and he has high status within the university. His entrance into the lecture room during Act 1, Scene 4 could be marked by a use of stillness among the students as they watch on in awe 'as this guru walks towards the front'. The performers' actions here would help to build up the status of Dr Maudsley.

Now try this

List **three** characters from your performance text. Outline how you feel stance could be used to convey these characters at significant moments in the text.

When completing your list of characters, take time to consider why each one would hold a particular stance – you need to be able to justify this in your answer.

Movement and spatial awareness

Spatial awareness and a character's **movement** are two aspects of a performer's physicality that can be used to communicate with the audience.

A performer's use of movement

Movement is an essential form of expression. It is vital for any performer to consider:

- how they will move
- where they will move
- why they will move.

Movement often follows on from a character's **objectives** or **motivation** in a scene. The performer first needs to decide on the purpose of the movement before deciding on what form it will take.

> For example, in Act 2 of *The Crucible*, the character of Elizabeth is told that she has been accused of witchcraft. Her physical movements will express her fear and shock at this revelation.

Stanislavski's system

Stanislavski's system:

- ✓ refers to an approach to acting that tries to achieve a **naturalistic style**, in that the performers try to recreate a sense of 'real life' on stage

- ✓ makes movement and physical responses key to the performance. Staging a play in this way requires careful consideration of the reasons behind each movement in order to communicate the performance in as 'real' a way as possible

- ✓ works well with a play such as *The Crucible*, which is written in great detail by playwright Arthur Miller.

Turn to page 17 to read about a character's aims and objectives, another part of Stanislavski's system.

Movement – This connects to **stance, stillness, facial expression** and **body language**, as movement can encompass all of these elements. The **quality** of a performer's movement can convey a great deal about a particular character.

The use of movement and physical skills

Spatial awareness – This describes how a performer may use space on stage and what this might reveal about their character's **personality**. Rudolf Laban referred to this as a person's **kinesphere** – namely the 'space around them'. It is linked to **proxemics**, which describes how space is used on stage.

The importance of movement

Movement can be significant in certain scenes on stage.

> For example, during a very heated discussion in Act 3 of *An Inspector Calls*, Eric realises that his mother, Mrs Birling, had turned Eva Smith away when she went to her for help. Eric becomes very agitated. Here, movement becomes significant: the performer playing Eric needs to make use of physicality as well as voice to clearly communicate his feelings towards his mother at this point.

Using spatial awareness

How a performer uses space around them may convey a strong message to an audience.

> For example, in *Twelfth Night* Olivia teases Viola (dressed as Cesario) in their first meeting in Act 1, Scene 5. When Olivia finally reveals herself to Cesario, lifting her veil and speaking the line 'we will draw the curtain and show you the picture', she could move towards Cesario in order to see the response, as well as to tease. The spatial awareness of the performer playing Olivia will need to be well thought out here.

Now try this

Describe **two** ways you would use movement to convey a particular moment in your performance text. Explain why you would use this type of movement.

Some moments in your performance text will require more significant uses of movement than others. Make sure that you outline clearly where this is the case.

Personality and purpose

Understanding and interpreting characters is a large part of approaching plays. A performer will consider the character's **personality** and **purpose** in order to understand their role in more depth.

Bringing character to life

All performers must understand the personality of the character they will act on stage. Personality:

👍 determines a character's thoughts, feelings and behaviour

👍 can explain what characters say and why.

For example, the character of John Tate in *DNA* has an overbearing personality, which comes across as though he is bullying the others. In Scene 3 he is aggressive and angry, and it is easy to recognise John's place within the group by his behaviour and how the others respond to him. As the group responds to the situation that unfolds, John becomes a leader rather than a follower.

National Theatre performer Jack Gordon's portrayal of the aggressive personality of John Tate, from *DNA*, at the Cottesloe Theatre in 2008.

Personality – These are the characteristics or qualities that describe an individual's **distinct character** or way of **behaving**.

Interpreting character

Purpose – A character's purpose in a play often **drives** his or her behaviour; it can explain why they act the way they do. Purpose often connects with **aims and objectives**. Turn to page 17 for more on aims and objectives.

Understanding a character's purpose

To find out more about how a character acts on stage, it is useful to consider what their purpose in the play might be.

In Gogol's *Government Inspector*, the character of Khlestakov changes his purpose once he becomes aware of the Mayor's mistaken belief that he is in fact the actual inspector. The character becomes focused on carrying on the deception throughout the rest of the play and gaining as many benefits from the 'act' as possible. This is an example of how a character's purpose can change; it also highlights how the purpose of the character can lead the decisions that are made.

Understanding a character's personality

Considering a character's personality often helps in developing an understanding of their character.

For example, in Miller's *The Crucible*, the character of Proctor is seen as having a proud, strong and stubborn personality. This comes across in many of the earlier scenes in the play, but it becomes more and more relevant as he is imprisoned in court on suspicion of witchcraft. Even up to the final scene, Proctor stays strong and committed to his beliefs. His personality is conveyed clearly in the way the character acts throughout the play, and the performer playing Proctor must understand these qualities to portray the character accurately.

Now try this

Choose **one or two** of the lead characters from your performance text. Describe their personality. Find specific examples of how this is shown through their behaviour or what they say.

Remember to look for evidence within the performance text to support your judgement about a character's personality.

Motives, aims and objectives

When approaching play texts, as well as understanding a character's purpose, a performer needs to consider the **motives**, **aims** and **objectives** of the character they are portraying.

Understanding a character's motivation

A character's motivation often leads them to move or use actions in a certain way. Motive often explains the reasons behind a character's actions.

> For example, in Act 3, Scene 4 of *Twelfth Night*, Malvolio decides to wear cross-gartered yellow stockings and smile wildly at Olivia because he believes this will encourage her to love him. This is the **motive** behind his unusual behaviour.

What other motives may explain behaviour in the performance texts? For example:

- *The Crucible*: character – Abigail; motive for accusations of witchcraft: love for Proctor.
- *Government Inspector*: character – the Mayor; motive for giving loans to Khlestakov: fear of receiving a negative report.

See page 15 to read about using movement to suggest a character's motivations.

Motives – The character's deeper motivation and the underlying reason why they act in the way they do. Motives are behind a character's aims and objectives.

Interpreting character

Aims and objectives – A character's aims are their immediate and conscious goals; their objectives describe how they will go about achieving those goals.

> Aims and objectives can be seen as the 'stepping stones' to a character achieving their motive. For example, a character may want to be admired for being successful in life, with the aim and objective of impressing at a job interview and being offered a higher status job.

Aims and objectives in practice

Stanislavski suggested that all humans have aims and objectives that drive them. He asked his performers to work out what their character's aims and objectives were as part of the rehearsal process.

> For example, in *An Inspector Calls*, J.B. Priestley describes the entrance of the Inspector, but he allows the performer playing this role to think about the Inspector's aims and objectives. In the opening scene, the character explains that he likes to work methodically to avoid confusion. The performer must decide whether the objective here is to challenge the others in the room, to frighten them, or maybe to make them feel uneasy. Perhaps it is to test their responses. The objective chosen will change how the line is spoken and the portrayal of the Inspector.

Motive can shape actions

Understanding a character's underlying motive is important for the performer when deciding how they will act in the play.

> For example, consider the character of Alex, from *100*. At the start of the play, what motivates him to behave so aggressively and angrily towards the other characters, particularly the Guide? Then, as the play progresses and reaches its climax, why does Alex become desperate and fearful? The performer playing Alex must attempt to understand the character's perspective on his own situation as well as his relationships with the other characters. This will help the performer to understand the motives behind Alex's behaviour, which will help to make the portrayal of the character more convincing.

Now try this

Choose **one** line of dialogue from your performance text and assign different objectives to it. Note how this changes the outcome of the line and the interpretation of the character.

> Make sure you choose a line that can be interpreted in different ways.

Development and relationships

When approaching play texts, it is essential for a performer to explore the character's **development** throughout the play, as well as their **relationships** with others.

Exploring character development

A performer approaching a character in rehearsal needs to consider how that character develops throughout the play. Character development within a play can be achieved by different factors in the action.

For example, consider the character of Winston from *1984*. A performer portraying Winston needs to chart how the different stages of the play affect the development of Winston's character – from his fear of the Thought Police to his falling in love with Julia. The development of Winston's character is central to the plot of *1984* and reflects the intentions of author George Orwell, as well as playwrights Robert Icke and Duncan Macmillan, who adapted Orwell's novel. Without the development of Winston's character, the final betrayal of his love towards the end of the play would not be so powerful.

The performer Sam Crane – seen here in a production at the Playhouse Theatre, London – would have needed to consider how the character of Winston develops.

Character development – This outlines how a character develops throughout the 'action of the play'. It can be shown by events during the course of the play or by referring to events that took place before the start of the play's action begins.

Interpreting character

Character relationships – In all of the performance texts, character relationships are important to character development. Performers may also consider a character's relationship with the audience in texts, particularly if the character speaks a soliloquy.

How and when a character develops

Characters can **evolve** (develop) in texts. It is important that a performer is aware of **when** these changes take place.

For example, the character of Malvolio changes significantly in *Twelfth Night*. For instance, in Act 3, Scene 4, he enters wearing yellow stockings. Malvolio behaves in a very pompous way, full of self-importance for his place in the household. However, by the end of the play Malvolio has been imprisoned and is feeling very sorry for himself. As he leaves the stage he says angrily, 'I'll be revenged on the whole pack of you.'

Conveying a character's relationships

Once a performer is aware of their character's relationships, the next step is to communicate them to an audience.

For example, in *Blue Stockings* the character of Tess is caught in a dilemma over her passion for learning and her love for Will. Their relationship is central to the development of Tess's character. Her relationship with Will deepens as the play progresses, as he comes to increasingly support the women students' right to graduate. The performer playing Tess needs to show how Tess's relationship with Will deepens, culminating in an emotional scene at the train station towards the end of the play.

Now try this

Choose **one** character from your performance text and **one** important relationship they have with another character. Explain how this relationship affects the character you are focusing on.

Use quotations from the performance text to support your ideas.

Research and impact

When understanding and interpreting character, a performer may explore and **research** the **character's past** as well as considering the **impact** of the character on the audience.

Researching a character's past

It is often useful for a performer approaching playing a character to research the character's past and find out any details or secrets that may help the performer understand the role better. Much like a detective, a performer can investigate and look for **evidence** to build up a clearer understanding of the role.

For example, a performer playing the role of Leah in Dennis Kelly's *DNA* may consider why she talks a lot, often non-stop, especially in scenes with Phil. The performer may question why Leah is so talkative and look for clues that explain why.

Mitchell's 'private moments'

The director Katie Mitchell spends a great deal of time in the rehearsal process improvising key moments in a character's **backstory**. This way of working involves researching as much detail and information about the play as possible, in order to understand how the character fits into the world of the play. Mitchell calls these backstory improvisations 'private moments', and they provide the performer with a unique insight into the character. The improvisations are often influenced by moments from the text or how Mitchell and the performers interpret the character.

Research – This is the work a performer does to understand the character they are playing in more depth. This may mean researching the historical time period during which the play is set as well as considering the intentions of the playwright.

Interpreting character

Impact on the audience – Different characters can affect the audience in different ways, for a number of reasons. A performer must consider what the impact of their character's behaviour will be, and how this will be conveyed at different moments in the play. For example, Adam in *DNA* may draw sympathy from the audience at the end of the play when it is discovered that he suffered alone in a forest. As another example, the character of Abigail in *The Crucible* is angry and manipulates the other girls, which may make the audience feel negatively towards her.

Researching the time period

Understanding the time in which a play is set may affect a performer's understanding of a character.

For example, *An Inspector Calls* is set in 1912, before the outbreak of the First World War in 1914. A performer playing any of the characters would need to research the time period carefully, including looking at what was happening socially in the location where the play is set (an industrial city in the North Midlands). This will help them to build a clear picture of the **context** in which the characters act and behave.

Impact on others

A performer will need to understand how their character can affect the audience and other characters at different moments in the play.

For example, in the play *1984*, the character of O'Brien is a powerful party member with high status in the world of the play. The impact of this can be seen in the way other characters respond to him. During O'Brien's interrogation of Winston – a key moment in the play – the performer portraying O'Brien must consider the impact he wants to have on the other performers as well as on the audience.

Take **one** character from your performance text. Consider how a performer might use research to build a broader picture of this character. List the areas the performer might research.

Remember to look for clues in the text that suggest what may have happened to the character before the action of the play began.

Still images and asides

A performer may use a number of possible techniques or approaches on stage to enhance a performance. Audience **asides** can be used to communicate important information directly to the audience, and a **still image** can be used to capture an important moment.

The use of asides

An aside can be used to communicate a line of dialogue with an audience while omitting other characters on stage from hearing. This technique is often used in Shakespearian plays.

For example, *Twelfth Night* has many instances of an aside. The technique is used frequently in Act 2, Scene 5, where Sir Toby, Sir Andrew and Fabian hide in a box tree after setting up a trap for the unsuspecting Malvolio with a fake love letter from Olivia. As Malvolio imagines telling Sir Toby what to do, Toby exclaims in an aside 'Shall this fellow live?' This is a secret conversation with the audience and adds to the comedy of the scene, as Malvolio is oblivious to Sir Toby's presence.

Sir Toby's aside in Act 2, Scene 5 of *Twelfth Night* is a perfect example of this technique being used effectively in performance. This was done in the RSC production of *Twelfth Night* in 1997.

Aside – A character's moment of **discussion** with the audience. Aside often works well when one character wishes to **connect** with the audience without wanting the other characters on stage to hear.

Performance skills

Still image – Sometimes known as a **tableau** or a **freeze frame**, this is a moment in time that has been stopped, with the performers still on stage. Still image can be a powerful, visual way of connecting with an audience.

Use of still image in performance

Still image is a technique that can mark an important moment or engage an audience through the performers' use of physical skills.

For example, in Scene 1 of *The Crucible*, the Reverend Parris kneels at his daughter Betty's bed, praying, after she has been caught dancing in the woods with Abigail and the other girls. The dance itself could be presented as a series of still images as the play begins, helping to paint a picture for the audience of what has caused this response from Parris. This would be a highly visual way of presenting the event to the audience.

Turn to pages 12–15 for more on performers' use of physical skills.

Where an aside isn't written down

Although many plays use asides, particularly Shakespearian texts, performers may wish to add their own aside into a scene.

For example, in *100*, many sections are written in a stylised way, which can be performed using simple props. To support this style, a performer could use **direct address**, speaking to the audience rather than to other characters on stage. For example, when Sophie recalls her memory from when she was 12, there are other performers on stage, and Sophie's lines are not specifically highlighted as an aside. However, the performer playing Sophie could speak the lines so as to ignore the other cast members, connect with the audience and indicate that this section is a flashback.

Now try this

Choose **one** key moment from your performance text. Outline how still image could be used to highlight or visually represent this moment to the audience. For example, it could help to explore or respond to what is happening on stage.

The moment doesn't necessarily need to happen 'within' the time of the play itself. It may be that a still image helps to add context to what is happening at that moment in the play. For example, in *100*, the opinions the Elders have about Ketu's theories could be presented through still image.

Monologue and physical theatre

The use of a **monologue** may explain a character's thoughts or feelings. **Physical theatre** can be used to capture a moment using the body in performance.

Using monologue

A playwright typically uses monologue:

👍 to impart information from one character to others on stage

👍 as a way of connecting with an audience.

When a character is alone on stage and delivers their thoughts or feelings out loud, this is known as a **soliloquy**. Shakespeare made particular use of soliloquy in his plays.

For example, a good instance of soliloquy in *Twelfth Night* is Viola's famous 'I left no ring with her' speech, at the end of Act 2 Scene 2. This soliloquy cleverly reveals the dilemma that Viola finds herself in, as she begins to realise that Olivia has fallen in love with her as Cesario. The soliloquy is often delivered directly to the audience, so helping to build a **connection** between character and spectator.

Modern soliloquys

Soliloquys aren't only used in older, classical plays.

For example, Dennis Kelly makes use of the technique in *DNA*, through the character of Leah. At points throughout the play, the characters of Leah and Phil are left alone on stage. Leah then proceeds to speak her thoughts and feelings aloud, with Phil present but not responding to what she is saying. The performer playing Leah must decide how she will approach the delivery of these monologues – particularly as she receives no feedback from Phil. For example, will she become more exasperated as the monologue continues?

Physical theatre – A distinct style of theatre where a performer uses movement and physicality in a visual way to communicate with the audience.

Performance skills

Monologue – A speech that a performer delivers on their own. A monologue can be spoken to other characters on stage or directly to the audience.

Using physical theatre in performance

Physical theatre can be used at particular moments of a play to communicate with the audience.

For example, in the opening scene of *Government Inspector*, the Mayor gathers important people from the town in his house. There is a sense of fear and anxiety as the Mayor delivers the news of the Government Inspector's arrival. The Mayor also makes reference to 'a premonition I had last night' of seeing 'two black rats', which seems to suggest bad news is on the horizon. The performers could use physical theatre to communicate this moment of ensemble performance and visual imagery to an audience.

Approaching a monologue in performance

Monologue is an important technique used as a form of communication by the playwright, so a performer needs to consider how they approach monologue carefully.

For example, one of the most prominent monologues from *An Inspector Calls* occurs in Act 3, when Inspector Goole delivers an impassioned speech in response to Mr Birling's untimely offer of money. The Inspector's monologue reflects his (and the playwright's) views on social injustice. The performer delivering this monologue must make use of voice and physical skills, making careful choices about which words and gestures to emphasise, to bring the Inspector's lines to life.

Now try this

Find **one** monologue from your performance text or **one** moment from your performance text where physical theatre could be applied. Outline how you would approach this speech or moment – what would you intend to communicate to your audience, and how?

Be clear about where monologue occurs in your performance text. Try to understand why the playwright has chosen to use this device at that moment in the play.

Narration and multi-role

Narration is one device that helps to tell the story of the play, while the technique of **multi-role** can allow a performer to communicate a number of different characters.

Using multi-role in performance

Multi-role can:
- 👍 provide an effective way of telling a story with a small company of performers
- 👍 be a device to tell the story, so that the audience can focus on the story's message
- 👍 be achieved through the use of costume and physical and vocal skills
- 👍 be an effective way to engage an audience.

Multi-role can be achieved through various acting techniques or design elements.

A Brechtian technique

Multi-role is often referred to as a **Brechtian technique**, as it was a key idea of the theatre practitioner Bertolt Brecht. Brecht wanted his audiences to focus on the message of the play rather than becoming too attached to any particular character. Brecht believed that a performer can 'distance' him or herself from a role they are playing by portraying a number of roles to an audience in the same play.

In *100*, multi-role can be used to help create the wide range of different locations and events that feature in the characters' memories. In the original production, there were only five performers, even though there are many more characters in the play, giving the production a more **non-naturalistic** or **stylised** feel. In this way, the audience will be aware they are watching theatre and so will not become too attached to individual characters – the play becomes more about the theme or message than about the characters' individual stories.

Multi-role – When a performer plays various roles on stage in one play. Multi-role can include performers playing different genders and personalities. These changes are often portrayed through an adjustment in the performer's costume, physicality and voice.

Performance skills

Narration – The process of telling a story. It can take many forms, including a character narrating sections of the play, or the playwright using a specified narrator or narrators to carry out a specific role in the play.

Narration in performance

Narration can take many forms and require particular skills in performance.

For example, the play *1984* opens with a voice that acts as a narrator telling the story of Winston. The performer playing the voice cannot be seen, so the performer's vocal skills are vital here in delivering the words clearly and with the most appropriate tone. This narrative device works well on stage, as *1984* is an adaptation of a novel. The invisible voice returns at the end of the play, and a performer playing this role would need to consider how the delivery changes at this point.

Multi-role performance

Multi-role demands particular performance skills in order to make the approach work successfully.

For example, in the Young Vic 2011 production of *Government Inspector*, many members of the cast played more than one role. The performer Steven Beard played the roles of Dr Gibner, Waiter and Shopkeeper. This would have required the performer to create three separate characters, with three different approaches to physicality and voice. Playing these different characters also meant the performer had to think carefully about how he developed each role throughout the performance.

Now try this

Find **one** moment from your performance text where you feel it would be appropriate to use either narration or multi-role. Outline how you would approach this technique and why it would be useful.

Remember to base your choice on what would work within the context of the play.

Mime, flashback and flash forward

Mimed sequences can help to tell a story of a play, while **flashback** and **flash forward** allow a playwright to change the time period in the same text.

A performer's use of mime

Mime is a useful technique that requires a performer to communicate without voice. Though many of the performance texts are 'naturalistic' in style and form, mimed sequences can help develop certain scenes.

Performers such as Steven Berkoff and Jacques Lecoq wanted to make mime a component of body language and communication, rather than just relying on mime to display a gesture. In this sense, mime can be used in every role to enhance the communication of the character, rather than as a separate technique.

> For example, near the beginning of *100*, Alex recalls a motorcycle race and the race itself is 're-enacted'. This would be very difficult to represent in a naturalistic way on stage but it could be staged as a mimed sequence. If the performers playing Alex and the other racers use mime, they will have to convince the audience they are racing motorcycles at high speed.

> The use of mime was made famous by the French 'white-face' mime artist Marcel Marceau, who created 'Bip the Clown' in the 1940s.

Mimed sequence – This is a moment in a play that relies solely on the use of **non-verbal communication** such as body language, physicality and facial expressions.

Performance skills

Flashback and flash forward – The use of flashback and flash forward moves the action in a performance backwards or forwards in time.

Using mimed sequences

Mimed sequences are often given in the text as stage directions. Therefore, rather than being used as a stand-alone technique (such as physical theatre), mime can be incorporated into staging a moment from a text.

> For example, there are several mimed sequences in Jessica Swale's *Blue Stockings*. During the men's card game at Trinity College in Act 2, Scene 8, there is also a stage direction that includes moments of mime: '*They take it in turns to put a card down from the three they've picked. It's fast... They get excited...*' As there are no lines of dialogue at this point, the performers might mime laughter or gestures, as though the characters are holding a conversation.

Using flashback and flash forward

Changes in time within a play can be an effective device to help engage an audience. The use of flashback and flash forward can help communicate character background and development.

> For example, towards the end of *1984*, the character of Winston is threatened with having a cage of rats set on his face. As the scene progresses, he becomes more and more desperate and the scene builds towards a crescendo of tension. Within a quick snapped blackout, the playwright uses a flash forward to take Winston into a café in sunshine after this very dark scene. The performer portraying Winston could show his confusion at the change in scene, as well as his relief that his nightmare is over.

Now try this

Outline how you could use a mimed sequence to enhance **one** moment from your performance text. Be clear about how the mimed sequence would help to tell the story of the play.

Remember to think about the aims and intentions of the playwright.

Symbolism and split scene

The technique of **split scene**, which allows two scenes to be shown at the same time on stage, can be central to a performance, as can the use of **symbolism**.

Using split scene in performance

Directors and playwrights often favour split scene as it enables two scenes to run alongside each other at the same time. When split scene is used, performers must be focused on their own scene and their part of the stage, as the technique doesn't work if the two 'worlds' overlap.

For example, in Act 3, Scene 4 of *Twelfth Night*, Sir Toby and his friend Fabian persuade Viola and Sir Andrew that each wants to fight the other. This is a set up, so it is important that the performers playing Fabian and Sir Toby are able to have the conversations with Viola and Sir Andrew on the same stage, but separately from each other. Here, split screen is ideal.

In this 2014 production of *Dealer's Choice* at the Royal & Derngate, Northampton, split scene was used to run two separate scenes on stage.

Split scene – Also referred to as **cross-cutting**, this is where two scenes are cut between each other on stage at the same time. The idea is very similar to a filmic device that moves between scenes in a seamless way.

Performance skills

Symbolism – Ideas, images or suggestions are used to represent thoughts, emotions or qualities. Symbolism can be obvious at times but can also be fairly complex in performance.

For example, in *1984*, Big Brother is a **symbol** of always being watched or monitored by the state.

Using symbolism on stage

Performers can deepen their understanding of their roles in a play by developing an awareness of the play's symbolism.

For example, in *An Inspector Calls*, J.B. Priestley uses characters as symbols for political ideas: the Inspector is symbolic of Priestley's socialist views (that all wealth should be shared equally), while Mr Birling represents capitalist ideas (that only a few individuals will profit within a free economy).

The symbolism within a play can also be communicated to the audience through the set.

In director Stephen Daldry's original production of *An Inspector Calls*, the Birlings' house physically collapsed on stage, symbolising the characters' lives caving in on them.

Skills required for split scene

Split scene can work very effectively when staged well. It requires performers to make careful use of the following practical skills:

- **Proxemics**: careful and precise use of space
- **Physical skills**: carefully chosen eye contact, movement and body language.

The performers' skills become even more important with cross-cutting, as one of the scenes will need to stay frozen in a **still image** while the other scene continues.

Remember to think about the aims and intentions of the playwright.

Now try this

Find **one** moment in your performance text where you could use either symbolism or split scene to enhance the performance. Explain your choices.

Caricature and choral speaking

Performers can approach a role by exaggerating the characteristics of that role, creating a **caricature** that is often larger than life. A performance can also be developed through the use of **choral speaking**.

The use of caricature in performance

A performer using caricature will make use of physical and vocal skills that push their character into becoming a **comic** or **grotesque** version of itself.

For example, in *Government Inspector*, caricature could support a powerful portrayal of the Mayor's character. The Mayor's panic and anxiety could be exaggerated through the performer's use of large gestures and frenetic body language. As the play progresses and the Mayor grows more desperate, the performer could make the Mayor's behaviour more out of the ordinary. The Mayor's voice could become louder and more high pitched, his gestures wild and his facial expressions wide as he tries to 'cover' the shortcomings of the town. His behaviour would become larger than life.

When caricature is effective

It is useful to consider how caricature will work in the context of the style of your performance text. Caricature:

- ✓ works particularly well in a **stylised** form of theatre, rather than in **naturalistic** theatre (which is based on the development of 'real' or 'believable' characters)
- ✓ fits well with the performance texts *Government Inspector* and *100*, both of which lend themselves to **non-naturalistic** approaches. *Government Inspector* is often described as a grotesque comedy and *100* includes many **Brechtian** elements such as multi-role, larger-than-life characters (such as the Guide) and asking challenging, personal questions.

Caricature – A performer can decide to use caricature to play a character in an exaggerated way, so creating a character that is a larger-than-life version of the original.

Performance skills

Choral speaking – This is when more than one person speaks or reads text at the same time. It can **emphasise** or **underline** key moments on stage.

When character becomes caricature

The use of caricature will suit certain styles of theatre and particular characters.

For example, although the character of Malvolio in *Twelfth Night* may not have been written as a caricature, there are many performers who have approached the role by creating a comic, grotesque version of him. In the production at Shakespeare's Globe in 2012, the performer Stephen Fry achieved this through his use of large gestures and heightened vocal skills. This choice makes sense, as the character of Malvolio acts and behaves in an exaggerated way.

Using choral speech

The playwright may specify the use of choral speech, or it may be chosen by a director.

For example, during Ketu's memory in *100*, the Elders warn Ketu to abandon his ideas and theories as they are frightening people in the village. The warnings are severe and threatening, becoming more intimidating towards Ketu with each line and making it clear that they want him to stop telling people the Earth is round. The performers or director may use choral speech to emphasise the importance of this warning, to make the audience aware that it is much more than a simple piece of advice.

Now try this

Explain where the use of either caricature or choral speech could enhance your performance text. Base your ideas on the context or style of the text as a whole.

Remember: when answering a question such as this, your decision may depend on your own interpretation of your performance text.

The director

A **director** has **overall creative control** over the entire production and is usually involved from the very start of the project. From selecting a text and making decisions about genre, form and style, to auditioning the performers, working with designers and rehearsing the show, the director must make sure every piece of the production fits together in a way that is consistent and **engages the audience**.

Overall creative control – The director must have a **strong vision** for how the production will look in performance. This overall focus begins in the pre-production stages and continues all the way through to the actual run of performances.

Working with designers – Creating a successful overall vision will often rely on costume (including make-up), lighting, set and sound. The director will work with the designers from the start of the process to ensure their ideas are consistent with the rest of the production.

Organising rehearsals – It is the director's job to make sure that the rehearsals are well structured and that the rehearsal period is effective and efficient.

Ensuring consistency – The director is responsible for making sure that all the different elements come together smoothly. Consistency is the key to a much more effective experience for the audience.

The role of the director

Instructing the performers – This will include blocking (positioning the performers on the stage) and working with the performers to select how they deliver lines, move on stage and develop relationships between the characters.

Identifying genre, style and form – This is closely linked to the overall vision for the production. The director will choose the way the production will be performed.

Understanding the themes of the play – Before rehearsals start, a key task for the director is to make sure they have a deep understanding of the themes and issues in the play and how these will affect the production.

Selecting the message of the production – The director may concentrate on one specific message of the play or choose to emphasise a range of different points.

Pre-production

- ✓ Many of the key decisions about a production, such as its genre, style and form, will be made long before rehearsals start.
- ✓ Much of this work will be led by the director, who will spend a lot of time **reading and rereading** the play, usually several times over.
- ✓ The director needs a **detailed and in-depth understanding** of the play – including its **themes, issues and messages** – in order to decide what to highlight for an audience.
- ✓ This close understanding of a play can be gained from the whole text, including **stage directions**, and even **notes from the playwright**.

Important decisions

For example, in *DNA*, the character list and setting notes are left very open by the playwright, Dennis Kelly. While characters' names and genders are given, a note suggests that these can be altered as desired.

In the example of *DNA*, where the playwright offers a huge amount of flexibility, there are instant decisions to be made about the casting.

A director will need a detailed understanding of the play in order to consider how any changes would affect the overall vision. For example, what would the **impact** be if a character were cast as a different gender? How would this affect the way in which the audience understands the narrative?

Now try this

What are the most important skills a director should have? Explain why you have chosen those particular skills.

 Think about the different responsibilities a director has towards the production overall.

Messages and subtext

One of the first things a director needs to establish is a **clear vison** for the whole production. This involves making a range of decisions, including identifying the **genre** and **style** of the production, as well as deciding on the **key messages** to communicate to the audience. See page 28 to find out more about genre and style.

Key messages

Plays often carry a strong message, sometimes more than one. A director may choose to expand on key messages in their production of a play.

For example, *An Inspector Calls* has a very strong central message relating to the responsibility of society. So, a director preparing a production of *An Inspector Calls* might decide to emphasise the power of the younger generation or the dangers of ignoring wider social problems.

The social class structure, symbolised by the set, collapses in the National Theatre's 2009 production of *An Inspector Calls*.

Subtext

Subtext describes the unspoken thoughts and messages behind the text. Characters may say one thing but mean the complete opposite. Clues as to the play's key messages, and the context of those messages, may be given both in the spoken words and in the stage directions.

In this production of *An Inspector Calls*, the director, working closely with the set designer, has chosen to emphasise the breakdown of the social structure by having the Birling house literally collapse. This theme is heavily hinted at in the actual text, but it was the director who made the decision to represent it in this way.

In this example from *Government Inspector*, the Mayor is terrified that the Inspector will discover his corrupt ways. However, when they first meet, the Mayor has to pretend he is delighted to see the man he believes is the Inspector. Equally, Khlestakov (who is not really the Inspector) thinks he is about to be arrested for not paying his hotel bill. Therefore, the audience is clear that the message here is about misunderstanding and confusion.

The real feelings of the characters can be found in the stage directions and the spoken words.

The Mayor and Dobchinsky enter. They all look at each other, attempting to hide their fear. The Mayor stands to attention.

Mayor May I humbly welcome you to our town.

Khlestakov Say again?

Mayor You are incognito – I mean, you are welcome. Most utterly warmly welcome.

Khlestakov ... Thank you.

Mayor I must firstly apologise for intruding on you like this.

Khlestakov Not at all.

(From *Government Inspector* by Nikolai Gogol)

Now try this

Find **one** example in your performance text of a character saying or doing the opposite of what they actually mean. How could a performer communicate this clearly to the audience?

Select an example where the character has a significant impact on the action. Be clear about the context and why the character might be pretending or hiding something.

Genre and style

Genre and style are terms that are often used to mean the same thing. However, **genre** refers to the type or category of theatre, while **style** refers to the way it is performed. So a genre may be performed in a range of different styles.

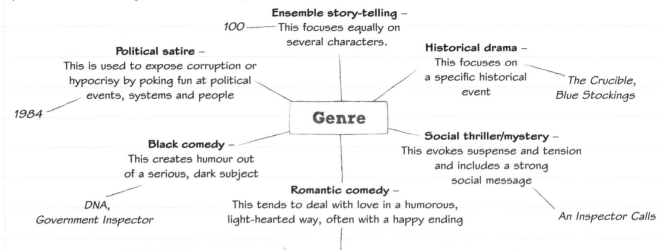

Ensemble story-telling –
100 —— This focuses equally on several characters.

Political satire –
This is used to expose corruption or hypocrisy by poking fun at political events, systems and people
1984

Historical drama –
This focuses on a specific historical event
The Crucible, Blue Stockings

Genre

Black comedy –
This creates humour out of a serious, dark subject
DNA, Government Inspector

Social thriller/mystery –
This evokes suspense and tension and includes a strong social message
An Inspector Calls

Romantic comedy –
This tends to deal with love in a humorous, light-hearted way, often with a happy ending
Twelfth Night

The performance texts for Edexcel GCSE Drama have been categorised according to these genres. Which genre does your performance text belong to?

Comedy and tragedy are the two most fundamental genres. Both can trace their origins back to Ancient Greek theatre.

Style

Theatre can be performed in many different styles. New styles and forms are created as theatre evolves and when existing styles are combined to create a new style. One of the most exciting elements of theatre is the creative development of ideas. This ensures that plays that may have been performed many times can still feel fresh and contemporary.

Director Nicholas Hytner chose to set this 2013 National Theatre production of *Othello*, a tragedy, in the modern British Army. This is an example of a **naturalistic** style.

Popular contemporary styles

The most popular contemporary styles include:

1. **naturalism** – imitates real life, from the style of acting to detailed, realistic sets and costume
2. **epic theatre** – developed by Bertolt Brecht; often contains a moral or political message; uses techniques designed to alienate the audience, emotionally detaching audience members from the action and encouraging a rational, intellectual response instead
3. **physical theatre** – very immersive style of theatre, which mainly uses the body and movement to represent ideas, emotions and relationships
4. **expressionism** – non-naturalistic style; focuses on communicating and evoking strong emotional reactions; frequently uses exaggeration; influenced Brecht's work.

Now try this

Think about your performance text. Make a list of the play's main themes and issues. Which styles would help you to bring out these themes and issues most effectively?

 Try to identify clues and evidence in the performance text to support your ideas. See pages 68–83 for more about the performance texts.

Types of staging

Once the director has decided on the central message of the production and chosen the genre and style, he or she can make key decisions about the **practicalities** of staging the production.

Proscenium arch (also known as **end-on staging**)

👍 Excellent sightlines for the audience

👍 Very common type of staging and easy to use effectively

👎 The audience may feel quite distant from the action.

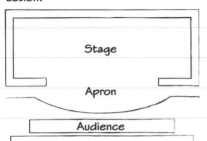

Thrust stage

👍 Brings the action into the audience

👍 Use of a **back wall** (providing a defined end to the stage space and a place to attach set to) can help with the set

👎 Sightlines and audience awareness (the audience's ability to see the performers) can be an issue.

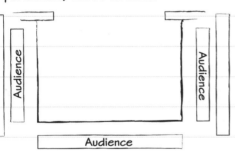

Theatre-in-the-round

👍 Can create a very intimate performance space

👍 Presents interesting opportunities to use a **naturalistic style** of performance, as the performance space is not just aimed in one direction

👎 Can be difficult to use scenery without affecting sightlines.

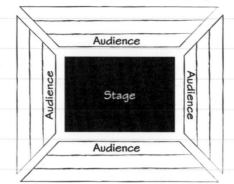

Traverse stage

👍 Can be a very intimate type of staging

👍 Provides opportunities for less naturalistic styles, as audience members can see each other

👎 Can be difficult to use large and extensive sets.

Types of staging: pros and cons

Selecting the type of space in which the play will be performed is central to many other directorial decisions. For more about types of staging, turn to page 61.

Promenade theatre

👍 Each scene can be specifically designed and created

👍 Relationship between the performers and the audience can be improved owing to the potential **proximity** (closeness) between the two

👎 Management of the audience members may become difficult, as they are moved from location to location.

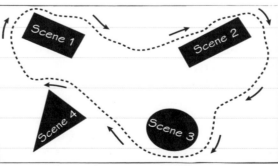

Dotted line = direction of audience

Now try this

Choose **one** scene from your performance text. Think about how you would stage the scene in different settings. Choose **one** type of staging and give an example of how this might affect the vision and message of the production.

Always keep the perspective of the audience in mind when making decisions about staging your production.

Consistency and communication

To help produce the impact required in a production, a director aims for **consistency of style** and **clear communication** with the audience. The director must always try to balance all the elements carefully, to make the production as effective as possible.

Unity of convention

Once the genre, style and type of staging have been identified, a director must work hard to ensure there is a consistency across the whole production. For example, combining traditional costumes with a modern set, or blocking a scene for an 'end-on' stage but using theatre-in-the-round staging, may cause confusion for the audience and a misunderstanding of the message. The aim is to achieve **unity** (wholeness) of convention.

A **dramatic convention** is a technique – the way something is done. The conventions used in a production need to work together to achieve a consistent overall style. Conventions can include still image, audience aside, simultaneous different locations, mime and narration.

The RSC's 1993 production of *Julius Caesar* used **promenade theatre**, enabling the audience to get very close to the action. Consistency will have been vital to ensure a fluid production. Here, a contemporary stretcher and floor covering reinforce the modern costume.

Audience awareness

A director must consider:

- the **impact** the staging of the production will have on the **audience**

- the implications for **audience awareness**, which must also be planned carefully; knowing exactly where the audience is positioned will help a director decide on the positioning of set and props, as well as the blocking of performers. See page 38 for more on blocking.

- the **communication** of the central message or messages of the play.

Audience awareness is ensuring the audience is able to see what is happening on stage.

Communicating with the audience

The audience needs to be given a lot of information regarding all aspects of the plot. Time, location, character, situation, mood and atmosphere are just some of the elements that be must clear and help provide **context**.
The director, often working with designers, the production team and performers, must decide how to combine lighting, set, costume, sound and performance skills to convey ideas quickly and effectively to the audience.

For example, to get across the idea of a wild, outdoor location at night, a director might choose a stark, simple set with a rustic doorway leading to an indoor location. When this is combined with blue and white lighting, the audience will quickly understand the setting.

Now try this

Choose **one** scene from your performance text. List the key information you want your audience to know in order to understand the play's narrative and themes.

Be selective and stick to key details. This will help you to avoid overloading the audience with information.

Purpose

As well as deciding on the central message of a play, the director must also be very clear about its **purpose**. Knowing why the play was written, and what it is designed to do, is vital when making decisions about the wide range of production elements.

The importance of purpose

☑ Plays exist for many different purposes – for example, to teach or entertain.

☑ While a playwright may have a very specific reason for writing a play, a director may have a different purpose driving their production.

☑ To ensure a production is successful, a director must understand the original purpose of the play. This will help them to define the purpose of their particular production.

To educate – From Theatre in Education (TIE) to soap opera, the immersive (deeply engaging) experience of theatre can be very effective in educating audiences on a wide range of issues.

To influence – Throughout history, theatre has influenced people to change their opinions or to take action in response to an issue or problem.

To entertain – Theatre has always provided a form of entertainment and it can be a very effective form of escape from the demands of everyday life.

The purpose of theatre

To empower – Theatre can demonstrate how to challenge the existing situation. For example, the ideas of theatre practitioner Augusto Boal helped to empower many people around the world to change their lives for the better.

To challenge – Satire and metaphor have been effective tools in challenging the political establishment and can also act as a warning about possible future developments.

To understand – Plays can explore situations that are beyond the experience of the audience. This opportunity to examine challenging themes and issues can help people to develop emotional intelligence, empathy and understanding.

To question – By presenting different situations and examining the consequences of actions, theatre can encourage audiences to ask questions about what is right and what is wrong.

Satire uses humour to highlight or criticise something/someone. **Metaphor** is when a phrase, person or object is used to represent something different. For example, the witch trials in *The Crucible* are a metaphor for the McCarthy trials in 1950s America.

Didactic theatre

- Didactic theatre is most commonly associated with **Bertolt Brecht**.
- Its central purpose is to communicate a moral or political message.
- It is designed to educate and encourage the audience to have an intellectual response to the issues presented in the play.

For example, Brecht's play *Mother Courage and Her Children* has a strong **anti-war message** and is considered by many to be one of the most powerful plays of the 20th century.

Gaining a deeper understanding

Theatre can challenge audiences to gain a deeper **understanding** of what it is to be human and to see things from a range of different perspectives. By examining themes and issues through characterisation, audience members can be taken on a journey and witness a range of experiences normally beyond their own reality.

For example, Sarah Kane's play *4.48 Psychosis* gives a challenging insight into mental health issues, helping audiences to develop a greater understanding of this difficult area.

Now try this

What is the central purpose of your performance text? What impact might this have on your overall staging of the production?

Research your performance text and identify its central theme. Then decide how to present your ideas to an audience using a range of production elements and theatrical styles.

Managing the audience

One of the most difficult things a director must do is **manage the reaction of the audience**.

Managing audience reaction

When the reaction of the audience is managed effectively, it is far more likely that the play's **purpose** will be successfully drawn out. A director needs to:

☑ consider the audience's **perspective** (view) on the action

☑ find the **climax** and **anti-climax** in the play.

> Managing the audience's reaction is, in part, linked to the play's structure.

The classic pantomime joke of having characters looking for something that is directly behind them has made audiences laugh – and shout – out loud for many generations.

Perspective

What the audience can **see** is important.

A director might **manipulate** its reaction by giving it:

- a wider **view** of action that is not visible to the characters on stage, as in the example on the left
- a **wider insight** than the characters.

> For example, the issue of **mistaken or false identity** is central to the plot of *Twelfth Night*, where Olivia falls in love with Viola, thinking she is a man ('Cesario'). The humour comes from that fact the audience knows the truth and sees Viola/Cesario try to resolve the situation without giving up the disguise.

Climax

Climax is the point where the **build-up** of tension reaches tipping point and the tension is released, often in an explosive way.

> For example, in Act 2, Scene 11 of *Blue Stockings*, the growing sound of the angry men builds tension. As they finally burst onto the stage, the sudden silence is threatening, suggesting that something is about to happen. The climax is reached as Lloyd throws Mrs Welsh down. The stillness on stage as Mrs Welsh lies on the floor shows that Lloyd has gone too far.

Anti-climax

Like climax, **anti-climax** is about tension that is built up and then released. However, with anti-climax, the resolution is less powerful or significant than expected, so the sense is one of disappointment or decline.

> In Act 3 of *The Crucible*, Elizabeth Proctor lies in an attempt to save her husband, John, unaware that he has confessed to his affair with Abigail. This dramatic anti-climax can be managed with careful positioning of the performers, giving the audience a much wider visual perspective than Elizabeth.

When answering this question:
- select a moment from your performance text that is pivotal to the plot, where you want the audience to have a significant reaction
- be very clear about the reaction you want the audience to have, and your reasons for this
- consider how you will get the audience to react in that way. What elements and techniques will help you control their reaction? Do you need to start building up tension earlier in the scene?

Now try this

Choose **one** key moment in your performance text. As a director, what is the reaction you want to get from your audience? Explain how you will achieve this.

Choosing location and time

As theatre evolves, directors are always looking to **reinterpret** plays and put their own creative mark on productions. Different directors might set the same play in different **locations** or **time periods**, making their decision carefully to emphasise a specific message for a target audience.

Location

Playwrights are often very specific about the **location** of the play. This may be particularly relevant for historical dramas, where the plot is based on real events.

However, there are many instances where a director will decide to change the location. Whenever directors choose to do this, there must be very clear and **justified reasons** for the decision, so that the central message of the play is not diluted and remains clear.

In a 2004 production of *Macbeth*, theatre company Out of Joint changed the location from Scotland to central Africa in order to highlight the devastating impact civil war was having on the population there in the early 21st century.

Time

Directors will also experiment with setting plays in different time periods or even making a play **timeless**.

In this 2013 production of *Romeo and Juliet*, the modern-day setting takes the central message of division and expands on the reasons behind it.

Why change the location?

There are many reasons why a director may choose to change the location of a play or scene. For example:

1. to make the play more **relevant** for a contemporary audience
2. to make a **political** or **moral point** about a contemporary issue
3. to **reflect** better the original playwright's message – which may no longer be appropriate in the original setting
4. to provide a more **local** setting for the audience.

Why change the time?

As for location, the time period in which a plot takes place can have a powerful effect on the central message the director wishes to **convey** (get across). The time might be changed for a number of reasons, including:

1. to make a strong **historical** point
2. to show how things **might be** in the future if things don't change
3. to show that the central message is **timeless**
4. to engage a contemporary audience and make the play more **relevant**.

Now try this

As a director, think about your vision for a production of your performance text, and the central message you want to convey. How might different locations be appropriate for your performance text?

Make sure you can clearly justify all the points in your answer.

Contexts

A play's **social, cultural and historical contexts** can have a huge effect on the way a director chooses to interpret the text.

Why contexts matter

A play's contexts are one of the aspects a director will consider when making decisions about how their production will look. They also influence decisions about the **key message** or messages the director wants to **communicate** to the audience. Turn to page 27 for more about deciding on key messages. Contexts can be:

 social

 cultural

✓ historical.

> The social, cultural and historical contexts in a play are usually interlinked.

Social context

Example: *100* explores the themes of life and death, and raises powerful questions about what is really most important in our lives.

> **Social context** refers to the way in which **ordinary society** was functioning at the time the play was written. It can also refer to the way in which everyday people receive and react to the play (for example receiving the play with anger, then trying to shut it down).

Example: *Twelfth Night* explores relationships and how humans of all social standings have the same emotions and desires.

Example: *DNA* explores youth culture and questions the role of group pressure in actions being taken too far.

Cultural context

Example: *Government Inspector* explores political corruption, where the audience can witness the downfall of the politicians.

> **Culture** is the way in which different sections of society can express a **mutual** (shared) **identity**. Understanding the cultural context of a play can provide deep insights into the text's hidden messages and why those themes and issues need to be expressed.

Example: *An Inspector Calls* shows how the audience has a moral responsibility to other human beings.

Example: *Blue Stockings* makes the audience question how much our culture values/ discriminates against women.

Historical context

Example: In *The Crucible*, Arthur Miller uses the historical events in 17th-century Salem to make a political point, highlighting the concerns of many US citizens about the McCarthy trials of the 1950s.

> This considers significant **historical** events taking place at the time the play was written. In some cases, a play might directly reflect these events. Other plays use historical events as a **metaphor** to highlight issues and events that occurred when the play was written.

Example: The play *1984* asks challenging questions about how freedom can be defined and what restrictions are placed on individuals by modern society, focusing on how technology can be used to monitor our movements and lifestyle choices.

Now try this

What are the social, historical and cultural contexts in your performance text? Explain how these contexts influence your interpretation of the play? See pages 68–83 for more about the performance texts.

> You need to show a good understanding of the context in which your performance text was originally created and performed, as well as what the playwright intended.

Mood and atmosphere

The **communication of ideas** is key to the success of any production. It is crucial that the central message of a play is communicated to the audience, but **how** that message is conveyed is equally important. The **mood** and **atmosphere** of a production can help to deliver the central message in a way that is easily understood, so a director must therefore make careful choices about these.
For more about communication, see page 30. For a reminder about the messages in a production, turn to page 27.

Mood

The **mood** of a scene or whole production is:

- ✓ about how that scene or production feels
- ✓ linked to the **emotions** being communicated
- ✓ **created by the director, performers and performance elements all working together.**

Vision, message, location and contexts are all important in creating mood.

Atmosphere

The **atmosphere** of a production:

- ✓ is closely linked to mood
- ✓ refers more to the emotions of the audience
- ✓ **is what the audience feels as a result of the mood of the scene.**

See pages 27–34 for more about the elements that can contribute to mood and atmosphere.

Humour

Humour can be created in many different ways. The mood of the characters on stage may be very different to the atmosphere the audience is experiencing.

For example, in the sitcom *Fawlty Towers*, the hotel is badly run and the characters' relationships are dysfunctional. The characters are often under stress or in distress, yet the director, designers and performers manage the mood so that the atmosphere felt by the audience is a comic one.

The absurd, slapstick humour of the Reduced Shakespeare Company productions generates high levels of comedy, creating a positive and happy atmosphere for the audience.

Mystery and anger

A mysterious mood can be created through:

- careful use of lighting
- simple staging
- performances that show the characters' emotions, such as fear.

The combination of these elements will create an atmosphere that is dark and filled with **tension**.

Theatre is also often used to encourage people to take action. By using high emotions to create a mood of sympathy or **anger**, the atmosphere can be one of **activation**.

This 2013 production of *Trash Cuisine* by Belarus Free Theatre asks difficult questions about capital punishment.

Now try this

1 Choose **one** scene from your performance text. As a director, what mood would you want to convey? Explain which performance elements would help to convey this to the audience.

2 Now explain how the audience might react to this mood and what kind of atmosphere would be created.

Be clear about what you want to convey and select a range of production elements and performance techniques to communicate this to an audience. Ensure your ideas are consistent and remember to justify your answer with examples from the performance text.

Style

Initial ideas about the visual **style** of a production are also the director's responsibility. Decisions about style will quickly influence the way the production develops and a director may choose to follow a **naturalistic** or **abstract** approach. For more about style, turn to page 28.

Naturalistic set design

A **naturalistic style** is a look and feel that resembles real life. It is the director's job to decide on the style of a production. If the director chooses a naturalistic style, it is then the job of the designers to make sure that style is realised.

For example, to support a naturalistic style for a scene outside a house, designers might focus on small but important **details** such as a tree, complete with leaves, or a washing line.

See pages 41–47 for more about costume design.
For more about lighting design, turn to pages 48–54.
See pages 55–62 for more about set design.

Naturalistic costume design

Costume is also vital in **representing** the style of a production. Like set, costume communicates visually with the audience, and can convey huge amounts of information very quickly.

The late 19th-century costumes in this 2013 production of Ibsen's *Ghosts* contribute to the naturalistic style. Notice the **consistency** between costume and set: the furniture reflects the same era and status of the characters.

Abstract set design

Directors are always trying to find new ways of communicating the ideas and themes within a play. They will often work with the designers to find fresh and interesting ideas to help them develop an **abstract** style.

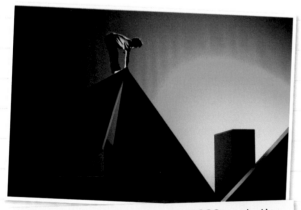

The abstract set design for this 2009 production of *Les Sept Planches de la Ruse* makes effective use of lighting and levels.

When something is **abstract**, it doesn't try to represent real life directly. Instead, it attempts to express ideas and feelings about something through elements such as colour and shape.

Abstract lighting design

Effective use of lighting can:

👍 make a significant contribution to the style of a play

👍 crystallise the style and transform a production, particularly if used in **collaboration** with other design elements.

For the lighting designer to achieve the required effect, a director must consider carefully the type of impact they are looking for.

Epic theatre, physical theatre and expressionism use types of abstract style.

Now try this

As a director, explain which style you would choose for a production of your performance text. Suggest at least **two** ways the designers could help to achieve this.

Justify your style choice and link this to your overall vision for the production. Remember, as a director you only need to come up with the initial ideas.

Presenting location and time

Early in the process of visualising a production, a director needs to think about how the play should **look** and **sound** to the audience. As with the style of a production, the director should have strong **initial ideas** that can be discussed and developed throughout the production period. Specialist designers then complete the detailed design work. See pages 41–67 for more about costume, lighting, set and sound design.

Interpreting location

Some playwrights give an indication of the **location** in which a scene should be set. Others avoid specific detail, leaving it to the director and designers to create the location in a way that fits the **style** of the production. Different styles can therefore lead to very different interpretations of location.

For example, the 'wood' location in DNA could be approached differently to fulfill a different directorial vision. For instance, the floor space might have been covered with grass and leaves for a more naturalistic feel.

Sometimes, a director may choose to set the whole play in a different location to the one originally intended by the playwright. For more about this, turn to page 33.

Presenting location

In Dennis Kelly's *DNA*, three different locations are given: a street; a field; a wood. How these locations are presented, though, is very open to interpretation.

This 2012 production of *DNA* uses **projection** on to narrow **flats** (flat pieces of stage scenery) and a bare stage to set the scene.

Plays are set in a particular time periods for various reasons. This may be for historical accuracy, or because the playwright is using the piece as a metaphor for contemporary events, but wishes to distance the audience members from their own experiences.

Presenting time

As with location, a director might choose to set the play in a different **time period** – and this may affect the style of the production. For example, directors often move Shakespeare's plays around in time (and location). They might do this to emphasise a particular aspect of the text or to make the play more relevant to a contemporary audience. See page 33 for more about choosing a time period.

For example, different productions of *Twelfth Night* have been set in various time periods, allowing directors to put their own spin on this versatile comedy. For instance, in 2006 the Auckland Theatre Company set *Twelfth Night* on a tropical island in the 1950s; in 2015, Bedlam's production set the play in a modern, post-college era.

This 2011 production of *Twelfth Night*, from The Original Theatre Company, is set in India in 1947, in the last days of the British Empire. Notice the impact of the choice of time on the style of the production.

Now try this

Decide which locations and time periods are important in your performance text. Give **two** ideas about how you could represent location and time in your initial ideas for your set.

Make sure your suggestions are consistent with your overall vision and the central message you want to communicate.

Blocking

The key to communicating the message and themes of a play to an audience often relies on the performers. A director must work carefully and in collaboration with the performers to create maximum impact for the audience.

Blocking

Blocking is where the director positions the performers on the stage. Successful blocking will achieve several different things.

1. It will establish the desired **dramatic effect**, emphasising the relationships, events or emotions of the characters.

2. It will allow **lighting** to be used effectively.

3. It will create clear **sightlines** for the audience, ensuring the action is visible from all angles and that all opportunities to convey the narrative are taken. Blocking is closely linked to proxemics. Turn to page 39 to find out more.

Careful blocking in this 2009 production of *An Inspector Calls* provides **depth** and **focus** on stage as well as creating an ominous atmosphere.

Areas of a stage

To understand how blocking works, it is helpful to be familiar with the different areas of a stage. Different types of **staging** require different considerations in terms of blocking and **audience awareness**. Go to page 29 for more about different types of staging.

Here are the areas of a traditional 'end-on' stage.

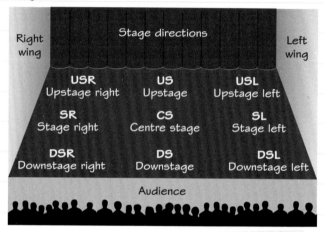

Notice how the areas – such as 'stage left' – are from the perspective of the performer, not the audience. Using the correct terms in rehearsals helps performers understand quickly and effectively what the director has in mind.

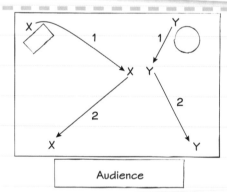

A very simple stage plan, with arrows to indicate where performers X and Y move from and to.

The value of a stage plan

When a director has fully considered the blocking, it is important to make a **record** of what has been decided. This will help not only the performers, but also the production and design teams as they develop their ideas.

A stage plan can be of great use to the whole production team, providing a clear and permanent record of the decisions that have been made.

Choose **one** key scene from your performance text. Consider which characters are on stage. Explain where you would position them to create the maximum impact for your audience.

Remember that even characters in a scene who have no lines to deliver can have a strong impact. Think about the relationships between the characters on stage as well as their status.

Stage business, relationships and proxemics

A director must work with performers on how to approach the text and their characters. For example, a director will help a performer to understand their character's **backstory** and **relationships**, as well as to develop the character's mannerisms as part of **stage business**.

Stage business

Stage business focuses on the **smaller**, more **detailed** movements or gestures a performer can make to convey the central message of the production or specific character traits.

How a character eats or drinks is worth considering. For example, gulping might suggest greed or haste, whereas sipping could suggest politeness or nervousness.

Playing with a mobile phone might suggest a character is absorbed in a world of their own – or is deliberately ignoring what is going on around them.

A character fiddling with their hair or clothing, or drumming their fingers, might give the idea of boredom, impatience or nervousness.

A character who wears glasses might remove them and point with them to suggest they are angry or trying to make a point.

Relationships

Relationships are fundamental to the development of **conflict** and **tension** – and therefore drama – in plays. A director must have a strong understanding of all of the relationships in a play, and how these affect each character throughout the piece. This may involve researching a character's history or background for the time period before the action of the play begins. This is known as a character's backstory, and can help to add context. You can find out more about backstory on page 19.

Proxemics

Proxemics, or **spatial positioning**, needs careful consideration from the director. This is about where a performer should stand in relation to other performers and any objects in a scene. Proxemics:

- is closely linked to blocking and the representation of relationships
- can have a powerful impact on what the audience understands about the message and emotions on stage
- requires consideration of what the audience can actually see. Carefully planned **sightlines** can give the audience a lot of contextual information.

For example, in *The Crucible*, when Proctor and Abigail are alone for the first time, a director may position them relatively **close** to one another, to hint at their past relationship. As it becomes clear that Proctor is no longer interested in restarting the affair, the **proxemics** will change: a director is likely to increase the space between the characters. If Proctor is positioned downstage and Abigail upstage, but both face the audience, the sightlines will mean the audience can see the anguish on John's face when Abigail taunts him about his wife. For more on proxemics, turn to page 13.

Now try this

Choose **one** key scene from your performance text and **one** character in that scene. List appropriate stage business that would help to convey the characterisation and reinforce the message of the play.

Consider the smaller, personal gestures and movements a performer would use to represent their character. Link this with the context of the scene.

Characterisation and style

Some of the most important decisions a director will make are about **how** a performer interprets a role and the **style** in which the role should be interpreted.

Characterisation

Characterisation is the way a performer plays a role. A performer will often have very strong opinions about how a role should be interpreted. However, the director will also have ideas, and these will relate to all of the different elements considered throughout this section on the role of the director. The most effective progress will often be made when the performer and director work together and discuss ideas.

A director must have an overall vision for each character.

- Who are they?
- Where have they come from (physically and emotionally)?
- Are they a comic or a serious character?
- What is the function of the character within the play as a whole?

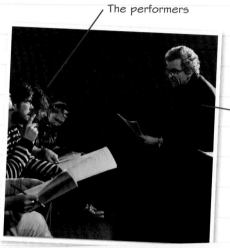
The performers

The director

Before the rehearsal period starts, a director will meet with all members of the cast and crew to outline their vision and ideas. When meeting with the performers, the director will explain what is required from each character and, in general terms, how that character should be portrayed.

Consistency of style

Consistency is the key to success, and the director must always make sure that the development of the characters is in line with the overall style of the production. See page 28 for more about style.

A performer

The director

A director and performer discuss characterisation during rehearsals. Because the performer will be constantly trying to develop their character, discussions like this will happen throughout the entire rehearsal process. Similarly, the director, being the central decision-maker, will also work with the costume and set designers to ensure the selected style is applied consistently across all aspects of the production.

An ongoing process

Characterisation and performance style continue to be the responsibility of the director all the way through the rehearsal process. Even in the **dress rehearsal** or in the early stages of the production run, a director might be:

- suggesting different ways to deliver a specific line or to emphasise a specific moment in a relationship
- reminding the performers about the central message of the piece. The central message, like style, can affect the approach to characterisation.

For example, if the style is expressionism, a character might need to use exaggerated physical gestures to help portray key information to an audience.

Now try this

Choose **one** character and **one** scene from your performance text. As a director, consider **two** ways in which you might direct a performer to play the role at this point in the play. Then select the approach you prefer and give reasons for your choice.

Be clear about what you would like the audience to understand about the character (in terms of personality, motives, relationships with others, and so on). Then provide **two** contrasting options about how you might ask a performer to play the role.

The costume designer

A costume designer must be able to support the overall concept of the performance and communicate key aspects of the play and character to an audience.

Working with the director – From the start of the production process, the costume designer needs to be aware of the director's overall vision for the performance and make suggestions, using specialist knowledge of costume design, that are consistent with the director's vision.

Creativity – The costume designer needs to be able to use costume to represent symbolically key moments of the play and the play's different characters.

Problem solving – The costume designer needs to be able to work systematically to avoid and resolve problems in all stages of costume design and manufacture.

Working with performers – The costume designer needs to ensure the costumes fit, create the desired look and can be used practically on stage, for example allowing the performer to move freely. They will need to make any necessary adjustments.

Producing preliminary designs – The costume designer will need to create initial ideas for the costume design. The director will check that the proposed costumes are consistent with the overall vision for the play and support the work of the play's other designers (such as set, sound and lighting designers).

The role of the costume designer

Working with costume makers – The costume designer needs to find the right materials for each costume and make them to the highest standard.

Researching – The costume designer needs to carry out careful research to check that the costume designs are appropriate for the specific time period or location of the play.

Understanding the themes of the play – The costume designer needs to ensure that the costumes represent the play's themes to an audience. For example, threadbare costumes in 1984 would represent the harsh life faced by some of those living under the regime.

Understanding the overall message of the performance – The costume designer needs to understand how the costumes reflect the message of the play and the different characters. For example, high-quality, black costumes would suit the high status of Puritan judges in The Crucible.

Pre-production

The costume designer works with the director and other designers long before rehearsals start.

To help shape the production, the costume designer needs to:

✓ have a clear and full understanding of the play

✓ share and develop ideas about the text, themes, issues and characters.

For example, a play about the Hillsborough disaster might include the following helpful information for a costume designer:

- The opening scene is set in a casualty ward in Sheffield, in 1989.
- The play cross-cuts between the events of 1989 and the inquests of 2014 to 2016.
- The stage is often very busy so there must be a clear contrast between the football fans, medical staff and police officers.

Using the stage directions

Two Ambulance Workers, *in uniform, carry a stretcher. On the stretcher is an unconscious Liverpool* Fan *wearing a blood-stained, 1989 Liverpool FC away top. They are followed by a* Police Officer, *also in uniform.*

The clues to the time period and the types of characters can be found in the stage directions.

For example, a play about the Hillsborough disaster might include the following helpful information for a costume designer:
- The opening scene is set in a casualty ward in Sheffield, in 1989.
- The play cross-cuts between the events of 1989 and the inquests of 2014 to 2016.
- The stage is often very busy so there must be a clear contrast between the football fans, medical staff and police officers.

Now try this

What do you think are the most important skills a costume designer should have? Explain why you have chosen those particular skills.

Costume and context

If a performance is to flow and be consistent, it is vital to ensure that the costume designs fit with the play's overall design concept. Therefore, each costume-design decision needs to be considered in the wider context of the performance as a whole.

General design concept

While a playwright might indicate how the play should be set, directors often look for new, creative approaches.

At the start of the production process, a director works closely with a team of designers. Each designer must be clear about the overall design concept and work to achieve it.

Fundamental elements that may influence the overall design concept are:

- the location in which the play is set
- the time in which the play is set
- the style of the production
- the genre of the play
- the space used to stage the production
- portability (whether the production is touring).

Symbolism

Costume design is effective when it conveys messages about the plot and the characters to the audience. These messages can be very obvious or quite subtle.

Symbolism is where the costume (or part of a costume) represents something more than its surface meaning. See page 27 for more on symbolism.

Costume can be used to:

- show social status or wealth/poverty
- show a change in a character's fortunes
- show location, such as a tropical island or snow-bound Siberia
- indicate the time period of the play
- represent themes
- create mood and atmosphere.

Status

A character's **status** can be clearly represented through different combinations of materials, colours and accessories.

- **Higher status** can be indicated through neat, expensive, clean and well-fitting clothes.
- **Lower status** can be shown through dirty, torn, damaged and ill-fitting clothes.

In the Comedy Theatre's 2000 production of Harold Pinter's *The Caretaker*, the contrast between Davies's lower status as a tramp and Aston's higher status is symbolised through costume.

Character traits

Costume can be used to show how a character behaves or feels, and their personal habits. For example, if a character is depressed, they may take little care in their appearance and personal hygiene, and look scruffy and dirty. If a character is trying to impress someone, they may take great care about how they look.

Costume and context

Costume is key to communicating the social, historical and cultural context to an audience. It makes clear the wider context in which the play is set and therefore allows the audience to gain a deeper understanding of the play.

Now try this

Select a character or characters from your performance text. List key information about the character or characters and consider how each of those elements might be symbolised through costume design.

Aspects of costume

For this course, costume design does not just refer to the clothes worn by the performers. It can also refer to the accessories, hair, make-up and masks. For more on accessories and masks, turn to page 45. To find out more about hair and make-up, go to page 46.

Character type and location – The type of character or location may require that certain materials are worn. For example, Dr Maudsley in *Blue Stockings* is a pompous academic, a member of the aristocracy and delivering a formal lecture, so he would be dressed in a cap and gown with a rich, formal suit underneath, all of which would reflect the fashion of the late 19th century.

Pros and cons – Each different type of material has its own benefits and drawbacks. For example, cotton and wool can be very hot to wear, although they can be easily dyed.

Ease of care – Costumes need to be robust, as they will be used repeatedly.

Noise – Will it be too noisy? For example, the noise a full suit of armour makes could be distracting for the audience.

Materials and practicality

Authenticity – It is important to consider whether certain materials were available during the time period in which the production is set. For example, until the invention of modern synthetic dyes in the mid-1800s, the colours of fabrics were limited.

Ease of use – How easy is it to get the costume on and off?

Heat – Will the costume become too hot under stage lighting?

Weight – Will this hinder movement?

Length and size – Will it get in the way?

Effective costumes must be practical for performers to use on stage. So it is important to consider the types of materials used. See page 44 for more on different materials and page 47 for more about practicalities.

Accessories

A costume designer must consider the accessories a character might need, such as a bag, a handkerchief or a watch.

Make-up

Make-up provides visual clues about character. Costume designers must consider how much to use and the style required.

Different genres may need different styles, for example:

- a pantomime dame, often played by a man, may need lots of heavy make-up

- a naturalistic play may use minimal make-up to highlight facial features and minimise glare from the lights.

Make-up can also help to represent injuries or wounds; illness or health; and non-human or deceased characters.

Masks

Some playwrights make deliberate use of masks, for example to represent dream/nightmare sequences.

A costume designer could include masks for a variety of reasons, in naturalistic and non-naturalistic productions.

When choosing masks, the costume designer must consider:

- the impact required
- whether to use a full- or half-face mask
- colours
- the expression of the mask
- how the mask will affect a performer's vision and, if necessary, speech.

Hair

Hairstyles can be an effective addition to costume. They can:

👍 show the fashions of the time period in which the play is set

👍 help represent other important elements of a character, such as:

- age (grey hair may represent old age)
- status (is the style well-kept or unkempt?)
- situation (what has been happening to the character?).

Now try this

Take a character in a key scene from your performance text. Explain how you would use hair, make-up and accessories (including masks if appropriate) to represent the key elements of the character in that scene.

Materials and colours

The choice of materials used in costume design can have a significant impact on how effective the end results are. Key messages such as character **status** can be communicated through colour in costume design.

Cotton
- 👍 Easy to dye or alter
- 👍 Cheap and easy to replace
- 👎 Can rip easily and is slow to dry when wet

Wool
- 👍 Strong
- 👎 Can be very hot under stage lights
- 👎 Becomes heavy when wet and may be itchy

Velvet
- 👍 Gives a very luxurious look for high-status characters
- 👎 Can be expensive

Lace
- 👍 Excellent for enhancing costume
- 👎 Is often finely detailed, a feature that cannot be appreciated by audience members at a distance

Leather
- 👍 Can provide an authentic look for specific eras and genres
- 👎 Can be difficult to alter and gets hot under stage lights

Metal
- 👍 Can give an authentic look to some costumes
- 👍 Modern metals can be a lot thinner (and lighter) than older varieties
- 👍 Can be used for accessories
- 👎 Polished metal can reflect the lights and dazzle the audience
- 👎 Can be noisy and heavy

Plastic/PVC
- 👍 Lightweight alternative to leather or metal when sprayed (for example, for armour)
- 👍 Does not make excessive noise
- 👎 Not breathable so can become sweaty

Materials used in costume design

The use of colour in costume design

The careful use of **colours** can help to provide the audience with **strong visual information**. Different colours can mean different things and so **colour symbolism** must be considered in the context of the play's whole design.

Colours and symbolism

- Pink – compassion, love, femininity
- Grey – boring, plain, oppression, routine
- Red – danger, blood, passion, love, fear
- Brown – earth, dirt, nature
- Green – nature, growth, innocence, progress, jealousy
- Purple – royalty, high status, power
- Blue – opportunity, depth, strength, truthfulness, water, cold
- White – purity, innocence, goodness, faith
- Black – night, evil, high status, mystery, death
- Yellow – light, joy, youth, energy

For example, in *1984*, Julia wears a narrow scarlet sash. This symbolises the Anti-Sex League, but the deep red colour also represents her own passion and love for Winston.

Now try this

Choose **one** character from your performance text. Explain how you would use colour in the costume design to communicate the character's status to an audience.

Colour, while being only one aspect of consideration for costume designers, can be a very important visual aid to the audience. Carefully consider the use of colours in the costume. What would these colours communicate to an audience?

Accessories and masks

The clothing worn by the performer often makes up the majority of the costume. Adding accessories provides detail and finishing touches, and makes the costume effective and successful.

Accessories

These:

- include a huge range of items that provide detail and even more clues to the character and narrative
- could be part of the worn costume, such as a **sword** or a **handkerchief**, or carried by the performer, such as a **bag** or **umbrella**
- add **depth** and detail to the character, highlighting or emphasising **specific traits** or information for the audience.
- should always be **consistent** with the rest of the costume (unless for a specific reason, for example a plot twist).

Designers need to consider the **time** frame, **location**, wealth and **status** of the character and ensure all accessories are **practical** for the performer to use.

Siân Phillips as Lady Bracknell in a 2014 production of *The Importance of Being Earnest*. Note the effective use of accessories – umbrella, handbag, gloves, earrings and hat – to complete the look of authority, high status and wealth.

Masks

Masks can:

- provide a range of opportunities for designers and directors to create interesting ways of communicating specific ideas and characters to an audience
- provide a character with anonymity
- help to portray death or some other 'otherworldly' qualities
- help to create a contrast between different groups of performers, for example, between a chorus and the main protagonists
- be used to show human performers playing animals, such as in *The Lion King* or *The Valkyrie*.

Remember, the use of masks is not appropriate to every style and genre; they should be used carefully.

In the 2014 Gods and Monsters Theatre production of *The Valkyrie*, the performers wore symbolic masks to create a team of horses. This effective method provided the performers with:
- huge flexibility in terms of movement and being able to use voice effectively
- the possibility of playing multiple roles
- the ability to portray the key narrative in a simple, controlled and yet creative way.

Now try this

Take a character from a key scene in your performance text. Explain the accessories you would use help to communicate the key aspects of the character in that scene to an audience.

Be very clear about your reason for including each accessory, and think how it will enhance the audience experience.

Make-up and hair

The use of make-up and hairstyling can have a dramatic impact on an overall costume.

Make-up

Make-up can provide a finishing touch to a costume and help to enhance the character being portrayed.

- In a **naturalistic** performance, the make-up tends to be quite **subtle** and will often use soft colours. Eyeliner, foundation and blusher may help to provide definition to faces.

> Without make-up, a performer's face can appear 'washed out' under bright stage lights.

- Make-up can be used to create **wounds** or **scars**, helping to communicate important moments in the narrative.

> For example, in the play *Macbeth*, when the ghost of Banquo appears to Macbeth at the feast, the wounds and injuries from his murder can be made clear to the audience visually.

- In some performances, more **abstract make-up** may be appropriate. For example, in *Twelfth Night*, the fool, Feste, may use clown-like make-up to indicate his role more clearly.

The pale skin created by white make-up and the deep, dark eye sockets, emphasised by black eyeshadow, gives The Woman in Black a haunted, deathly look in Stephen Mallatratt's 1989 adaptation of the novel. This, when combined with the gothic costume and clever use of lighting, creates a terrifying effect that has had a profound and chilling impact on audiences for many years.

> Theatre forms from various different cultures use make-up extensively, such as Japanese Kabuki Theatre and Indian Kathakali Theatre.

Hair

Hairstyles communicate clear messages to an audience. The chosen hair design needs to complement:

- the **style** of the production
- character **type** and **age**
- the **era** in which the play is set.

Aspects of hair design include the following:

- **Hair colour** can be altered through use of **dyes**.
- Hair can be **cut** into specific **styles** or even shaved off completely.
- If longer hair is required for a role, **extensions** can be added or **wigs** can be used to quickly create new styles. Baldness can also be created using specialist bald 'wigs'.

> If a play is set over a short period of time, such as *An Inspector Calls*, which takes place over the course of one evening, the characters may only need one hairstyle. In the case of *The Crucible*, which takes place over several months and where Proctor begins with very high status and ends up in prison, a change in hairstyle could help to show his loss of status.

> Wigs enable a performer to change styles quickly within a performance. For example, in *Twelfth Night*, Viola could use a wig to 'become' Cesario, then remove it to reveal her true identity at the end.

Now try this

Select **one** character from your performance text. Consider how you would design their make-up and hair for a key moment in the play. Explain your ideas.

> Consider whether a character would benefit from several different hairstyles throughout the performance or from keeping the same hairstyle.

Practicality and safety

More traditional or original materials can now be represented by modern ones, which can help to make costumes far more **practical** for the performers on stage. A costume designer must also consider important **health and safety** issues in order to keep the performers and audience safe during performances.

Practicality

A costume must enable the performer to work effectively, efficiently and comfortably on stage. The costume:

- must give the performer a clear field of vision so they can see what is on stage
- must allow the performer to move and speak freely, so the audience's experience is not disrupted
- needs to be light enough to allow the performer to move without draining their energy or distracting them
- needs to prevent the performer from becoming excessively hot under strong stage lights
- must not be noisy or in any other way distracting to the audience.

For more on the choice of materials used in costume design, turn to page 44.

A suit of armour made from leather and sprayed plastic gives a very convincing look in the RSC's 2015 production of *Henry V*. These materials make the costume quiet, light and easy to put on, and do not restrict movement in the way metal would.

Health and safety

As a costume designer, there are several things to consider with regard to health and safety.

 Make-up and hairstyles (including products and wigs)

- Care must be taken to ensure that products do not cause **allergic reactions**
- All products must be **flame retardant**.
- Make-up needs to be kept **clean** and care must be taken to avoid **cross-contamination** (germs spreading when the same make-up products are used on different people).

 Clothing and accessories must:

- be flame retardant
- not create a trip hazard
- not be too heavy
- have no sharp edges (for metal/plastic elements).

Care must also be taken that:

- they do not impede movement or vision
- they do not impede breathing or hearing
- materials and dyes do not cause allergic reactions
- where possible, clothing is frequently washed or cleaned.

It is vital that the costume design, including any accessories, hair and make-up, does not put the health and safety of the cast, crew or audience at risk during a performance.

 Now try this

Take a character in a key scene from your performance text. Explain the practical considerations you need to take into account in order to make the performer's costume usable on stage.

Think about how you will make sure the performer is as comfortable as possible while also communicating the scene's message to the audience.

The lighting designer

The **lighting designer** has a major responsibility for designing and conveying the **mood** and **atmosphere** of a performance. They work collaboratively with other designers to help communicate the director's intentions.

The role of the lighting designer

Working with the director – The lighting designer will work with both the director and other designers to ensure ideas are consistent with the creative vision for the performance.

Creative lighting control – The lighting designer must have a clear vision for how the lighting will look in performance and must consider what is possible on stage.

Visual consistency – The lighting designer must ensure the lighting is consistent with all other production elements, to ensure a smooth experience for the audience.

Problem-solving – The lighting designer needs to work to avoid and resolve technical or creative issues that arise.

Selecting colour, shade and tone in the lighting – The lighting designer will select and design colours, levels and angles to communicate specific emotions and ideas to the audience at key moments of the performance.

Creating a lighting plot – The lighting designer will work with a lighting team to ensure the design is created and realised as closely and as practically as possible.

Understanding the themes of the play and the style of the performance – The lighting designer must ensure the design team has a clear understanding of the themes and issues in the play and how these could be communicated to the audience.

Pre-production

The director and wider creative team make a lot of decisions before rehearsals begin. Sometimes the lighting designer will be involved in decision-making from the start, particularly if the lighting plot for the production is going to be challenging practically and is central to the overall feel and tone of the production.

Key elements a lighting designer considers

- 👍 Colour
- 👍 Atmosphere
- 👍 Location
- 👍 Effect
- 👍 Angle
- 👍 Mood
- 👍 Symbolism
- 👍 Time
- 👍 Position

Look at the visual impact of this scene from a production of Joe Masteroff's *She Loves Me* (2016). Consider how blue lighting has been used to convey the evening and how the focus on the performers is enhanced for the audience by the use of a spotlight.

In this production, clear decisions have been made about the use of **colour**; the deep blues suggesting a warm summer evening are contrasted with the deep yellows of the lights inside the buildings. The attention of the audience is directed towards the performers, not only by their position on stage, but also by the use of a soft-edged **spotlight**, **angled** high above the stage and positioned in front of the performers. The **direction** of lights and strong use of colour help to convey both the time of day and a feeling of romance, as the characters on stage kiss.

Now try this

What do you think are the most important skills a lighting designer should have? Explain why you have chosen those particular skills.

Try to consider the different responsibilities a lighting designer has towards the production overall.

Colour, symbolism, mood and atmosphere

Lighting can have a strong impact on a performance – it is essential in communicating key information, and well-designed and effective lighting can support and improve the audience's experience. A lighting designer needs to consider how colour and levels of light can be used to create mood and atmosphere.

Colour

Lighting provides an opportunity to use a vast range of **colours** to enhance a performance. Colours:

- are highly **symbolic**
- can convey situations and emotions clearly to an audience.

See page 44 for more on the symbolism of different colours.

For example, a red light could be used to highlight the passion between two characters. A blue light could be used to emphasise the cold and unnerving atmosphere of woods at night.

Mood and atmosphere

Altering the **level of light** and combining the light with various colours can help to significantly change the **mood** and **atmosphere** of a scene.

- A **low lighting level**, with dark blues, greens or reds, can make the stage very **eerie** and filled with dramatic tension.
- A **high lighting level** of warm, coloured light can produce a very **happy** and **energetic** feeling on stage.

For more on mood and atmosphere, turn to page 35.

The **level of lighting** is how bright or dim the lighting is on stage.

Bright, warm colours, such as yellow and orange, are used at a high level in this National Theatre 2011 production of Richard Bean's *One Man, Two Guvnors*. This creates a happy, positive atmosphere, which emphasises the comedic elements of the play. This is especially effective against a blue (cold) backdrop.

In Nigel Bryant's 2010 stage production of Charles Dickens's *A Christmas Carol*, when the ghost of Marley appeared, pale low-level lighting, using light greens mixed with a blue-tinted white light, contrasted with the darkness. This conveyed a chilling and frightening atmosphere.

Now try this

Select a key moment from your performance text. Decide what mood and atmosphere you would like to create. Discuss which colours and levels of lighting would help you achieve your objectives.

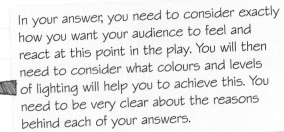

In your answer, you need to consider exactly how you want your audience to feel and react at this point in the play. You will then need to consider what colours and levels of lighting will help you to achieve this. You need to be very clear about the reasons behind each of your answers.

Style, location and era

The selected style of a production will have a strong influence on the style of lighting used. The lighting must be consistent with the director's aims and enhance the performance for the audience. Lighting choices can also help to present the location and era (time period). See page 36 for more on style.

Style: naturalism

A **naturalistic style** is a look and feel that resembles real life. If the selected style of a performance is **naturalism**, then it is important that the lighting reflects this.

- Colours will tend to be quite **neutral** and **evenly spread**.

- The lighting will also need to support other design areas, such as sunlight coming through a window – just as it would in reality.

This highly naturalistic set – from Katie Mitchell's 2014 production of Anton Chekhov's *The Cherry Orchard* – is complemented by the naturalistic lighting. A single ceiling light is enhanced by the blue moonlight coming through the (unseen) windows.

Style: abstract

When something is **abstract**, it doesn't try to represent real life directly. Instead, it attempts to express ideas and feelings about something through elements such as colour and shape. In an abstract performance the lighting:

- may be much more **symbolic**

- will use colours to represent **emotions**.

Strong colours may represent characters or locations, rather than a physical set.

Here, an abstract impression is created through the use of a deep orange colour and backlighting to create silhouettes. Symbolically, this scene might represent the energy and fire of the warriors' fight.

Location

Lighting can be used to convey the **physical** location of a scene, including:

- whether it is **indoors** or **outside**
- the **type** of location (such as a railway station, garden, palace, school)
- the **activities** that take place there.

For example, in Act 1, Scene 8 of *Blue Stockings*, the lighting in Tess's room at night would be relatively bright and cosy, representing the artificial light used indoors. By contrast, the lighting used for the orchard would need to convey the sense of a cold, moonlit night outside, perhaps with shadows from the trees.

Era

Lighting can also be used to indicate the **time period** in which a scene is set.

For example, in *The Crucible*, the lighting in the prison needs to reflect the era in which the play is set. A prison cell in Salem in 1692 would be dark and dingy, lit by small windows and burning torches or candles. By contrast, a modern 21st-century prison cell would have larger windows, allowing more natural light into the cell; it would be lit using artificial electric light, which would give a brighter, even spread of light.

Now try this

Select a location from your performance text. Consider how you would represent the location using lighting. Give reasons to support your ideas.

 Consider the time of day and the style of your performance when creating your lighting design.

Types of lantern

Different types of lighting can produce a range of effects to enhance the audience's visual experience of the performance. There are four key types of lighting used by designers and technicians: **profile spotlight**; **soft-edged spotlight**; **floodlight**; and **parcans**.

Key lighting types

1 **Profile spotlight**

👍 Produces a sharp, clearly defined edge

👍 Excellent for highlighting specific performers or areas

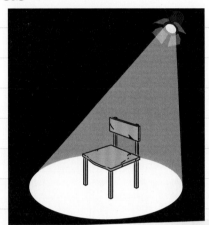

Here, the spotlight creates a stark contrast with the unlit areas of the stage, ensuring the focus of the audience is directed towards the empty chair.

2 **Soft-edged spotlight**

👍 Enables the lighting of precise areas

👍 Easier to blend into other lighting effects

Soft-edged spotlights are combined with floodlights in the lighting for this scene from a 2004 production of Schiller's *Don Carlos*. Although all areas of the stage are lit and the edges of the spotlight cannot be identified, it is still clear which areas are being highlighted.

3 **Floodlight**

👍 Provides a lot of light to a wide area

👍 Useful for general lighting of stage areas and backdrops

👎 Lack of control prevents lighting of specific performers

Some floodlights, known as Codas, include three or four floodlights to support colour mixing.

4 **Parcans**

👍 Versatile lamp that provides a narrower focus than a floodlight

👍 Best used for lighting large areas and providing intense colours

👎 Lack of control prevents lighting of specific performers

Parcans were used to mix reds and blues together, giving a warm, late-night feel to this party scene in a 2016 production of Masteroff's *She Loves Me* at the Menier Chocolate Factory in London.

Now try this

Choose **one** – or a combination – of the lighting design techniques mentioned on this page, and explain how it could be useful in a production of your performance text.

Consider the effect you want to create for your chosen scene and then decide which lighting technique – or combination of techniques – will help you achieve this.

Lighting angles

It is not just the type of light a designer uses that is important, but also the **position** from which the light is directed. By placing lamps in a variety of locations, both light and **shadow** can be manipulated to give some very interesting effects.

High front light

High front light and **downlight** are the most common position for lighting, placing the lamps **above** and **in front of** the performers. This provides a clear and **natural effect**, which imitates similar angles we have become used to (such as the sun or streetlight). Additionally, if a downlight is placed directly above a performer, it can create mysterious shadow effects.

The clear, bright lighting from above helps give the impression of an office in daytime for this 2013 National Theatre production of *Othello*.

Up-light

An effectively used **up-light** can direct shadows and create high levels of **suspense**, making its use perfect for building **tension** or **horror** scenes.

In this scene from *The Woman in Black*, the up-light highlights the woman's pale skin and deep, dark eye sockets, giving her a haunted, deathly look. The shadows cast on the woman's clothing and the background enhance the effect.

Backlight/silhouette

Backlight can be used to create **shadows** and, at times, obscure the audience's view, creating a very **mysterious effect**. It can also effectively imply morning or evening, times when a low sun often reduces visual clarity.

Shadow is where a backlight is used to project something or someone onto a screen between the object/person and the audience.
Silhouette does not use a screen. Rather, the backlight prevents the audience seeing detailed features of the person/object.

Shadow theatre can be incredibly effective, enabling performers to communicate many different ideas.

Side light

Lighting a scene from the **side** can produce an **abstract** effect. It may imply a different **location** off-stage, or as with backlighting, can use shadow to give a feeling of mystery.

Mixing white with blue, the use of side lighting in this production of *An Inspector Calls* helps to provide **depth** and **focus** on stage as well as creating an ominous atmosphere.

Now try this

Think of **one** key moment in your performance text. Consider how some of the lighting angles described above might help to enhance or communicate your ideas about that key moment to an audience.

Consider what you want the performance to convey at this point and then decide which lighting angle would help you design the most effective impact for your audience. Consider colours and lighting levels to help make the most of the lighting angles you have chosen.

Gels, barn doors and gobos

Light can be manipulated in a range of ways to create different effects. **Gels** and **colour changers** can alter the colour of bright white light; **barn doors** help to shut out light from specific areas of the performance stage; and **gobos** produce patterns and shadows in lighting.

Gels

Gels are sheets of coloured plastic that can be placed in front of a lantern to alter the colour of the light. These can be cut to the required size and shape. A **gel holder** holds the gel in place.

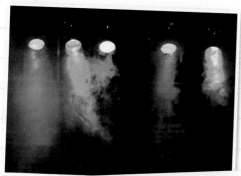

Gels help to change the colour of bright white light, so providing a range of colour lighting options for the lighting designer.

Colour changer

A **colour changer** is a powered **reel** that contains a range of gels. The reel can be **controlled remotely**, enabling one lantern to produce different colours. This provides a wider range of possibilities for a lighting designer.

A **reel** is a cylinder on which flexible material – in this case plastic gels – can be wound.

In a **colour changer**, a roll of gels, joined together, scroll across the lantern, enabling the colours to be changed remotely.

Barn door

A **barn door** is made of metal and consists of **four hinged flaps** fitted in front of a lantern. The flaps can be positioned to block the light from reaching specific areas of the performance stage. They provide the lighting designer with another level of control over the positioning of lights.

Lighting can be directed by moving the barn doors in (which blocks off light) or out.

Gobo

Gobos are **small discs** that are placed in front of a light. **Patterns** and **shapes** cut into the discs are projected onto the stage in the form of **shadows**. This helps to convey a sense of location and adds extra depth to a lighting design.

This tree and leaf effect gobo provides an indication of both location and time, as well as making the space interesting to look at.

Now try this

Select a key moment from your performance text. Explain how you might use a gobo to enhance the performance for the audience.

Gobos can indicate specific locations. They may also enhance a mood or atmosphere.

Structure and focus

Lighting can support the structure of a play by indicating the beginning and end of scenes as well as changes in location or situation. These changes in the lights can occur suddenly or more gradually.

Structure and focus in a scene

One of the subtlest ways to indicate the structure of a scene is through effective use of lighting. For example:

- **Fading the lights up** from a **blackout** indicates to the audience that the play or scene is starting.
- Similarly, **fading the lights down** to a blackout may indicate the play or scene is ending.

However, it is also possible to support techniques such as **split scene** more effectively by using lighting. Lighting two different parts of the stage and then **cross fading** between the two can indicate two different locations or time periods. This will help the audience to understand any change in scene.

Cross fade – Similar to a fade, a cross fade occurs when one lighting state gradually fades out while the next lighting state fades in. This allows smooth transitions between different lighting states.

State – This refers to which lights are being used at any one time.

Blackout – This signifies all the lights going out at once and can be a strong signal at the start or end of a scene, an act or a whole play. Blackouts can also create a sudden moment of tension, leaving the audience in total darkness. However, they should be used sparingly so they do not disrupt the pace and flow of the performance for the audience.

Fade – This technique gradually brings in or takes out a lighting state. The exact amount of time required for a fade can be pre-determined and programmed into the lighting desk. Therefore, a fade can be fast or it can happen very gradually over a long period – for example, to represent a sunrise over a whole scene.

States, cues and light changes

Snap – This is where the lighting suddenly changes from one state to another. A snap can be used effectively to create tension or to signify a change of situation in a performance; for example, when a character goes from being part of a scene to directly addressing the audience.

Cue – This is the indicator of when the next lighting state should take place. Often, the cue will be a specific line the performer says or a move the performer makes.

By using pools of light and keeping areas of the stage dark, this lighting designer has helped indicate two zones of focus. By fading up one section and fading down the other, the attention of the audience can be effectively directed to the required part of the stage.

Select a scene from your performance text and consider where you would like to focus the audience's attention. Discuss how you could use lighting successfully to achieve this.

Remember to consider the layout of the stage as well as what is happening before and after the scene. You can then consider how to use levels and colours of lighting, as well as areas of shadow or darkness.

The set designer

The **set designer** is responsible for creating the **physical location** in which the performers work. The **set** helps indicate where scenes are set and conveys **important messages** to the **audience**. The set designer works **collaboratively** with other designers to help communicate the director's intentions.

Creative intentions – The set designer must have a clear vision for how the set will look in performance and consider what is possible in the chosen performance space.

Working with the director – The set designer will work with both the director and other designers to ensure ideas are consistent with the overall creative feel of the performance.

Creating a set design – The set designer will work with a construction team to ensure the set design is created and realised as closely and as practically as possible.

The role of the set designer

Visual consistency – The set designer must ensure the set is consistent with all other production elements, to ensure a smooth visual experience for the audience.

Selecting levels, space, entrances and exits – The set designer must select and design the most effective use of space, levels and entrances/exits to communicate specific locations and ideas to the audience at key moments of the performance.

Understanding the themes of the play and the style of the performance – The set designer must ensure the design team (including the set builders) has a clear understanding of the themes and issues in the play and how these could be communicated to the audience.

The work of a set designer pre-production

The director and the wider creative team make many decisions before the rehearsals begin. Sometimes the set designer is involved in decision-making from a very early stage, particularly if the set for the production is going to be complicated and integral to the overall feel and tone of the production.

Key elements a set designer needs to consider

- 👍 Space
- 👍 Materials
- 👍 Colours
- 👍 Location
- 👍 Levels
- 👍 Entrances/exits
- 👍 Symbolism
- 👍 Time

Using the playwright's stage directions

[*The dining room of a small, Victorian, end-of-terrace house, once surrounded by fields and now on the outer fringes of the retail area of a small, provincial town. Some of the furniture is new, modern but with hint of the traditional in its design. Other items are worn, and in need of repair or replacement. The numerous bookcases, which dominate the room, are overflowing with books, reflecting the owner's occupation as a writer. The dining table itself, and several side tables, are similarly buried in books and manuscripts. A small desk under the tall window holds a lamp and a laptop computer, with several mugs and the remains of a meal.*]

Here, the playwright has been detailed in outlining a vision for a scene, which will be helpful to the set designer.

While some playwrights offer very little information, others outline their ideas very clearly. For example, in Act 1 of *An Inspector Calls*, J.B. Priestley includes a great deal of detail. This makes it clear that he wants the set to **reflect** both the **era** (1912) and the substantial **wealth** of the family, in order to provide the audience with an instant context. The domination of the dining table gives a very clear indication as to the room in which the action takes place, as well as conveying to the audience what the Birling family are doing.

What do you think are the most important skills a set designer should have? Explain why you have chosen those particular skills.

Try to consider the different **responsibilities** a set designer has towards the production overall.

Style and genre

Very often, the **set** is the first thing an audience sees. Therefore, the **initial impression** of the set needs to provide the audience with a sense of the **style** or **genre** of the performance and help place the rest of the production in **context**. For more on genre and style, turn to pages 28 and 36.

Naturalistic set design

A naturalistic set strives to look as **realistic** as possible. A set designer will spend a great deal of time researching, designing, creating and sourcing elements such as furniture, wall coverings and flooring, so they look exactly as they would in **real** life.

This highly naturalistic set is from Katie Mitchell's 2014 production of Anton Chekhov's *The Cherry Orchard*.

Abstract set design

An abstract set tends to be much more **symbolic** and **representative** than a naturalistic set. A set designer will consider

the play's themes and issues and seek to use the set design to convey these to the audience.

The set for the 2011 National Theatre production of *Frankenstein* combined strong symbolic elements, such as an array of light bulbs, to represent the electricity used to bring the Creature to life.

Set design for physical theatre

Physical theatre often relies heavily on the set to help support the performers and style of production. The set may need to be **adapted** so it provides opportunities for the performers to use the space in **unusual ways**, from different directions and at different levels.

In Franz Kafka's play *Metamorphosis*, the main character (Gregor) wakes to find he has transformed into a huge insect-like creature. This 2013 set for the play, at the Lyric Hammersmith, has built in **grip points**, allowing the performer to move around the whole set in an insect-like way.

Minimalist set design

Minimalist sets tend to be brought right **back to basics**. However, the set designer may decide to make what is there extremely **symbolic**. It may also be that, while there is a lack of physical material on stage, the use of colour plays a prominent part in **conveying ideas** about the performance.

A single bench on an empty stage under a single light is all that is needed for this 2006 production of *Come and Go* by Samuel Beckett, at the Barbican Centre, London.

Now try this

Consider all of the different scenes and locations in your performance text. Which style would you use for your set design? Give reasons and examples to support your ideas.

Remember to remain **consistent** with the **style** of your production when creating your set design.

Colours, location and time

The use of **colour** in a set can help give the audience vital **clues** about a performance, such as the play's key moments. The set is also central to establishing the **location** of the action, as well as the **time period** in which the action takes place.

Colour and set design

The colours used within a set can help to enhance the performance. Colours are highly **symbolic** and can convey situations and emotions clearly to an audience.

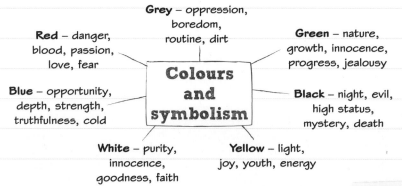

Grey – oppression, boredom, routine, dirt

Red – danger, blood, passion, love, fear

Green – nature, growth, innocence, progress, jealousy

Blue – opportunity, depth, strength, truthfulness, cold

Colours and symbolism

Black – night, evil, high status, mystery, death

White – purity, innocence, goodness, faith

Yellow – light, joy, youth, energy

See page 49 for more on colour, symbolism, mood and atmosphere.

The pale grey used in this 2012 set for English National Opera's production of *Jakob Lenz* emphasises the cold and wild environment.

Location

Depending on the style of the production, the set can represent the location (or locations) in various different ways.

A designer must consider the following.

- How much space is available?
- What is the style/genre of the production?
- Are multiple locations required in a short space of time?
- Are locations repeated?
- In what era is the play set?
- What mood/atmosphere should the location communicate to an audience?

For example:

- In *Twelfth Night*, Olivia's house is repeatedly used as a location.
- *DNA* uses the same three locations – a street, a field and a wood – in a cyclical way.
- *An Inspector Calls* only has one location but is clearly set in 1912.
- *Blue Stockings* is set in a clearly defined era and has relatively short scenes set in many different locations.

Time period

As directors reinterpret plays for specific **target audiences**, the role of the set designer is vital in helping the audience to understand the **context** of a performance. The use of furniture or construction styles from specific eras can provide helpful clues about when – as well as where – the performance is set.

While not a **naturalistic** set, the stone balustrade used in this 2009 production of a reworking of the story of *Romeo and Juliet* represents a traditional setting for Bellini's *I Capuleti e i Montecchi*.

Now try this

Take a key scene from your performance text. What are the key themes/issues in the scene? How could you represent these themes/issues to your audience by using colour within the set design?

Remember to consider how the colour of the set can help to represent the **mood** and **atmosphere** you want to convey to your audience.

Practicality, health and safety

A set designer needs to make sure the set is **practical** to use for both the performers and crew. The **construction** of the set must also take into consideration the **health and safety** of the performers, the crew and the audience.

Practicality

An effective set not only needs to look good, it must be practical for the performers to use. A designer must consider whether there is enough space for the performers to:

- move around without **tripping** over
- step up **levels** easily
- be able to get to **different parts** of the set quickly and safely.

In this 2016 production of *The Go-Between* at the Apollo Theatre, London, the designer carefully positioned the chairs to provide as much space as possible for the performers, as well as options for entrances and a clear **focal point**.

Touring productions

Designing a set for a touring production presents a range of additional challenges. The designer must consider:

- the **different venues** that will be visited
- how to make the set **portable**
- how to make the set as simple to **construct** or **strike** as possible.

This 2013 set for *Treasure Island* at the Exeter Phoenix is easily transported and quick to put together. It also gives a clear sense of location and is creatively **adaptable** for the whole of the performance.

Health and safety

It is vital that the set design, including props, does not put the **health and safety** of the cast, crew or audience at risk during a performance.

Can the set be **moved/changed** easily, without injury to cast or crew?

Are all materials used on set **flame retardant** and resistant to heat (from the lighting)?

Is anything on set a **trip hazard**?

Is the set easy to **clean** and **maintain**?

Health and safety aspects a set designer must consider

Is everything on set **secure and stable** – could it fall or collapse?

Does any part of the set have **sharp edges** (especially metal/plastic elements)?

Are all **levels** of the set **secure**, to prevent falling? Does any part of the set **impede** performers' movements, vision, breathing or hearing?

Could any materials used on set trigger **allergic reactions** or are they **dangerous substances** (such as asbestos)?

Now try this

Design a set for a touring production of your performance text. Describe how you would make the set as portable as possible, without affecting the quality of the overall design.

Remember that a touring production will visit different locations that will have a range of facilities and staging limitations, so the set design needs to be as adaptable as possible.

Props and stage furniture

Props and **stage furniture** can provide the audience with important information about character, location and situation.

Props

Props (short for 'stage properties' or 'theatrical properties') are moveable items a performer uses on stage. The term can refer to any object that is part of the performance, but it does not include costume or scenery.

> Props help to enhance the performance for an audience.

Props must:
- be designed with the **overall costume style** in mind
- **complement** the main costume design
- be **consistent** with the main costume in terms of colours and materials
- be **practical** to use on stage
- be **safe** for the performers, crew and audience.

> Props are most effective when they help to communicate key information.

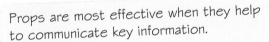

Stage furniture

The term stage furniture refers to parts of the set that the performers can use or move during the performance, but which cannot be defined as personal props.

Like props, stage furniture can play an important role in communicating key information to an audience. This can include:
- the **location** of the action
- the **time period** in which the play is set
- the **style** of the production
- the **status** of the characters.

> For example, the action in *Blue Stockings* takes place in 1896 at Cambridge University, one of the most prestigious and well-resourced educational establishments in the world. In the library and classroom scenes, a production reflecting this original setting and time period might feature desks, chairs and tables from the era, as well as a large number of books.

Communicating through props

Information that can be communicated through the use of props includes:
- **time period** (for example, this could be shown through the use of a digital watch or a pocket watch)
- the **status** – or changing status – of a character
- a specific **location** (for example, handcuffs can be used to show that a character is in prison; sunglasses could be used to suggest a sunny, tropical island)
- the play's **themes** and **issues** (for example, books can be used to indicate the theme of education and learning)
- **specific character traits** (for example, a sword could be used to show that a character has high status or is violent).

> Props are often detailed and can provide the **finishing touches** to a character – these are known as **personal props**. They can help a performer to find the **nuances** in their character, which in turn helps to bring the character to life.

In this scene from the National Theatre's 2009 production of *War Horse*, personal props such as tin hats and rifles are combined with stage furniture – a camouflaged netting draped over an early 20th-century horse-drawn plough. Together, the props and stage furniture provide a powerful naturalistic and symbolic First World War setting for the audience.

Now try this

Select a character from your performance text. As a designer, explain how you would use props to communicate key information about the character to an audience.

> Make sure you have a clear idea about what you need the audience to understand about the character and their situation or context.

Levels, entrances and exits

Careful consideration of **levels** and where characters can **enter** or **exit** the performance space can help to provide the audience with important clues about the narrative and reinforce key messages.

The importance of levels

Levels can convey:

👍 power 👍 status
👍 perspective 👍 variation.

Levels are vital to help the audience understand the **relations between characters** and who has the **power**.

- An effective set design may include a variety of levels, which can open up a range of possibilities for the performers.

- The **perspective** of the audience can also provide opportunities to use levels to build up **tension**, by enabling it to see things some characters cannot, such as a character hiding or running away.

This 2011 ballet production, *The Peony Pavilion*, adapted from a play by Tang Xianzu, uses levels for dramatic effect. Here, the performers' safety will have been a key priority for the set designer.

Entrances and exits

- Ensuring the performers can **enter** and **exit** the performance space quickly and **safely** is vital.

- It may also be important for the **audience** to understand exactly **where** characters have come from or where they are going to.

For example, in *DNA*, Brian exits with Adam to take him back to his 'hedge'. When Brian returns, it is clear where he has been. He then leaves again with Cathy, with the intention of suffocating Adam with a plastic bag. Although the actual location is not explicitly mentioned, the dialogue, coupled with using the same exit, suggests to an audience that they are going to the same place.

In this 2014 Old Vic production of *The Crucible*, Act 1 takes place in an upstairs room in Reverend Parris's house. The set designer has ensured the **stage directions** have been understood, and indicates this by including a staircase from under the stage. To support the style required, a simple wooden handrail is included, protruding just above the floor level. This also provides an important **safety aid** for the performers and can be **retracted quickly**.

Comedy often relies on **confusion**, which can be greatly aided by having lots of entrances and exits.

- A set designer must have a complete knowledge of the text to ensure that each scene can be placed in **context**.

- It is also important to have **consistency** when using the entrances and exits, to support the narrative. For example, if an exit is established to lead to a specific location, it should remain being used for that location.

Now try this

Take a key scene from your performance text. How many entrances and exits are required for your scene and where should they be located? Give reasons for your answers.

 Remember to consider the scene in the **context** of the whole play.

Types of staging and terminology

It is helpful to know and use the correct **technical vocabulary** when indicating exactly where a performer should be positioned and when discussing space and levels. It is also important to consider the **type of stage** or performance space you are using. For more on proxemics, or spatial positioning, turn to page 39.

Note how left and right are from the **perspective of the performer** and not the audience.

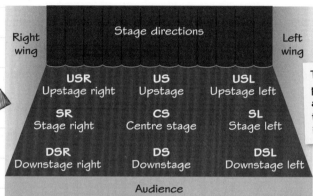

	Stage directions	
Right wing		Left wing
USR Upstage right	**US** Upstage	**USL** Upstage left
SR Stage right	**CS** Centre stage	**SL** Stage left
DSR Downstage right	**DS** Downstage	**DSL** Downstage left
	Audience	

This diagram indicates what each part of a traditional **proscenium arch stage** is called. Using these terms will help make your ideas clear.

Different styles of staging

There is a range of different types of staging. Here are three of the most popular.

Theatre in the round
👍 The audience **surrounds** the performance space, often creating an intimate atmosphere and giving everyone a clear view.
👎 It can be difficult to use scenery without blocking **sightlines**.

Thrust stage
👍 Can be very **intimate**, bringing the audience and performers close together.
👎 Scenery can block **sightlines** and so can only be used in specific parts of the stage or when the stage is limited in size.

Traverse theatre
👍 As with the thrust stage, this type of stage can be very **engaging**, bringing the audience very close to the action.
👎 The sightlines for the audience need to be carefully considered when using scenery or props. Performers need to carefully consider **audience awareness** when positioning themselves on stage.

Now try this

Choose **one** type of staging and explain why you think this would be an effective style for a production of your performance text. Consider what impact your chosen type of staging will have on an audience.

A set designer needs to be aware of the pros and cons of each type of staging. For example, if the performance is set 'in the round' then using large flats would block the view for some of the audience.

Symbolism, semiotics, spatial consideration and depth

The set designer has the opportunity to **convey** huge amounts of **information** to an audience. At times, that information may be very obvious. However, at other times, through careful use of **symbolism** and **space**, the set may offer **subtle clues** as to what is going to happen.

Symbolism

The set can instantly represent key **themes** and **issues** to an audience.

In the Lyttelton Theatre's 2016 production of *The Plough and the Stars*, a play set against the 1916 Easter Rising in Dublin, a decaying, derelict house represented not only the physical violence and the damage it caused, but also the breaking and failing relationships between the characters as the events of the play unfolded.

See page 27 for more on how the set can be used to symbolise key themes in a play.

Semiotics

Semiotics – the **interpretation of signs** – is a subtle yet powerful way in which a set can convey ideas and themes to an audience.

In the National Theatre's 2014 production of *The Curious Incident of the Dog in the Night-Time*, the set's electronic lit-up network **signified** the way in which Christopher's mind worked to make connections.

Spatial consideration

Performers need enough space to be able to work without being **limited** by the set. So a set designer must carefully consider the needs of the performers in terms of:

* the space they need to work
* exactly where the performers are able to stand.

This set design for the 2012 performance of Ibsen's *The Lady from the Sea*, at the Rose Theatre, Kingston, uses broad **open** spaces, gentle curves and **wooden flooring** to suggest the play's Scandinavian setting as well as the rolling effect of waves.

Depth

In order to provide an audience with a more **immersive** experience, theatre designers have experimented with depth on stage for generations.

In this 2015 production of *Macbeth* at the Young Vic, the long corridor was cleverly designed to become narrower further upstage, giving the **impression of depth**. This helped to provide a clear **focal point**, which was emphasised by the doorway at the end.

Now try this

Consider the set design for your performance text. Explain how you could use the space and set to convey the themes and narrative effectively to an audience.

⬅ When considering how to make the most effective use of stage space, try to use all of the available dimensions, including **width**, **depth** and **height**.

The sound designer

The **sound designer** works with both **music** and specific **sound effects** to enhance the production in various ways. The use of sound can **signal** many different things to an audience and can have a powerful impact on **mood** and **atmosphere**.

Creating a sound plot – The sound designer will work with a sound team to ensure the design is created and realised as closely and as practically as possible. If the sound is to be produced live, then the sound designer also needs to work with the musicians and/or performers to ensure the correct type of sound is produced at the right time.

Production consistency – The sound designer must ensure the sound is consistent with all other production elements to ensure a smooth experience for the audience.

Understanding the themes of the play and the style of the performance – The sound designer must select and design the most effective use of sound effects, music, volume levels and other audible aspects of the production to communicate specific ideas and emotions to the audience at key moments of the performance.

The role of the sound designer

Working with the director – The sound designer will work with both the director and other designers to ensure ideas for the sound design are consistent with the overall creative feel of the performance.

Creative audio control – The sound designer must have a clear vision for how all audio will sound in performance and consider what impact this will have on the audience.

Selecting volume, style and tone in the sound effects – The sound designer will select and design levels and styles of music, and even the specific location in the performance space from which the sound is produced (for example, speakers behind the audience). This helps to communicate specific emotions and ideas to the audience at key moments.

The work of a sound designer pre-production

The director and the wider creative team make a lot of decisions before the rehearsals begin. Sometimes the sound designer is involved in decision-making from a very early stage, particularly if the **sound plot** for the production is going to be complicated and integral to the overall feel and tone of the production.

Key elements a sound designer needs to consider

- 👍 Volume
- 👍 Mood and atmosphere
- 👍 Location
- 👍 Special effects
- 👍 Tone
- 👍 Symbolism
- 👍 Time

A room in the Duke's palace.
Enter DUKE, CURIO, lords; musicians attending.
DUKE If music be the food of love, play on;
Give me excess of it, that, surfeiting,
The appetite may sicken, and so die.
That strain again! it had a dying fall;
O, it came o'er my ear like the sweet sound
That breathes upon a bank of violets.
Stealing and giving odour. Enough! no more;
'Tis not so sweet now as it was before.

(*Twelfth Night*, Act 1, Scene 1, lines 1–8)

For example, the opening of Shakespeare's *Twelfth Night* gives the sound designer the opportunity to have an **immediate impact** on the overall performance. Orsino's opening line – 'If music be the food of love, play on…' – instantly indicates that the Duke is listening to music; Shakespeare also refers to musicians in the stage directions.

A sound designer will understand that Orsino, being a powerful duke, will need to be supported by quite regal, stately music, reflecting his high **status**.

The next consideration is the **mood** the music creates for an **audience**. Orsino is feeling sad, and declares unhappily that his love for Olivia is unrequited. Therefore, the music should reflect this, providing a melancholy start to the play.

What do you think are the most important skills a sound designer should have? Explain why you have chosen those particular skills.

Try to consider the different responsibilities a sound designer has towards the production overall.

Music and sound effects

Music and sound effects can be either **recorded** or played **live** by performers on stage. Music has an incredible power to **stir emotions**, so careful use of music can have a profound impact on the performance and can help to convey mood and atmosphere. Similarly, sound effects can provide the audience with **context** and **clarity** for what is happening on stage.

Live music

Live music has been used for generations and recorded sound is only a relatively recent invention. Today, live music can add a **vibrant dimension** to a performance or indicate a specific **cultural** style.

A sound designer/composer works with the director from an early stage of the project to ensure the music supports specific parts of the performance.

A drummer plays live on stage to support the action in this 2016 Young Vic production of *Battlefield*.

Live sound

👍 Can be completely **integrated** into the performance
👍 Can be perfectly **timed** to fit into the actual performance
👍 Can sound much more **authentic**
👎 Can be **inconsistent** and differ each time
👎 Can add extra **strain** on the performers
👎 May need **additional crew/performers**, costing more

Recorded sound

👍 Will be **consistent** in every performance
👍 Can be re-recorded until **perfected**
👎 Relies on **technology**
👎 May be difficult to adapt **timing** to the performers
👎 Is less 'authentic', so there is some loss of quality overall

Music and mood

Music can be used to **emphasise** subtly what is happening on stage. For example, mysterious music could be played when the Inspector arrives at the Birling house in *An Inspector Calls*.

Underscoring is when music is played **quietly underneath** the dialogue. It is vital that the music does not prevent the audience from hearing what the performers are saying.

For example, when Tess in *Blue Stockings* first rides a bicycle, the stage directions indicate, *'When she is out of sight, there is an almighty crash and a yell.'* This tells the audience that Tess has not mastered cycling. Here **both recorded** sound (for the 'crash' sound effect) and **live sound** (Tess yelling in pain and shock) could be used together, with the 'crash' acting as the cue for the performer playing Tess to call out.

Sound effects

- Sound effects can be either recorded or created live. This may depend on the **style** of the performance. (For example, a naturalistic piece would most likely benefit from recorded sound effects, whereas an abstract performance could use live sound effects produced on stage in front of the audience.)

- They can be used to **reflect** not only what is happening **on stage** but also events taking place **off stage**.

- Several recorded sound effects can be **merged** together to create a single, larger effect. For example, separate effects of a car quickly accelerating can be mixed with the sound of tyres squealing as they search for grip, followed by the sound effect of a loud crash as the vehicle collides with something.

Now try this

Choose a key moment from your performance text. Discuss how you could use music and/or sound effects to convey the required atmosphere to an audience.

Consider whether live or recorded sound would be the most appropriate way of producing the sound effect you want.

Atmosphere and time

Sound and music can help create a powerful **atmosphere**, build to a crescendo, and give very strong clues as to the time period in which a scene is taking place.

Using sound to convey atmosphere

Sound and music are extremely effective when conveying the atmosphere required for a specific scene or moment. A sound designer, working with the director, will:

- identify moments where the sound can **enhance** the action on stage for an audience
- decide what **sort** of sound is required (music, sound effect or a combination).

In Act V of *Twelfth Night*, joy replaces the sadness and grief experienced by the key characters of Viola, Olivia and Orsino at the play's opening. Many of the characters pair up, resulting in several marriages. This can be effectively supported with harmonious and uplifting music, providing the characters with an opportunity to dance, and reflecting the joy and festivities at the weddings. This happy, vibrant music will also **contrast** with the sad music played at the beginning of the play.

The chilling tension-filled atmosphere as the Woman in Black suddenly appears under cold lights on a shadow-filled stage can be enhanced by sound effects and music. For example, quiet, choral-style music, played on low-pitched stringed instruments, would reflect the style of the lighting design. This quiet and chilling sound could then build to a frightening climax, ending in a blood-curdling scream. Repeating this effect throughout the play would put people in the audience on the edge of their seats – as they would know the Woman in Black was coming but would be unsure as to exactly when she would appear.

Music will often imply that the drama on stage is building to a **climax**, making the audience think that something is going to happen and putting them on edge.

For example, using a carefully constructed **crescendo** of music, **tension** can be built quickly and strongly in a horror scene, even when the performer is silent.

Time

Music and sound effects can quickly help to establish the **time period** in which a play is set.

For example, if a production of *Government Inspector* is set in the **1980s**, you might decide to play **pop music** from that era when changing scenes. This would help provide a smoother transition and support the production decisions made by the director.

- The music may be contemporary to the chosen period.
- Specific sound effects can be used to indicate a certain time period.

For example, in a production of *Blue Stockings*, to indicate a 19th-century setting, it would be appropriate to use the sound effect of a steam train at the beginning and end of the play. The sound of a modern train horn or station announcement would **contradict** the established time period.

Now try this

Choose a key moment from your performance text. Discuss how you would use music and sound effects to convey the required atmosphere to an audience.

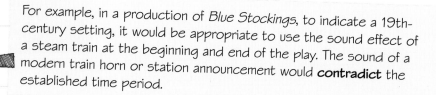

First, decide what you wish to **convey** to an audience. Then put the scene into the wider **context** of the whole play.

Location and genre

Music and sound effects are often associated with **specific locations** and **genres**. A sound designer can use this knowledge to their advantage and help provide the audience with strong clues regarding the context of a production.

Location

The sound designer has an important role to play in helping the audience understand where a play is set. The sense of location can be represented by effective use of sound.

For example, the play *DNA* moves between three different and distinct locations – street, field, wood. However, as the change between locations is quite quick, the various design elements, including sound, must come together promptly, to help portray the location of each scene. For instance:

- to represent the street, you could design the sounds of vehicles moving or children playing
- to represent the field, you could use the sound of distant birdsong
- to represent the wood, you could have much louder birdsong and the wind whistling through the trees.

New Orleans is the setting for Tennessee Williams's play *A Streetcar Named Desire*, and is famous for jazz and blues music. Playing a blues trumpet throughout the performance would be an effective way of indicating through sound that New Orleans is the location for the play.

In *1984*, for example, a sound designer might create a loud, metallic, uncomfortable sound effect to indicate Winston's torture. Once the meaning of this abstract sound is established, the audience will understand the situation and its emotional, personal impact.

Genre

Sound effects and music can provide a clear indication of a production's **style** and **genre**.

Genre refers to the type or category of theatre (such as historical drama or political satire), while style refers to the way it is performed (such as physical theatre or expressionism).

If the text is **naturalistic**, you may choose to use naturalistic sound effects, such as the sound of a steam train or a car door being slammed shut.

For example, the opening of a naturalistic production of *An Inspector Calls* could be supported by a **string quartet** playing late 19th-century or early 20th-century music. The play's period and genre (social thriller) could be indicated through the use of tense music contemporary to the era and appropriate to the status of the characters.

If the production is more **abstract**, you could use a sound effect, such as a loud 'swish' noise to represent someone looking through a pile of papers, or music that represents a specific style, such as atonal music (clashing chords and notes) to represent confusion or conflict.

This production of *The Taming of the Shrew* has been transported from 12th-century Italy in the 1940s. The use of an acoustic guitar instantly supports the style and location of the performance and helps the audience place the play in context.

Now try this

Explain how you would use music or sound effects to indicate the location of a particular scene or scenes in your performance text.

Consider whether you want to convey a general location or something very specific to your audience. Remember to consider the time in which your performance text is set, as this may affect the types of sounds you can include.

Sound equipment and levels

As **technology** has developed, a wide range of options for producing sound effects and music has become available. Advances in technology have also provided the opportunity to control **volume levels** with increased precision, helping sound designers to have greater **impact** on the audience.

CD player – A reliable and flexible way of storing sound effects and music. However, they are now relatively old technology. Although CD players provide excellent sound quality, they can also become scratched and stop working.

MP3 player – Modern technology that can store a huge amount of data (depending on the memory size). They produce high-quality sound and are very portable. Data can be backed up for security.

Speakers – An output device that enables the sound to be heard by the audience, cast and crew.

Sound equipment

Laptop – Can provide specific editing software and dedicated audio programs to help produce improved sound quality and play sounds/music.

Amplifiers – These allow the sound from a mixing desk or player to be increased to fill a larger space. They also improve/maintain the quality of the sound produced.

Mixing desk – This allows multiple devices to be 'mixed' together through different channels. It also allows you to control volume and sound quality for individual sounds/music.

Sound effects can be quickly and effectively created and recorded using modern **computer software**.

Sound effects are readily available from the **internet**.

Sounds can be recorded live and then digitally manipulated using **editing software**.

Important: Make sure you are not breaking any **copyright** rules when using material produced by other people (for example, when you download something from the internet).

Volume levels

Effective use of the **mixing desk** is crucial: ensuring volume levels are correct is very important.

- If the volume of one sound effect or piece of music is too loud, the audience may be unable to hear any dialogue or other important sound effects.
- If the volume is too quiet, the audience or performers (who may be relying on sound for an important **cue**) may not be able to hear properly.

Speaker placement

A sound designer can create various effects.

- Placing the speakers behind the audience and using those speakers for foreboding music or footsteps can make the audience think there is something behind them. This use of **rear speakers** can contribute massively to the atmosphere of the piece.
- **Surround sound** (literally surrounding the audience with sound) can produce an **immersive** experience, allowing the audience to feel very much part of the performance.

Mixing desk with speakers.

Now try this

Take a scene from your performance text that you feel could be enhanced with sound effects. Consider where you might place the speakers in relation to the audience, to help support your ideas and immerse the audience in the production.

Don't forget to consider the **volume levels** of your sound design. If the speakers are close to the audience, this may have an impact on what they can hear from the stage.

1984: overview

You need to consider the ways in which performers, directors and designers create impact and meaning for an audience. Understanding the context and subtext of the play will help you make key decisions about the messages you wish to convey. You also need to consider how each character has an impact on the plot.

> Only revise pages 68 and 69 if your performance text is *1984*.

Context

You must make reference to the context in which the text was created and performed.

> George Orwell wrote the novel *1984* at a time of deep political instability. There are strong parallels with our lives today, which are similarly dominated by screens. Social media has a huge impact and advertising messages can be targeted at individuals using information gathered from online activity. Facts can been manipulated to cover up the truth. Different areas of the media are controlled by powerful individuals who are able to present specific perspectives on news stories. Robert Icke and Duncan Macmillan recognised how the novel had relevance today and wrote the play to highlight the central question asked in the introduction – 'Can you trust evidence?'

Key information

Written by: Robert Icke and Duncan Macmillan (based on the novel by George Orwell)
First performed: Nottingham in 2013
Set in: Airstrip One, post-2084 (with cross-cutting)
Structure: one act with no interval

Themes

State vs individual – Winston's struggle against the Party is inspired by his desire for greater personal freedom.
Reality or fiction – The Mother makes the point that maybe the Party has not been overthrown, but has just made it look that way.
Fact or interpretation – The structure challenges the audience to consider whether it is watching events from Winston's perspective, or the interpretation of the diary the group are imposing on events.
Power – The Party, represented through O'Brien, has absolute power over the people it governs.
Love – Winston and Julia's emotions are the motivation for their actions against the Party.
Trust – Winston trusts Charrington and O'Brien, but both are working for the Party and betray him.
Sanity/psychology – O'Brien tells Winston that he will make him sane again. At the end of the play, Winston thanks O'Brien.

Central characters

Winston	Works at the Ministry of Truth, where he must change historical documents. He is fascinated by the past and becomes increasingly angry and despondent with the Party. He is spurred into action by his love for Julia.
Julia	Meets Winston in the canteen at work and secretly passes him a note, asking him to meet her. She is the catalyst for action, but something of a mystery. Who is she exactly?
O'Brien	A double agent. Actually a Party member who tortures Winston, to 'cure' him.
Martin	O'Brien's servant. Says very little, but is supportive of the regime.
Syme	Expert in Newspeak. Works with Winston. O'Brien implies Syme has been 'unpersoned', using this as a link to dupe Winston.
Parsons	Lives next door to and works with Winston. His daughter is fully indoctrinated into the Party. She informs on him, leading to his execution.

Now try this

Go through the play and find examples of each of the themes above. The examples may be individual lines, small or longer sections of text, or stage directions.

Consider how the production elements of the early 21st century would have affected the original production. You will need to refer to this context in your answer to Question (b) (i) in the exam.

1984: plot

This retelling of George Orwell's *1984* cleverly turns the original novel into a history book. It takes inspiration from the little-read appendix at the end of the book and reimagines the text as if set deep into the future. However, the constantly cross-cutting keeps the audience asking questions about the reality and truth throughout the whole performance.

Overview

A mysterious group of people are discussing a book from history. It is Winston's diary from 1984 – a time when the Party was in control. Winston can be seen throughout the discussion and it is possible that this discussion is occurring in his own mind. The plot unfolds and it becomes clear that Winston is increasingly frustrated by the Governing Party and by his own part in the system. A meeting with Julia leads him to take action, although he is quickly captured and 'rehabilitated' by O'Brien using torturous methods. The structure of the text is deliberately confusing, with often short, repeated scenes and echoes of previous events. This means the audience is never quite sure of the order in which things happen. It is also never clear if all of the events actually happened, or if Winston has imagined them.

Opening section

The scene opens with a narration as Winston writes in his diary. The lights change and we see a group of people reading over his shoulder. However, it is clear they are from the future, looking back at his words. They discuss what the book could mean and how it makes them feel, posing challenging philosophical questions about why Winston was writing and who his intended audience was. Different voices speak and there is a power cut. When the lights are restored, time returns to Winston's present. A child blows a whistle loudly, proclaiming Winston a Thought Criminal. Disorientated, Winston asks the Mother where he is.

Middle section 1

Suddenly, Winston is in an antiques shop, where he buys the diary and discovers an unused room. At work, Winston discusses Newspeak with Symes, and Parsons proudly tells how his 7-year-old daughter – the same child from earlier – handed over what she believed to be a spy. Winston takes part in 'Two Minutes Hate' where a 'Thought Criminal' confesses his crimes and is executed. Julia passes Winston a note and they meet in secret and begin a relationship. Winston returns to the antiques shop and rents the unused room. Julia and Winston continue their relationship. She produces food and discovers rats have gnawed the bed. Winston reveals he is terrified of rats. A disagreement arises between them about how they should deal with the situation.

Middle section 2

A sudden scene change and Winston is back at work. O'Brien approaches him, implies he is part of a rebellion and asks Winston to meet him at his apartment. Both Winston and Julia go and commit themselves to the Brotherhood. Later, Julia and Winston are in bed. He is reading the book given to him by O'Brien. Suddenly, they are surrounded by noise and uniformed men, who arrest them both. Winston is tortured by O'Brien, who reveals himself to be a member of the Party and not part of the rebellion.

Closing section

O'Brien claims he is curing Winston of his insanity. His techniques of both physical and mental torture have a profound impact on Winston, until he no longer knows what to believe. Winston finally betrays Julia as he is threatened with starving rats being released on his face. He is psychologically destroyed. As the lights change, the original group emerge, still questioning whether Winston existed or not and whether he suffered from false memories. The Mother asks whether the Party really did fall – or whether they structured the world to make it appear that way.

Now try this

Find out some key facts about how personal data is collected and used when you go online (such as how personal browsing history is shared with marketing companies). Consider how this may have affected the first performance of *1984* in Nottingham in 2013.

Read the play's Foreword. Are there any connections between the themes and issues in the play and modern society?

An Inspector Calls: overview

You need to consider the ways in which performers, directors and designers create impact and meaning for an audience. Understanding the context and subtext of the play will help you make key decisions about the messages you wish to convey. You also need to consider how each character has an impact on the plot.

Context

You must make reference to the context in which the text was created and performed.

Only revise pages 70 and 71 if your performance text is An Inspector Calls.

J.B. Priestley was a deeply moral man. Between the two World Wars, he became involved in a political movement that called for greater social equality. This socialist movement played an important part in the emergence of the welfare state after the Second World War, when poverty was common.

This prompted Priestley to write a play through which many people could personally identify with Eva, and that might also encourage wealthy audience members to take some responsibility by giving financial support. In this way, the power comes with responsibility

Key information

Written by: J.B. Priestley
First performed: Moscow and Leningrad (now St Petersburg), 1945 (first London performance 1946)
Set in: Brumley, industrial city in the Midlands, 1912
Structure: three acts

Themes

Social status – Mr Birling is concerned about his social connections and how he can climb the social ladder.
Money – Sheila's marriage to Gerald will bring significant financial security.
Responsibility – Each character has to face the realisation that they have some responsibility in the death of Eva Smith.
Morality – Sheila and Eric know they have a moral duty to help those less fortunate.
Prejudice – Mrs Birling judges the father of Eva's child before knowing the facts.
Higher power – Who is the Inspector and how does he know so much?
Generation and gender – Mr Birling reflects the traditions of the past, while Sheila represents the future.

Central characters

Inspector Goole	The mysterious Inspector is able to pull apart every character with his apparent omniscience (knowing everything). He has little respect for the social status of those he questions, putting his duty first.
Mr Arthur Birling	Head of the Birling family and a man with traditional views. He is a hard-headed businessman, which has led to financial success.
Mrs Birling	Married to Mr Birling. She enjoys being regarded as a charitable woman, but her prejudices about the working classes reveal her true feelings.
Sheila	Daughter of Mr and Mrs Birling. She is engaged to Gerald and is initially regarded as selfish, but changes, realising her responsibility towards others.
Gerald	Son of a wealthy businessman and engaged to Sheila. While his instinct is to agree with Birling's approach, he also recognises his responsibilities to others. He initially treated Daisy honourably, but then took advantage.
Eric	Son of Mr and Mrs Birling. Regarded as a disappointment, he quickly recognises his responsibility and feels guilty about the way he treated Eva.

Now try this

Go through the play and find examples of each of the themes above. The examples may be individual lines, small or longer sections, or stage directions.

Consider how the **structure** of An Inspector Calls would have affected the original production. You will need to refer to this context in your answer to Question (b) (i) in the exam.

An Inspector Calls: plot

An Inspector Calls may initially seem to be a straightforward 'whodunit?', but its structure, combined with the moral questions it raises, posed significant challenges to British post-war audiences.

Overview

Brumley, North Midlands. Spring 1912. A dining room in a substantial suburban house. The Birlings are gathered to celebrate the engagement of their daughter Sheila to Gerald Croft, the son of a wealthy businessman. This engagement will see not only the union of two people, but also of two businesses, placing economics at the heart of the play. The evening is interrupted when a mysterious Inspector arrives and announces the suicide of a young woman called Eva Smith. Although initially it appears no one knew the girl, the Inspector's questions reveal that each family member had some contact with her. The Inspector highlights how their actions played a part in Eva's death, forcing them to question their responsibilities to others and to society in general.

Act 1   The Dining Room

The Birlings are celebrating Sheila's engagement to Gerald Croft. Mr Birling makes a speech focusing on the economic environment. The women leave the men to talk and Mr Birling reveals that he may be in line for a knighthood. Inspector Goole arrives and announces a young woman named Eva Smith has committed suicide. Mr Birling cannot see why he is being questioned about this, until the Inspector reveals that two years earlier he sacked her from his factory for asking for a pay rise. Sheila enters and is questioned about an incident at a shop where she used her influence to get the girl sacked, because she looked better in a dress than Sheila did. These actions again led Eva into poverty. When the Inspector announces that Eva also used the name Daisy Renton, Gerald is shocked. He admits to Sheila that he had a relationship with Daisy in the previous year.

Act 2   The Dining Room

The Inspector returns to question Gerald about his relationship with Daisy Renton. Before he can do so, Mrs Birling enters and tries to take control. Sheila warns her mother to stop, without success. The Inspector begins to question Gerald, who reveals that he initially tried to help Daisy escape the attentions of an older man. He arranged for her to stay in a friend's rooms and a relationship developed. When his friend returned, the relationship ended and she moved out. Sheila returns Gerald's engagement ring and Gerald leaves to get some fresh air. The Inspector now reveals Mrs Birling turned a pregnant and desperate Eva Smith away from her charity. Defensive, Mrs Birling claims the baby's father should take the responsibility and be publically humiliated. It is only then that she realises the father is her own son, Eric.

Act 3   The Dining Room

Eric confesses to his relationship with Eva, revealing he tried to give her money stolen from the factory. Eva refused it, despite her desperation. She wanted to protect Eric from shame, which is why she approached the charity for help. When Eric finds out his mother had turned her away, he becomes angry, blaming Mrs Birling for Eva's death. The Inspector again takes control, delivering a speech about the social responsibility everyone has to each other. He then suddenly exits, leaving the family in turmoil. As a sense of unease grows, Mr Birling telephones the Chief Constable to discover there is no Inspector Goole. Gerald phones the infirmary to discover that no girl has been admitted that day. Some of the characters remain disturbed by the evening's events while other family members celebrate. However, celebrations are short-lived as the telephone rings to inform them that a girl has committed suicide and an Inspector is on his way to question them all.

Now try this

Find out some key facts about British theatre in 1946. Consider how this may have affected the first London performance of the play in 1946.

Read the play's commentary notes. Are there any connections between the themes and issues in the play and modern society?

Blue Stockings: overview

You need to consider the ways in which performers, directors and designers create impact and meaning for an audience. Understanding the context and subtext of the play will help you make key decisions about the messages you wish to convey. You also need to consider how each character has an impact on the plot.

Context

You must make reference to the context in which the text was created and performed.

> Only revise pages 72 and 73 if your performance text is *Blue Stockings*.

The fight for women's rights grew during the second half of the 19th century. While the Suffragette movement is the most famous women's movement of the time, they were not the only section of society campaigning for equal rights. Several groups pushed for women to be allowed to receive education. The term 'bluestocking' was applied to an educated woman and, over time, the phrase became derogatory (insulting). Many people at the time believed it was unnatural for a woman to be educated – and certainly not to the same level as men.

While in many places today education is passionately encouraged for both genders, this is not the case everywhere. It is therefore interesting to note that the play is dedicated to Malala Yousafzai.

Key information

Written by: Jessica Swale
First performed: Shakespeare's Globe, London, 2013
Set in: Girton College, Cambridge, 1896
Structure: two acts, set against the backdrop of passionate gender protests

Themes

Gender – The women fight for their right to attend lectures and to graduate in the same way as the men.
Sacrifice – Mr Banks and Miss Blake lose their positions because they believe in equality and are unwilling to compromise on these beliefs.
Protest – The very fact the women are being educated is a protest against the established systems of the time.
Education – The women are challenged as to the value of education. They have been denied university education, so they consider it more precious than the men do; for the men, it is almost an expectation.
Balance – To promote progress, the arts and sciences should work together.
Choice – The dominant attitude was that a woman had to choose between an education or love. Tess indicates that it may be possible to have both.

Central characters

Tess Moffat	A student at Girton College. She has a strong desire to learn and question. Her attempt to balance education and a love interest puts strain on her progress.
Carolyn Addison	Strong-minded and a risk-taker, Carolyn has significant experience of the wider world and does not conform to the expectations of society.
Celia Willbond	Though initially she appears to lack confidence, she demonstrates how determined she is to succeed in her education.
Maeve Sullivan	Called a 'mystery', she represents the challenges women faced when balancing the desire for education with the expectations of supporting a family.
Mrs Welsh	Mistress at Girton College and lead campaigner for women's right to graduate. She is concerned about the impact of the Suffragettes.
Lloyd	A student at Trinity College, Cambridge, he expresses the views of many men that women should not be educated, and has a central role in the protest during the vote.

Now try this

Go through the play and find examples of each of the themes above. The examples may be individual lines, small or longer sections, or stage directions.

Research Malala Yousafzai's story. Consider how such issues might have affected the original production. You will need to refer to this context in your answer to Question (b) (i) in the exam.

Blue Stockings: plot

By the end of the 19th century, the fight for gender equality was becoming a full-scale rebellion in Britain. However, while the fight for gender equality tends to be associated with the Suffragettes, there were also protests in other aspects of society (such as the battle for women to have the right to graduate from university) that were just as powerful – and involved just as much risk (physical and social) to those who dared to speak up for equal rights.

Overview

Girton College, Cambridge, 1896. Traditional university education is reserved for men only. Many believe that education is dangerous for a woman: it would sap her energy, lead to ill health and limit her ability to be an effective mother. Therefore, women can learn, but they cannot graduate. Four young women enter Girton to study. As they battle for the right to graduate, they learn much about the world in which they live, the expectations of society and who is able to support their cause. The events place an additional strain on the women and the staff who support them, leading to sacrifices on both sides of the gender divide.

Act 1, Prologue to Scene 7

Dr Maudsley outlines why women should not be educated. The woman arrive for their first lesson and introduce themselves. Their lesson involves riding a bicycle, demonstrating a freedom they have not felt before. The men cannot believe what they see. The women attend a lecture given by the famous Dr Maudsley, who makes clear that he does not agree with women's education. Tess challenges his view and he throws her out, causing embarrassment and anger among the other students. The women comfort Tess while some of the men are angered by her behaviour. Later, with everyone working in the library, a note is secretly passed from Ralph to Tess and, as he leaves, he throws her a quick, knowing look.

Act 1, Scenes 8 13

Will tries to explain to Tess why he pretended not to know her and his concerns about her reputation. She is upset and demands he leaves. She meets Ralph in the orchard. He reads her a love poem and tells her he thinks women studying is excellent. He kisses her hand as he departs; Tess is elated. The women, barred from another lecture, address the importance of moral science and the arts. Maeve's brother, Billy, arrives and tells Maeve their mother has died so she must go home to care for her siblings. Mrs Welsh tells Maeve to leave, as she has a responsibility to the children. Mr Banks gives the men one of Tess's essays; they are stunned at such quality work by a woman. While Mrs Welsh addresses the Senate to argue for women to graduate, Maeve leaves Girton forever.

Act 2, Scenes 1 6

The promotion offered to Mr Banks is withdrawn when he refuses to stop teaching the women. Will confesses his love for Tess, but she tells him she is already in a relationship. Carolyn tries to attend a Suffragette rally but is stopped by Mrs Welsh, who is concerned that it might jeopardise the campaign for female graduation. Celia tries to help Tess prepare for her exam but Tess is thinking about Ralph. In an angry exchange between the men and women, Lloyd rants against the women and their right to an education.

Act 2, Scenes 7 12

Mr Banks has been sacked and Miss Blake has resigned. The men are celebrating and Ralph produces a ring, but the ring is not for Tess. Will is shocked and breaks the devastating news to Tess. The next day, the women sit their exam. Celia and Carolyn both pass, but Tess, distracted by the events, fails. She is sent home but can resit the following year. As the women wait for the result of the vote, a violent protest against women's graduation breaks out. The vote is lost. At the end of term, Tess and Will part, but there is some hope between them.

Now try this

Find out some key facts about the right to an education in different parts of the world in the early 21st century. Consider how this may have affected the first performance of the play in London in 2013.

Read the play's commentary notes. Are there any connections between the themes and issues in the play and modern society?

The Crucible: overview

You need to consider the ways in which performers, directors and designers create impact and meaning for an audience. Understanding the context and subtext of the play will help you make key decisions about the messages you wish to convey. You also need to consider how each character has an impact on the plot.

> Only revise pages 74 and 75 if your performance text is *The Crucible*.

Context

You must make reference to the context in which the text was created and performed.

During the early 1950s, the American people became terrified that Soviet spies were living among them, undermining national security. As a result, Senator Joseph McCarthy led a very public campaign to find communist sympathisers and have them tried in court. Many of the accused were ostracised (excluded from society) and found it difficult to find work. Some people saw this as an opportunity to settle personal disputes and to discredit those they didn't like. Arthur Miller saw parallels with what had happened in Salem in the late 1600s and wrote *The Crucible* as a warning of what might happen.

Key information

Written by: Arthur Miller
First performed: New York, 1953
Set in: Salem, Massachusetts, 1692 – a strict, Puritan society
Structure: four acts

Themes

Guilt – Proctor feels guilty about his affair with Abigail.
Responsibility – Abigail is responsible for pressuring the girls to accuse others.
Revenge – Putnam uses his daughter to accuse his neighbours of witchcraft so that he can buy their land.
Morality – Reverend Hale changes his mind about who is telling the truth.
Gender – The oppression of women in the Puritan society may have led the girls to explode into life through the forbidden excitement of dancing in the woods.
Race – When accused, the girls deflect the blame on to Tituba, the only person of lower social standing in Salem.
Status and power – The judges consider themselves superior to the villagers of Salem.
Individual vs society/the system – Proctor stands up against the rest of society to fight for what he believes in.

Central characters

John Proctor	Mid-thirties. Respected landowner. Married to Elizabeth, it is his affair with Abigail that, in part, provides the motivation for the events in Salem. A man of principle and filled with guilt, he is willing to stand up against the Establishment.
Elizabeth Proctor	Married to John. Highly respected and deeply religious, she has the highest moral standards. She finds it hard to forgive her husband initially, but softens towards the end.
Abigail Williams	Former servant girl to Proctor and influential leader of the girls. Her desire for Proctor fuels her actions, although eventually they run beyond her control.
Mary Warren	Proctor's servant girl. Much more timid than the others, she knows the girls are wrong. However, when she tries to stand against them, she capitulates under the intense pressure.
Reverend Parris	Minister of Salem. A self-centred character who causes division within the village.
Deputy Governor Danforth	A highly experienced judge with enormous power. His religious convictions and unwillingness to compromise prevent the truth from being discovered.

Now try this

Go through the play and find examples of each of the themes above. The examples may be individual lines, small or longer sections of text, or stage directions.

Consider how the production elements of the 1950s would have affected the original production. You will need to refer to this context in your answer to Question (b) (i) in the exam.

The Crucible: plot

Set against the backdrop of the Salem Witch trials of 1692 and written at a time of deep political and social mistrust in the post-war United States, *The Crucible* was hugely controversial when it was first performed on Broadway, New York in January 1953.

Overview

Salem, Massachusetts. 1692. The Puritan society is rocked when a group of young girls are found in the woods 'conjuring' the Devil. Such activity is punishable by death, so in an attempt to save themselves, the girls blame others. Innocent people are then accused of witchcraft, tried in court, and either hanged or imprisoned.

The play is based on historical events. Neighbours involved in unrelated disputes would accuse their rival of witchcraft using the excuse of witchcraft to win their argument. Those accused of witchcraft, could confess and they would then be sent to jail. However, because of their deep religious beliefs, those people believed they had broken one of the Ten Commandments and would therefore be sent to hell for eternity. It was thought that the Devil still possessed those who did not confess and so they would be hanged. This meant many people faced an impossible decision.

Act 1   Reverend Parris's house

After being discovered dancing and conjuring the Devil in the woods, Betty Parris, the daughter of the minister, is lifeless in bed. The townspeople spread rumours that the girls were experimenting with witchcraft and the girls are getting scared about being punished. Abigail Williams admits to John Proctor (with whom she had has an affair) that they were only playing, but deep divisions emerge between the villagers. As the situation spirals out of control, the girls blame a slave called Tituba to protect themselves.

Act 2   Proctor's house

Proctor's relationship with his wife, Elizabeth, is still strained, owing to his affair with Abigail. Their servant, Mary Warren, arrives, announcing she is an official of the court, which has been set up to try those accused of witchcraft. She says many people have been accused and that they may be hanged if they do not confess. Tensions rise as Reverend Hale arrives to question both Proctor and Elizabeth after her name was mentioned in court. As the scene concludes, it becomes clear that respectable women have been accused. Elizabeth is arrested after being accused by Abigail (who sees this as a chance to pick up her relationship with Proctor).

Act 3   A side room, adjacent to the Courtroom

Proctor takes Mary to the court in order to admit the girls are lying about being bewitched by people. The girls deny this, and put pressure on Mary to support them. In an attempt to discredit Abigail, Proctor admits to their affair. Elizabeth, who we discover is pregnant and therefore will not hang, thinks she is protecting her husband and denies the affair happened. The girls now accuse Mary who, terrified for her life, now accuses Proctor of bewitching her. He is arrested, destroying Abigail's plans.

Act 4   A cell in Salem Prison

It is just minutes before Proctor is due to hang. Under pressure from the villagers, the officials of the court try to persuade Proctor to confess by allowing him time with Elizabeth. Although he is struggling with his conscience, he does sign a confession. However, when he discovers his signed confession will be displayed in public, he rips it up and is led away to his execution.

Now try this

Find out some key facts about McCarthyism in 1950s America. Consider how this may have affected the first performance of the play in 1953.

◀ Read the play's commentary notes. Are there any connections between the themes and issues in the play and modern society?

DNA: overview

You need to consider the ways in which performers, directors and designers create impact and meaning for an audience. Understanding the context and subtext of the play will help you make key decisions about the messages you wish to convey. You also need to consider how each character has an impact on the plot.

> Only revise pages 76 and 77 if your performance text is *DNA*.

Context

You must make reference to the context in which the text was created and performed.

People often stereotype teenagers, encouraged in part by the UK media's portrayal of gang culture as part of teenage life. Yet, far from being uncaring and emotionally detached, the teenagers in *DNA* have a clear sense of right and wrong. They realise they have created a terrible situation, but they do not know how to handle it. The play does not have a specific moral message, but is constructed to engage the audience and make it ask questions. It also demonstrates how easy it is to make the wrong choice and to get dragged into trouble. At a time when the national media presents negative stereotypes of teenagers, the characters in *DNA* present a very different, perhaps more realistic, perspective.

Key information

Written by: Dennis Kelly
First performed: London, 2008
Set in: contemporary Britain
Structure: four acts

Themes

Responsibility – No one wants to own up or take responsibility for what has happened.
Status – John Tate and Phil gain a higher status in different ways; both use their power to control the group.
Bullying – Adam is bullied because of the need to be part of a group. The 'pack mentality' allows the bullying to get out of hand.
Truth – Although it quickly becomes clear that there is a need to confess what actually happened, the group works hard to cover up the truth.
Peer pressure – The collective pressure over individuals means the violence towards Adam continues. It also stops anyone telling the truth.
Consequences – The psychological impact of the events has profound and significant implications for each character.

Central characters

Phil	Often silent, he did not take part in the actual incident. However, he comes up with the complex scheme that attempts to cover up the truth of the matter.
John Tate	Leads the group initially. He threatens violence when challenged by Richard.
Cathy	Compromises the plan by getting a jumper from the sorting office, so providing evidence that leads an innocent man to be arrested. Shows violent tendencies.
Brian	Emotionally unstable, he cannot take the strain or pressure of lying. He becomes increasingly psychologically damaged as the play progresses.
Leah	Very talkative, but with little of value to say, she is often very self-centred. Her conversations often appear random and she acts as a counter-character to the often silent Phil. It is Leah who eventually challenges Phil and questions his plans.
Lou	Focused on the problem, Lou finds it difficult to see a solution. She initially shows traces of panic and is happy to look to the others for reassurance and answers.

Now try this

Go through the play and find examples of each of the themes above. The examples may be individual lines, small or longer sections of text, or stage directions.

The play was intended for performance by schools and youth groups. Consider how the production elements available to such groups may have affected the original production. You will need to refer to this context in your answer to Question (b) (i) in the exam.

DNA: plot

Set in a street, a field and a wood, *DNA* follows a group of teenagers as they attempt to cover up their part in a bullying incident that leads to the apparent death of the victim. However, the complicated plan is not executed smoothly and there are consequences for each character.

Overview

Present day. A group of teenagers have been picking on another boy, Adam. Things get out of hand and turn violent. The peer pressure grows until Adam, while walking on a grille covering a deep hole, is hit by a stone on the head and falls. The teenagers assume he has been killed and the group devise a complex strategy to cover up the events. However, things don't go according to plan and an innocent man is arrested. As events spiral out of control, the characters are faced with difficult choices and must confront the consequences of their actions. Even when a possible solution presents itself, the group discovers that it may be too late to go back.

One

Tension and mystery build as Mark tells Jan that someone is dead. Leah, talking at Phil, admits she is scared. The group gather together, led by John Tate. Mark and Jan outline how they were bullying Adam, forcing him to do things until he walked over a grille and, while having stones thrown at him, fell in. The group assume Adam has been killed. Phil concocts an elaborate plan involving a fictional postman to cover up what they have done. Later, Leah compares humans to bonobos.

Two

The group find out the police have arrested a postman matching the description they gave. Cathy reveals that she thought she was using her initiative when the jumper she took for the plan was actually from a postman at the sorting office. Brian refuses to go back to the police station to positively identify the arrested postman. Phil tells Brian he must go back to positively identify the postman, otherwise they will kill him by throwing him down the same grille.

Three

Cathy finds Adam alive. Leah threatens to run away but Jan and Mark persuade her and Phil to go with them. They meet Cathy, Brian and Adam in the wood. Adam has been living in a hedge and is mentally unstable after his traumatic experience. He explains how, despite being injured by the fall, he crawled out of the tunnel, and survived by eating leaves and drinking blood. Phil sends Adam back to the hedge with Brian. Brian returns and then goes back with Cathy to carry out Phil's next instruction – to kill Adam.

Four

Jan and Mark discuss that someone has gone, but it is not clear who they are referring to. Richard meets Phil, who has been sitting alone in a field for a number of days. Richard outlines what has happened to everyone and the effects the events have had on them. It is clear that there have been some significant changes in people's lives, such as John Tate becoming very religious and Brian developing significant mental health problems and having to take strong medication to help him. He does not mention Leah. Phil does not respond.

Now try this

Explain how peer pressure may cause some young people to get involved in bullying incidents. Consider how this may have affected the first performance of *DNA*, in London in 2008.

Read the notes at the back of your copy of the play. How might the questions asked affect your decision-making if you were staging this production? Are there any connections between the themes and issues in the play and modern society?

100: overview

You need to consider the ways in which performers, directors and designers create impact and meaning for an audience. Understanding the context and subtext of the play will help you make key decisions about the messages you wish to convey. You also need to consider how each character has an impact on the plot.

Context

You must make reference to the context in which the text was created and performed.

> Only revise pages 78 and 79 if your performance text is *100*.

Christopher Heimann and Diene Petterle originally intended to create a play about themes they had strong feelings about – for example, what is really important in life. Later, they began to prepare the piece for the Edinburgh Festival Fringe and Neil Monaghan joined them to help develop it. How would audiences react to the concept of having to choose a single memory to keep for eternity? What are the consequences of finding out that all other memories would be deleted? This was originally a devised piece that was later developed into a script.

Key information

Written by: Diene Petterle, Neil Monaghan and Christopher Heimann

First performed: Edinburgh Festival Fringe, 2002 (in this format)

Set in: A timeless Void in the afterlife, with flashbacks into different memories

Structure: One act with no interval

Themes

Priorities – Everyone in the Void is asked to consider what is the most important thing in the world to them before moving on.

Time – Each character has to make an important decision in a very limited amount of time.

Truth – The events help each of the characters to understand that everyone has a different idea of truth.

Consequences – Each character begins to see that their choices have consequences.

Belief – The play invites the audience to consider what might happen after life.

Central characters

Guide	The mysterious host who tries to keep control of the people in the Void. He provides advice, challenges each character and provides dark, puzzling warnings to those who do not listen.
Alex	A young man who is confident and thinks he knows his own mind. He is willing to argue his situation with the Guide but becomes increasingly desperate to find a suitable memory as the play progresses.
Ketu	Born and raised in a remote African village, Ketu has many scientific questions and ideas which have led his family and community to exclude him. The rejection of his firmly held beliefs and opinions lead him to take his own life.
Sophie	A young woman who has always pushed herself to work extremely hard and to be successful in her career. However, a tragic illness has dramatically cut short her life, leading her to question what she has actually achieved.
Nia	A curious young woman with an open mind. She is able to accept her situation far quicker than her partner, Alex. Her attempts to help Alex are not always successful.

Now try this

Look at the list of **themes** above. Go through the play and find examples of each theme. The examples may be **individual lines, small sections of text, stage directions** or **longer sections of the play.**

Consider how the limited production elements available in a small venue would have affected the original production. You will need to make reference to this context in your answer to question (b) (i) in the exam.

100: plot

Set in a 'Void', four people are greeted by a mysterious Guide. 100 explores what might happen after death and forces the audience to question what is important in life.

Overview

Four young adults have died. They arrive in a mysterious space – the Void – and are met by the Guide, who tells them what has happened and that they have a short amount of time to select a single memory from their lives. They have very little time to choose this memory, which will stay with them for eternity as they continue their journey into the afterlife. Each character relives important moments from their lives and is forced to consider whether these moments are the most important thing that ever happened to them. The Guide gives no clear answers but questions each person to help them choose their memory. As each character begins to understand what is important to them, the task becomes easier, although some characters find it hard to tell memory from fantasy. If a character cannot choose a memory in time, there are serious consequences.

Opening section

Ketu, Sophie and Alex arrive in the Void. The Guide then joins them and tells them they are dead. He explains that they must select one memory to take with them into the afterlife, which will be recorded with a camera. After some confusion, Alex offers a memory of a motorcycle race. During the memory, Alex's girlfriend Nia appears. She, too, has died. Nia reminds Alex that his memory of the race wasn't real, just imagined. Sophie then remembers a time when she was 12 and realised she wasn't beautiful. The camera does not flash as the memory is not important enough. The other characters start having ideas about what they could choose.

Middle section 1

Ketu remembers his discovery, in his rural African village, that the world is round and that the sun travels around it. The camera does not flash. Sophie explains that it is the Earth that orbits the sun, but Ketu is happy because he was right that the world is round. Alex and Nia try again to select a memory, concentrating on the moment they met in a park while looking after other people's children. They recall the tactics they used to work out if they were both single without actually speaking to one another. Alex is disappointed when he finds out that, although he knew immediately that Nia was 'the one', Nia just felt a strong physical attraction to him. As a result, Alex decides not to choose this memory.

Middle section 2

Sophie tries another memory, this time of her first job. While she is initially faced with gender discrimination and inappropriate advances from her male colleagues, she takes her chance to impress her boss at the Christmas party. From this point, she rises through the ranks, quickly becoming a manager and later winning a 'Manager Of The Year' award. The camera doesn't flash. The other characters and the Guide question her and Sophie recalls becoming terminally ill. She then remembers how she started to forget things. The camera flashes and Sophie disappears. The other characters are confused but Ketu begins to understand that the chosen memory must demonstrate what a person does with their knowledge or situation, rather than the knowledge or situation itself.

Closing section

Ketu returns to his memory of telling the villagers the Earth is round. The villagers react with laughter, fear and then by turning on him with spears. The Elders tell him to stop saying these things and his wife begs him to think about the consequences for her and the children. Ketu tries to stop but cannot continue pretending, so takes his own life. The camera flashes and Ketu disappears. Nia and Alex then try to find a memory and Nia realises it needs to be something they can really feel. They recall a lazy Sunday they spent in bed. The camera flashes and Nia disappears, but Alex remains in the Void. Alex desperately tries to find a memory as the Guide counts towards 100. Alex suddenly realises that he and the Guide are very alike, and the Guide has noticed this too. Time runs out and the Guide leaves the stage, leaving Alex in the Void.

Now try this

Find out some key facts about the Edinburgh Festival Fringe and how plays are staged there. Consider how this may have affected the first performance of the play in 2002.

Read the play's introduction. How could a production of the play make sure that the questions the play raises are clear to an audience?

Government Inspector: overview

You need to consider the ways in which performers, directors and designers create impact and meaning for an audience. Understanding the context and subtext of the play will help you make key decisions about the messages you wish to convey. You also need to consider how each character has an impact on the plot.

Context

You must make reference to the context in which the text was created and performed.

> Only revise pages 80 and 81 if your performance text is *Government Inspector.*

The physical size of Russia meant it was difficult for the authorities to control many of the more remote areas. Gogol recognised this and understood how those with power exploited it for their own gains and that corruption was rife. He used this situation to create a comedy, poking fun at the authorities and highlighting the need for reform. While the play initially caused controversy, Tsar Nicholas I (Emperor of Russia from 1825 until 1855) intervened and performances continued.

Key information

Written by: Nikolai Gogol
First performed: St Petersburg, April 1836
Set in: the 1830s, in a provincial Russian town
Structure: five acts

Themes

Corruption – The officials all admit to taking bribes.

Greed – Khlestakov takes money from everyone.

Deception – Khlestakov deliberately continues to pretend to be an Inspector.

Mistaken identity – The townsfolk believe Khlestakov is the Inspector.

Status and power – The Mayor is pleased when Khlestakov proposes to Maria, thinking he will rise up in society.

Reform – The dishonesty of the officials shows the need for political reform.

Bureaucracy – The complex systems of government make corruption easy.

Central characters

The Mayor	The corrupt leader of the town. He is rude, full of self-importance, and cares little about the citizens. He flatters Khlestakov to advance his career and climb socially.
Khlestakov	A minor government official who is mistaken for the Government Inspector. He wastes his money on drinking and gambling and arrives in town penniless. He maintains the deception for his own advantage.
Osip	Khlestakov's servant. He is mistreated and often bad tempered. He is not afraid to speak his mind, and is quick to take advantage of the situation. He reads the situation better than his master; it is he who suggests they leave.
Maria	The Mayor's daughter. She likes the idea of marrying a man of power and influence, and flirts with Khlestakov. When they are discovered, Khlestakov proposes to get out of his predicament, which delights the Mayor.
Postmaster	Although a relatively minor role, it is the Postmaster's unlawful habit of opening letters that provides the Mayor with significant information, such as the arrival of a Government Inspector and also the truth about Khlestakov.

Now try this

Go through the play and find examples of each of the themes above. The examples may be individual lines, small or longer sections, or stage directions.

Consider how the technology available in the theatres of the 1830s would have affected the original production. You will need to refer to this context in your answer to Question (b) (i) in the exam.

Government Inspector: plot

Set in mid-19th-century Russia in a remote provincial town, *Government Inspector* provides a satirical look at the corrupt mechanism of the ruling classes. The play was very controversial when it was first performed, as the ruling classes saw it as an attack on the way society was run.

Overview

The political and administrative systems in 19th-century Russia were inefficient and corrupt. The size of the country made it impossible to maintain effective systems to monitor town officials. Therefore, those in power took advantage of their position. Gogol poked fun at this state of affairs, although the play was only allowed to be produced after the direct intervention of Tsar Nicholas I.

Act 1 The Mayor's house

The corrupt Mayor receives news that a Government Inspector is coming. The officials panic, as they rush to cover up their dishonesty. The alarm increases when Bobchinsky and Dobchinsky arrive to say they have heard the Inspector is already there. They decide it is the man staying in the local inn. Everyone panics and the Mayor sends each official away, with (often absurd) instructions on how to make their departments look good. Anna, the Mayor's wife and Maria, her daughter, enter. Maria is keen to see if the Inspector might make a suitable husband.

Act 2 A room in the inn

Khlestakov and his servant, Osip, are starving. However, they have no money and the landlord will not give them any more credit. Khlestakov manages to persuade the waiter to bring up some tasteless soup and beef. As the waiter leaves, Osip sees the Mayor approaching. Thinking they are in serious trouble, they prepare themselves for the worst. However, because the Mayor thinks Khlestakov is the Inspector, he welcomes them warmly. Though surprised and confused by this, Khlestakov goes along with the situation and begins his tour of the town.

Act 3 The Mayor's house

Anna and Maria wait for news. Dobchinsky brings a note from the Mayor, who believes Khlestakov is an official from St Petersburg. Preparations are made for Khlestakov to stay at the Mayor's house. As Osip carries in Khlestakov's luggage, Mishka, the Mayor's servant, asks about Khlestakov, calling him 'General'. Osip takes advantage of this mistaken identity. Khlestakov arrives and meets the ladies. He plays on the deception, detailing his importance in St Petersburg. He goes to rest. The ladies are clearly taken by him and Osip reinforces the deception.

Act 4 The Mayor's house

Each official is individually introduced to the 'Inspector'. Each one, terrified, bribes Khlestakov. Osip is concerned and convinces his master to leave before they are discovered. Khlestakov writes a letter to a friend in St Petersburg, outlining the truth. A gathering of shopkeepers arrives with bribes, asking for action against the Mayor. As Khlestakov decides to leave, Maria accosts him. Anna discovers them in a 'compromising' position, so he proposes to Maria. The Mayor is delighted, believing his social standing will rise. Osip and Khlestakov, promising to return for the wedding, escape, never to be seen again.

Act 5 The Mayor's house

The Mayor, believing he has new-found power, threatens the officials and shopkeepers, all of whom fear his new status. The Postmaster enters. He has opened Khlestakov's letter and the truth is revealed to the whole town. Just as they realise they have been duped and the recriminations begin, a policeman enters with a letter from the real Government Inspector, demanding to see the Mayor immediately.

Now try this

Find out some key facts about political corruption in 1830s Russia. Consider how this may have affected the first performance of the play in St Petersburg in 1836.

Make time to research Gogol's personal life. Consider how this influenced his writing. Are there any connections between the themes and issues in the play and modern society?

Twelfth Night: overview

You need to consider the ways in which performers, directors and designers create impact and meaning for an audience. Understanding the context and subtext of the play will help you make key decisions about the messages you wish to convey. You also need to consider how each character has an impact on the plot.

> Only revise pages 82 and 83 if your performance text is *Twelfth Night*.

Context

You must make reference to the context in which the text was created and performed.

> At the beginning of the 17th century, society began to question the class system and religious ideals. This led to the rise in strict religious groups, such as the Puritans, who protested against the greater freedoms everyday people had. Additionally, during this period, the twelfth night of Christmas (6th January) was marked with raucous celebrations where the traditional master/servant relationships were often reversed. All of these elements are brought together in *Twelfth Night* and would have been recognised by Elizabethan audiences watching this play at the Globe Theatre in London, and other playhouses of the time.

Key information

Written by: William Shakespeare
First performed: (probably) London, circa 1601–02
Set in: Illyria
Structure: five acts

Themes

Love – Almost all the characters are motivated by (often unreturned) love.
Deception – Maria, Sir Toby and Sir Andrew play a cruel trick on Malvolio in order to get revenge on him for his threat to report them to Olivia.
Social status – Feste undermines both Olivia and Malvolio with his wit and logic.
Gender confusion – Viola disguises herself as a man in order to gain employment and security.
Ambition – Malvolio is motivated to woo Olivia because he believes that, by marrying her, he will become a rich count.
Madness – Feste makes Malvolio think he is mad; he pushes the prank too far.
Honour – Sir Andrew thinks that by challenging 'Cesario' to a duel he is fighting for honour, as well as for the love of Olivia.

Central characters

Viola	Shipwrecked, she disguises herself as a man ('Cesario') to work for Orsino, then falls in love with him. Olivia falls in love with 'Cesario'.
Orsino	Duke of Illyria. He is in love with Olivia, although his love is unrequited (not returned), which frustrates him. He eventually falls in love with Viola.
Olivia	A countess who is in mourning for her brother. She falls in love with 'Cesario', but when the true identities are revealed she falls in love with Sebastian.
Malvolio	Olivia's humourless steward. He is only interested in gaining status and spends time stopping others having fun.
Sebastian	Viola's brother. Believed drowned in the shipwreck, he has actually survived. When he arrives in Illyria, everyone confuses him for his disguised sister.
Sir Toby Belch	Olivia's uncle. A drunkard who enjoys having a good time. His plans are often badly thought out, creating more problems than solutions.
Sir Andrew Aguecheek	Friend of Sir Toby who is in love with Olivia and challenges 'Cesario' to a duel.

Now try this

Go through the play and find examples of each of the themes above. The examples may be individual lines, small or longer sections, or stage directions.

Consider how the technology available in the theatres of the 1600s would have affected the original production. You will need to refer to this context in your answer to Question (b) (i) in the exam.

Twelfth Night: plot

One of Shakespeare's most famous romantic comedies, *Twelfth Night* makes audiences laugh through the classic conventions of cross-dressing, love triangles and mistaken identity.

Overview

Illyria. When servants and fools no longer treat their masters with respect, social structures are tested. The play is filled with deception and confusion; each character is at some point unable to understand what is going on.

Two main plot strands form the narrative:

- the love triangle between Olivia, Cesario/Viola and Orsino
- the relationship between Malvolio and the others, leading them to trick him.

The increasing confusion leads to comic consequences, resolved only when the twins are together and Viola reveals her true identity, resulting in a happy ending for (almost) all.

Act 1

Orsino is in love with Olivia, who is grieving for her brother and is not interested. Viola, rescued from a shipwreck, becomes one of Orsino's servants, disguised as 'Cesario', a man. Olivia's uncle, Sir Toby Belch, introduces Sir Andrew Aguecheek to Olivia; Sir Andrew tries to woo her. 'Cesario' gains Orsino's trust, and is sent to Oliva with love letters. Viola falls in love with Orsino. Olivia's humourless steward, Malvolio, believes himself superior to others and insults Feste, the fool. 'Cesario' delivers the love message from Orsino, but Olivia falls in love with 'Cesario'. 'Cesario' leaves, but Olivia pretends he has left a ring behind and sends Malvolio after 'him'.

Act 2

Sebastian, Viola's brother, has survived the shipwreck and Antonio rescues him. 'Cesario' realises Olivia is in love with 'him' when Malvolio tries to return the ring. Feste, Sir Toby and Sir Andrew are drinking heavily and Malvolio threatens to tell Olivia. In revenge, Maria forges a love letter, supposedly from Olivia to Malvolio. 'Cesario', using a plot about 'his sister', tells Orsino of her love for him. Malvolio finds the letter and believes he'll marry Olivia. Obeying the instructions in the letter, he leaves to find some yellow cross-gartered stockings (which Olivia actually hates).

Act 3

'Cesario' visits Olivia, who declares her love for him. Sir Andrew, jealous of 'Cesario', is persuaded by Sir Toby to challenge 'Cesario' to a duel. Malvolio, dressed in the stockings, arrives to woo Olivia. She has no idea what he is doing and thinks he has gone mad. Sir Andrew and 'Cesario' warily prepare to fight. They are interrupted by Antonio, who thinks 'Cesario' is Sebastian. When Viola hears the name Sebastian, she realises her brother must still be alive and runs off to look for him. Sir Andrew thinks he has nothing to fear from 'Cesario' and promises to fight him.

Act 4

Sir Andrew attacks Sebastian, thinking he is 'Cesario'. Sebastian fights back and Sir Toby steps in to help Sir Andrew. Olivia stops the duel, thinking she is saving 'Cesario'. She takes Sebastian away and banishes Sir Toby. She suggests that she and Sebastian should marry (still thinking he is 'Cesario'). Malvolio is imprisoned by Sir Toby and Feste makes him think he is mad. Worried he has upset Olivia, Sir Toby suggests Malvolio be released. Malvolio writes to Olivia to explain his behaviour.

Act 5

Orsino, with 'Cesario', arrives to speak to Olivia. Olivia, thinking 'Cesario' is Sebastian, accuses him of breaking his promise of marriage. Orsino is livid when he thinks that 'Cesario' is to be married to Olivia. Sebastian enters, causing shock and confusion: for the first time, 'Cesario' and Sebastian are in the same place. As the true identities are revealed, Orsino proposes to Viola, Sebastian proposes to Olivia, and Malvolio's letter is read out. He leaves, bitterly angry that he has been tricked.

Now try this

Find out some key facts about life and important events in Shakespeare's England. Consider how these may have affected the first performance of the play in around 1601–02.

Reading the play's commentary notes. Are there any connections between the themes and issues in the play and modern society?

About Section A

Section A of the exam focuses on your performance text. You will need to answer a range of questions from the perspective of a performer, director and designer. To complete this section you will need to think about your performance text from the point of view of all three roles.

Navigating the exam paper

The paper will include questions for all eight performance texts.

> Remember: you only need to answer the questions for the performance text you have studied.

For each performance text, there are **three** questions.

- **Question (a)** will ask you to respond from the perspective of a **performer**.
- **Question (b)** will ask you to respond from the perspective of a **director**.
- **Question (c)** will ask you to respond from the perspective of a **designer**.

Planning your time

The exam lasts for 1 hour 45 minutes (105 minutes) in total.

There are 45 marks for Section A, which is worth 75% of the total marks. So you should spend about 75% of the exam time – about 75–80 minutes – on Section A questions.

See pages 103–110 for more about Section B.

Extracts from the performance texts

The questions for each performance text will focus on a specific extract of approximately 70–80 lines. The extract will be printed in a Questions and Extracts booklet.

You are allowed to make notes on the extract.
For each question you must:

- ✓ consider ways in which each of these roles can create **impact** and **meaning** for an audience
- ✓ focus on the selected extract
- ✓ show an understanding of the **context** of the extract.

Reading the question

Make sure you answer the question that is being asked and not the question you think you have been asked! It may help to underline the important aspects of the question, to help clarify exactly what you need to do.

- Which **role** are you being asked about (**performer, director or designer**?)
- What **skills** are you being asked to discuss?
- Are you being asked to give **a specific number of examples or ideas**?
- What do you need to include in your answer to **justify** your ideas?

Unseen extracts

Until you open the Questions and Extracts booklet in the exam, you will have no idea which part of your performance text you will be asked to write about. It is therefore important to make sure you are as familiar as possible with the whole play. Make sure you have thought about the text from the perspective of **all three** roles: **performer, director** and **designer**.

> You are **not** allowed to take your own copy of the performance text in to the exam.

Make sure you:

1 Find the extract for your performance text.

2 Remind yourself of the extract, including stage directions.

3 Briefly annotate the extract with your thoughts and ideas.

It is helpful to have a system in place for approaching the extract, the questions and your time in the exam. You can find out more about this on page 86.

Now try this

Choose **one** character from your performance text, and choose one scene in which that character appears. Explain **two** ways you would use **vocal skills** to play the character in this scene.   **(4 marks)**

Look at this exam-style question. Highlight the key words and write a brief explanation of what the question is asking you to do.

Section A questions

Each question in Section A asks you to focus on specific skills and roles. You also need to give **evidence** to support your answers.

Question (a)

This question:

- is from the **performer's perspective**
- will be in **two parts**.

Part (i) is worth **4 marks**. The question will focus on either vocal or physical skills. You need to:

- identify **two** techniques
- provide a **linked explanation** for each.

Part (ii) is worth **6 marks**. This question requires you to show how you would use performance skills to play a role. You need to:

- identify **three** techniques
- provide a **linked explanation** for each.

> **Explaining** means you need to give **reasons** for your answers.

> Section A questions test **Assessment Objective 3** (Demonstrate **knowledge** and **understanding** of how drama and theatre is **developed** and **performed**). So you need to show that you understand how to use performance skills to **communicate** specific ideas to an audience.

Question (b)

This question:

- is from the perspective of a **director**
- will be in **two parts**.

Part (i) is worth **9 marks**. You will be given a choice of production elements (such as costume, staging, set). You need to:

- refer to **specific aspects** of the production element and its **practical application**.
- make clear **links** between the performance element, extract and **context** of the extract across your answer
- provide examples to **justify** your ideas.

Part (ii) is worth **12 marks**. The question will focus on **directing a performer**. You need to:

- demonstrate how a director will work with a performer, providing **specific examples** of voice, physicality, stage directions and stage space
- **justify** your ideas with examples from the extract
- demonstrate an **understanding** of the **whole play**.

Question (c)

This question:

- is from the perspective of a **designer**
- will be in **one part**
- is worth **14 marks**.

You need to:

- select **one design element** from a list of **three**. These options will always be different from those in Question (b) (ii)
- show how you would use the design element to **enhance the production** for an audience
- illustrate your **understanding** of the **technical requirements** of the design element and how it can be **practically applied**
- **link** the design element to the extract, putting your ideas into a context
- **justify** your ideas fully using examples from the text.

> **Remember:** Directors and designers have different approaches. A director ensures the general design is **consistent** with the production's overall style and message. A designer provides **detailed** designs that **support** the director's ideas. For Questions (b) and (c), make sure your answers reflect this difference.

Now try this

Choose **either** Question (b) **or** Question (c) from above. List the technical vocabulary that will help make your answer to this type of question clear. Check you know exactly what each term means and how to use it with reference to your performance text.

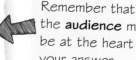

> Remember that the **audience** must be at the heart of your answer.

Approaching the extract

In the exam you will be working to a **time limit**. Therefore, it is important you approach the questions in a **structured**, systematic way. Spending a few minutes reading the question and making sure you fully understand the extract can save you a lot of time and help ensure you answer each question in detail and correctly.

Plan your time

Having a **plan** to follow in the exam will help you make the most of your time.

Each question is worth a different number of marks: the more marks available, the more time you should spend on the question. You have **105 minutes** in total.

Tackling Section A

1. **Open** the Questions and Extracts booklet to the performance text you have been studying in Drama.

2. **Read** the **whole extract** carefully, including all of the stage directions. **Skim** and **scan** for key characters, setting and action. Be clear who is saying each line.

3. **Read** the **questions** that relate to your performance text. Consider carefully what you are being asked to do. If it helps, make notes on the extract, planning your response to the question and thinking about the **context** of the extract.

4. Write your answer in the correct space in the Answer booklet, referring back to the text to **support** and **justify** your answer.

A possible plan

Here is a **possible outline** that breaks down the 105 minutes into each section. The timings are approximate, but broadly space out the time you have against the marks available for each question. It uses 9am as the start time of the exam.

09.00	Find the correct extract and read it carefully. Open the question paper and read the questions relating to your extract.	8 minutes
09.08	Answer Section A: bringing texts to life. **Question (a) (i)** – 4 marks.	4 minutes
09.12	Answer **Question (a) (ii)** – 6 marks.	6 minutes
09.18	Answer **Question (b) (i)** – 9 marks.	14 minutes
09.32	Answer **Question (b) (ii)** – 12 marks.	20 minutes
09.52	Answer **Question (c)** – 14 marks.	23 minutes
10.15	Answer Section B: live theatre evaluation. **Question 9 (a)** – 6 marks.	10 minutes
10.25	Answer **Question 9 (b)** – 9 marks.	15 minutes
10.40	Check all answers.	5 minutes
10.45	End of exam.	

Annotate the extract

Annotate the extract from your performance text as much as you like. Highlighting, circling or underlining words and phrases can help you **structure your answers** and make sure you stick to your point.

- ✓ Use a different coloured pen.
- ✓ Pay attention to the stage directions.
- ✓ Make sure you can still read the extract after you have highlighted something.
- ✓ Make brief notes in the margins if it helps.

Now try this

Construct your own plan for the exam. Think carefully about where you can gain the most marks and try to allocate the right amount of time to each question. When you have got a plan, apply it to different start times (for example, 12.30pm or 1pm), to help you understand when you would have to move on in the real exam.

When you are practising your answers, try to stick to the time limits you have planned, to help you prepare for the real thing.

Question (a) (i): vocal skills

Question (a) (i) asks you to **explain** how you, as a performer, could use either **vocal skills** or **physical skills** to play a particular character in a given extract. The question will make the skills focus clear. On this page, the focus is on **vocal skills**. See page 88 for a focus on physical skills.

Answering the question

Question (a) (i) is worth **4 marks**, so spend about **4 minutes** on this question. You will have to give **two** examples.

 Both choices have to **complement** each other and should show your ideas.

 You need to **explain**, not describe – state what you would do and say **why**.

 Fully **justify** your answer, showing **why** you have made your choices.

 Support your answer with **evidence** from the extract.

Worked example

You are going to play Julia. Explain **two** ways you would use **vocal skills** to play this character in this extract.   **(4 marks)**

Sample answer

1. I would use a rising tone of voice over the two lines, to indicate my growing frustration with Winston.
2. Linked to this, I would add a slight pause after the question 'Honestly?' and before 'It's boring.' to show I am asking a rhetorical question and provoking him further into the argument.

This question is about an extract from *1984*; prescribed edition, page 48, from line 14 (Winston) to line 28 (end of stage direction).

Keep focused on the action. Here, Winston and Julia are arguing, and the student has clearly picked up the tone of the scene.

Indicate the vocal skill you want to use, then justify your choice.

 Links You can find out more about **vocal skills** on pages 6–11.

The context of the extract

To decide which vocal skills would be the most appropriate, think about:

- the context of the scene
- who the character is
- where the extract falls within the whole play
- what has already happened.

Then use your knowledge of the character to decide what they are trying to achieve.

This question is about an extract from *The Crucible*: prescribed edition, page 108, lines 13–17.

Worked example

You are going to play Mary Warren. Explain **two** ways you would use **vocal skills** to play this character in this extract.   **(4 marks)**

Sample answer

1. I would use a wild and frantic tone, indicating my fear and desperation.
2. On the line 'Abby, Abby, I'll never hurt you more!', I would soften the sobbing in my voice, showing my change of loyalty.

Identify two examples and give a clear reason for both choices.

Now try this

Choose one character from your performance text, and choose one scene in which that character appears.

Explain **two** ways you could use **vocal skills** to play the character in this scene.   **(4 marks)**

Remember to give **two** examples of what you would do **and** explain why.

Question (a) (i): physical skills

Question (a) (i) might ask you to explain how you could use **physical skills** to play a particular character in a given extract. See page 87 for some advice on answering Question (a) (i), and for some worked examples based on vocal skills.

Worked example

You are going to play Sir Andrew Aguecheek. Explain **two** ways you would use **physical skills** to play this character in this extract. **(4 marks)**

This question is about this extract from Act 5, Scene 1 of *Twelfth Night*.

Enter SIR ANDREW AGUECHEEK.
SIR ANDREW For the love of God, a surgeon! Send one presently to Sir Toby.
OLIVIA What's the matter?
SIR ANDREW He has broke my head across, and has given Sir Toby a bloody coxcomb too. For the love of God, your help!

Sample answer

1. I would use a staggering movement to indicate that I was injured and in pain, and I would hold my head to show the location of my injury.
2. I would gesture off-stage to indicate that the injury took place there.

Examples can be simple, such as gesturing to indicate another character or location, as long as you say **why**.

Make sure your answer is relevant to the extract. Here, the student needs to show that Sir Andrew has been injured.

 Links See pages 12–15 for more about **physical skills**.

Paying close attention to the extract

Make sure you read the extract carefully. This will help you to keep your answer as relevant as possible. It can help if you annotate important words or lines in the extract when you read it. These could be from the spoken words, but also from the stage directions.

> Oh no. Hide! No, I can't hide...Fine. Let him in. They can throw me in prison but they won't break my spirit. (*Shouts.*) You hear? I'm ready. Take me away (*Holds his hands out to be handcuffed. Then suddenly cowers.*) No no, I don't want to go.

This question is about the extract from *Government Inspector* on the left, from the end of Act 2, Scene 3.

Worked example

You are going to play Khlestakov. Explain **two** ways you would use **physical skills** to play this character in this extract. **(4 marks)**

Sample answer

1. I would sweep my hand to my forehead, comically emphasising that I feel I am a harshly treated victim.
2. I would then fall melodramatically to the floor, showing that I have accepted that I am going to be arrested.

Now try this

Choose one character from your performance text, and choose one scene in which that character appears. Explain **two** ways you could use **physical skills** to play the character in this scene. **(4 marks)**

Remember to give **two** examples of what you would do **and** explain why.

Question (a) (ii)

Question (a) (ii) is broader than Question (a) (i). You will need to think carefully about what the question is asking you to communicate as a **performer**.

Answering the question

Question (a) (ii) is worth **6 marks**, so spend about **6 minutes** answering this question. Give **three** suggestions of how you would use **performance skills** to portray the character in the extract. For each example:

☑ indicate which skills you would use

☑ **justify** your answers, giving clear reasons.

Key tips

- Performance skills include both **physical** and **vocal** skills.
- Your ideas must also reference any **stage directions** included in the extract.
- Consider the **relationships** between characters, to help establish how and why the selected character might react and respond in the way they do.

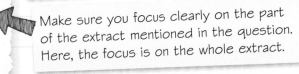 **Links** Turn to pages 16–25 for more on performance skills.

Worked example

You are going to play Tess. She is nervous and yet slightly braver and more curious than some of the other girls in this extract.

As a performer, give **three** suggestions of how you would use **performance skills** to show her growing curiosity from the start of this extract.

You must provide a reason for each suggestion. **(6 marks)**

This question is about an extract from *Blue Stockings*: from Act 1, Scene 1, from 'MR BANKS emerges on a bicycle. All four WOMEN step back in trepidation', to 'TESS. Eight miles in an hour! Woo!'

Sample answer

1. To show that Tess is 'a little braver' than the other girls, I would take a small, hesitant step forward to indicate that I am still unsure but am curious to find out what Mr Banks has planned for us with the bicycle.

2. As I try to get on the bicycle, I would fail to get my leg over the frame and would rearrange my skirt and look for help from the other girls. This would show that I have never ridden a bicycle before but am bravely determined to try.

3. I would deliver the line, 'Sir, I don't think it is ladylike to exert yourself' with a self-mocking tone, indicating that I have got over my inhibitions but I know this is not considered 'normal' or 'appropriate' behaviour for a woman.

 Make sure you focus clearly on the part of the extract mentioned in the question. Here, the focus is on the whole extract.

 Consider the subtext of the extract. How might this affect the way the character is played?

Think about a character's motives and status. This will affect the way the character behaves on stage, such as posture, vocal tone and gesture.

In this answer, the student has given **three** suggestions of how **performance skills** could be used to show Tess's growing curiosity. The student provides very detailed reasons for each suggestion made.

Now try this

Choose one character from your performance text and one scene in which that character appears.

As a performer, give **three** suggestions of how you would use **performance skills** to convey your chosen character's intentions to an audience in this extract.

You must provide a reason for each suggestion.

(6 marks)

Question (b) (i): costume

Question (b) (i) asks you about specific choices in the extract for a director. You need to discuss how you would use **one** particular **production element** to bring the extract to life. You will be given a **choice of three** of these production elements: **costume, staging, props/stage furniture, set, lighting** or **sound**. Here, the focus is on costume.

📎 **Links** For more on costume, turn to pages 41–47.

Answering the question

Question (b) (i) is worth **9 marks**, so you need to demonstrate **linked understanding** to the wider **context** of the play, as well as how costume affects **other production elements**. Consider:

☑ What do you want to **communicate**?

☑ What is the **context** within the wider play?

☑ Are there any **symbolic** aspects within other production elements that can be reflected in the costume?

☑ What **practical** considerations are there for those using the costume?

Worked example

As a director, discuss how you would use **one** of the **production elements below** to bring this extract to life for your audience.

You should make reference to the context in which the text was created and performed.

Choose **one** of the following:

- costume   • staging   • props/stage furniture.

(9 marks)

Sample extract

As a director, I would use stereotyped costume to show the audience the different types of shopkeepers approaching Khlestakov – for example, a baker wearing a white apron covered in flour, or a tailor in a suit draped with a tape measure. Each costume must clearly show the type of shop, but must also reflect the poverty the shopkeepers are complaining about. I would direct the butcher to wear dark trousers and a long white jacket with a full-length white apron heavily stained with blood – making it clear that he cannot afford to clean his apron or buy a new one. The dirt and blood will also indicate the difference in status between the poor shopkeepers and Khlestakov.

Remember to:
- fully **justify** your answers, using clues from the extract as well as your own knowledge of the performance text as a whole
- support your answer with **evidence**.

This question is about an extract from *Government Inspector*: from Act 4, Scene 8, line 40 ('Mishka goes. Outside, the sound of several footsteps, voices') to Act 4, Scene 9, line 5 ('It's the Mayor, Excellency.').

 Refer clearly to the **audience**.

 Think about how to **communicate** character type to the audience. Be specific. This answer suggests particular costume items, such as an apron covered in flour, to indicate each trade.

 Show a **linked understanding** to the wider **context** of the play. Here, the student highlights the difference in **status** between Khlestakov and the poor shopkeepers.

Now try this

Choose a character from an extract from your performance text.

As a director, discuss how you would use **costume** to bring this extract to life for your audience.

You should make reference to the context in which the text was created and performed. **(9 marks)**

 Try to fully **justify** your answers, using clues from the extract and also your own knowledge of the performance text as a whole.

Question (b) (i): staging

Question (b) (i) asks you about specific choices in the extract for a director. Here, the focus is on **staging.**

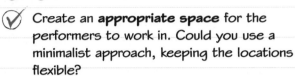 **Links** See pages 29 and 30 for more about staging.

When answering Question (b) (i) for staging

✓ Refer to **entrances** and **exits** for the performers and the impact this will have on the action on stage.

✓ Show **awareness** of the **audience** – where is it in relation to the action on stage? What about sightlines and using the audience space as part of the performance?

✓ Create an **appropriate space** for the performers to work in. Could you use a minimalist approach, keeping the locations flexible?

✓ Consider different **levels** and what these could represent. Could you use blocks or ramps to show different locations or the characters' different status?

Worked example

As a director, discuss how you would use **one** of the **production elements below** to bring this extract to life for your audience.

You should make reference to the context in which the text was created and performed.

Choose **one** of the following:

- costume
- staging
- props/stage furniture. **(9 marks)**

This question refers to an extract from near the opening of *100*, when the Guide enters.

Refer clearly to the **audience**, to put it at the heart of your response.

Use accurate and appropriate **technical vocabulary**, such as 'thrust stage' and 'upstage centre'.

Sample extract

As a director, I would want the staging to help emphasise the isolation of the Guide for the audience, clearly indicating he is separate to the other characters. I would use a thrust stage and have an entrance upstage centre for the Guide to use. This entrance would be raised higher, using a ramp, making the Guide seem instantly more powerful than the other characters and creating a focal point for the audience. It would also show how the Guide is isolated from the rest of the world. I would also scatter the boxes down stage, symbolising the confusion and disorientation of the other characters. This would also create a physical gap between the characters and the Guide, again highlighting the Guide's sense of isolation.

Create links between the themes and issues of the scene (here, the isolation of the Guide trapped in the Void) and the physical representation on stage (here, the isolation of the ramp from the rest of the stage).

Give clear reasons for your decisions. Here, the student explains clearly the reason for the positioning of the ramp.

This is an extract from a complete student answer. To complete this answer, you would need to demonstrate further how the chosen element (in this case, staging) could be used to enhance the production of the extract.

Now try this

Remember to take as much information as you can from the **stage directions.** Also include **evidence** from the extract and wider text to support and justify your answers.

Choose an extract from your performance text.

As a director, discuss how you would use **staging** to bring this extract to life for your audience.

You should make reference to the context in which the text was created and performed. **(9 marks)**

Question (b) (i): props

Question (b) (i) asks you about specific choices in the extract for a director. Here, the focus is on **props/stage furniture**.

 Links You can find out about props and stage furniture on page 59.

When answering Question (b) (i) for props/stage furniture

✓ **Refer to the time the play is set.** For example, *Blue Stockings* is set in 1896. Therefore, the men will carry pens from that time, and writing paper will not be lined. Characters may have a pocket watch rather than a wristwatch.

✓ **Refer to items that indicate the location.** For example, for *Blue Stockings* those items would be from a university science classroom, such as desks, test tubes, jars and other science equipment.

✓ **Refer to props that help indicate who each of the characters is.** For example, in *Blue Stockings*, Mr Banks, as the lecturer, may have a briefcase to carry his papers, or a folder, held by a ribbon, in which he carries the men's essays.

Worked example

As a director, discuss how you would use **one** of the **production elements below** to bring this extract to life for your audience.

You should make reference to the context in which the text was created and performed.

Choose **one** of the following:
- costume
- staging
- props/stage furniture.   **(9 marks)**

This question refers to an extract from Act 1, Scene 12 of *Blue Stockings*, from: 'MR BANKS (*referencing their essays*). These 'wonders of the human mind'. They're articulate, they're accurate. They're first class. But there's something missing' to: '*The* MEN *don't move; they are all reading the essay.*'

Sample extract

As a director, I would want to make sure that the audience clearly understands the status of the characters. For example, I would direct Mr Banks, who is a lecturer, to carry a leather briefcase. This would have a practical use, as a way of carrying the essays he hands back to the students. However, it would symbolise his status, as only fairly wealthy people could have afforded this kind of item in Victorian England. I would want the briefcase to be made of dark brown leather and covered with marks and scratches, to show it is old and well used. As the play is set in 1896, the briefcase would have a top opening with a brass catch, to represent the time period.

This answer creates a link between the **symbolic** and **practical** purposes of the briefcase, indicating that only certain people would have a need for such an item – as well as the money to buy one.

 Refer clearly to the **audience**, to put it at the heart of your response.

This is an extract from a complete student answer. To complete this answer, you would need to demonstrate further how the chosen element (in this case, props/stage furniture) could be used to enhance the production of the extract.

Now try this

Choose an extract from your performance text.

As a director, discuss how you would use **props/stage furniture** to bring this extract to life for your audience.

You should make reference to the context in which the text was created and performed.   **(9 marks)**

 Remember to refer to the **context** in which the text was created and performed.

Question (b) (i): set

Question (b) (i) asks you about specific choices in the extract for a director. Here, the focus is on **set**.

 Links Turn to pages 55–62 for more about set.

When answering Question (b) (i) for set

✓ Refer to the **time** and **location** of the play.

✓ Refer to the **style** of the piece. For example, a **naturalistic** set will include period furniture. A **minimalist** set will have much less detail but will still be highly representative.

✓ Consider the **entrance** into the room. Where could a door be positioned, for example?

✓ **Consider the levels.** For example, in *Goverment Inspector* the hotel room is likely to be **upstairs**.

✓ Consider use of **space** and the **type of staging** and how this would **affect** the set design and the **audience**.

✓ Always refer to **examples** from the text.

Worked example

As a director, discuss how you would use **one** of the **production elements below** to bring this extract to life for your audience.

You should make reference to the context in which the text was created and performed.

Choose **one** of the following:

• set   • lighting   • sound.   **(9 marks)**

This question is about these stage directions from *Government Inspector*, Act 2, Scene 1:

A room at the inn. Bed, table, suitcase, empty bottle, slippers, clothes brush, etc. Osip, Khlestakov's servant, lies on the bed, clutching his stomach.

Refer clearly to the **audience**, to put them at the heart of your response.

This answer refers briefly to stage furniture, indicating that the set is not operating in isolation.

Sample extract

As a director, I would want the audience to recognise immediately that the scene is set in an inn. This is important because Khlestakov and Osip are not local, unlike other characters. The stage directions give very specific details about the furniture that should be in the room. As the play was first performed in 1836, I would want the set to reflect the time period of the 1830s and the location. The town is in the middle of nowhere and unfashionable – this could be shown through a simple and slightly shabby set. For example, I would direct the bed to have old woollen blankets and stained pillows.

As this set is used only once, I would direct it to be raised to a high level, with open stairs. This would allow the audience to see first Khlestakov and then the Mayor arriving, building tension. I would position three flats upstage left. The flat furthest upstage would be parallel to the audience, but the others would be angled to create a funnel effect, giving an enclosed feeling.

This is an extract from a complete student answer. To complete this answer, you would need to demonstrate further how the chosen element (in this case, set) could be used to enhance the production of this extract, remembering to:

• indicate use of levels

• give specific examples of how to establish location for the audience, referring to furnishings, decoration, colours and materials

• justify your answers.

Use accurate and appropriate technical vocabulary to help identify key aspects of the set design such as 'upstage left'.

Now try this

Choose an extract from your performance text.

As a director, discuss how you would use **set** to bring this extract to life for your audience.

You should make reference to the context in which the text was created and performed.   **(9 marks)**

Consider **entrances and exits** and how they might represent different locations within the play. Refer to the **context** in which the text was created and performed.

Question (b) (i): lighting

Question (b) (i) asks you about specific choices in the extract for a director. Here, the focus is on **lighting**.

🔗 **Links** See pages 48–54 for more about lighting.

When answering Question (b) (i) for lighting

✓ **Refer to the time of day the extract is set.** For example, although *DNA* is set outdoors, the time of day and even the season can be shown through lighting.

✓ **Refer to items that indicate the location.** For example, in *DNA*, the woods can be represented with a leaf gobo and a mix of greens and blues to indicate the light passing through the trees.

✓ **Refer to the mood and atmosphere that lighting can produce.** For example, in *DNA*, the actions of the characters are sinister and secretive. Using lighting to create shadows and an eerie feeling, with blue and green gels, can enhance the fear factor for the audience.

Worked example

As a director, discuss how you would use **one** of the **production elements below** to bring this extract to life for your audience. You should make reference to the context in which the text was created and performed.

Choose **one** of the following:
- set   • lighting   • sound.   **(9 marks)**

This question is about an extract taken from Section 3 of *DNA*. If this is your performance text and you have the prescribed edition, the extract is from pages 47–50.

Refer clearly to the **audience**, to put it at the heart of your response.

Sample extract

As a director, I would want my audience to understand there are two different locations in this scene – the field and the wood. I would also use the lighting to symbolise the darkening mood as the characters enter the wood. For the field I would therefore use yellow and orange gels at quite a high light level. In contrast, I would use a combination of dark and light greens for the wood. I would add a pale yellow gobo of a speckled pattern to represent the sun shining through the trees.

I would direct a broad wash of greens and blues, mixed with some yellow for the wood, to represent emotions. For example, the fear of some characters could be symbolised with green, and blue could highlight how others are going along with the situation. A narrow, hard-edged spotlight on Leah and Phil would symbolise the intense pressure that Leah putting Phil under. For the second part of the scene, I would then use a smooth fade to move the focus to the other part of the stage.

Use accurate and appropriate technical vocabulary (here, for example, 'gels', 'broad wash' and 'hard-edged spotlight') to communicate your intentions and techniques clearly.

Justify each idea you give; here, the student explains how the hard-edged spotlight is symbolic of the pressure that Leah is trying to place on Phil.

This is an extract from a complete student answer. To complete this answer, you would need to further demonstrate how the chosen element (in this case, lighting) could be used to enhance the production of this extract.

Now try this

Choose an extract from your performance text.

As a director, discuss how you would use **lighting** to bring this extract to life for your audience.

You should make reference to the context in which the text was created and performed.   **(9 marks)**

What specific lighting do the **locations** require? What time of day is it? Is there a need to indicate an exit to a different location? What **mood** or **atmosphere** is required?

Question (b) (i): sound

Question (b) (i) asks you about specific choices in the extract for a director. Here, the focus is on **sound**.

 Links You can find out more about sound on pages 63–67.

When answering Question (b) (i) for sound

☑ Sound and music can enhance mood and atmosphere: a distant rumble of thunder may create an ominous atmosphere, while birdsong may lighten the mood.

☑ Music can reinforce the time period in which a play is set, if music from that era is used.

☑ Music can add atmosphere to a monologue: it could crescendo to build tension and reflect the power of the words.

☑ Sound may reference a play's specific situation, era, location or symbolic meaning.

☑ Sound and music may enable performers to indicate their status.

☑ Sounds can be used to indicate the style of the performance, for example, whether it is realistic or symbolic.

Worked example

As a director, discuss how you would use **one** of the **production elements below** to bring this extract to life for your audience.

You should make reference to the context in which the text was created and performed.

Choose **one** of the following:
- set • lighting • sound. **(9 marks)**

This question is about an extract from Act 3 of *An Inspector Calls*. If this is your performance text and you have the prescribed edition, see pages 55–56.

Sample extract

As a director, I would want the audience to understand the serious moral message in the Inspector's monologue. As the inspectors demands silence, I would direct a short pause and then a distant rumble of thunder. This sound effect would symbolise the approaching storm – the one in the characters' lives as well as the physical storm outside. This would build tension for the audience, and I would add to this with gloomy music that underscores the monologue and increases in volume during the final lines. The music would be played by a string quartet and would reflect the year in which the play is set – 1912.

The stage directions indicate a door slams as the Inspector leaves. I would also direct a repetition of the thunder effect as the Inspector exits, emphasising his mysterious character as well as the problems the Birlings are facing.

Refer clearly to the **audience**, to put it at the heart of your response.

Think about how sound and music can create a specific atmosphere – in this example, helping to build tension.

Use accurate and appropriate technical vocabulary, such as 'silence' and 'underscores'.

This is an extract from a complete student answer. To complete this answer, you would need to demonstrate how the chosen element (in this case, sound) could be used to further enhance the production of this extract.

Now try this

Choose an extract from your performance text.

As a director, discuss how you would use **sound** to bring this extract to life for your audience.

You should make reference to the context in which the text was created and performed. **(9 marks)**

Refer clearly to the **location** of the scene. Sound effects could indicate the context of the location. Techniques such as a **fade** and **cross fade** can help to alter the audience's perception throughout a scene.

Question (b) (ii)

Question (b) (ii) also asks you about specific choices in the extract for a **director**. You will need to discuss how a performer might play a particular **character** in the extract and in the play as a whole. You will need to think about **voice, physicality, stage directions** and **stage space**.

Answering the question

Question (b) (ii) is worth **12 marks**, so spend about **20 minutes** on this question.

- ✓ **Voice** – Focus on the delivery of specific lines and consider tone, pitch, pace and pause.
- ✓ **Physicality** – Consider levels, gestures, facial expressions, body language, posture and subtext.
- ✓ **Stage directions and stage space** – Consider the physical stage space and any restictions, levels and proxemics.

- ✓ Demonstrate your understanding of how a director would work with a performer.
- ✓ Discuss a range of options and pick the best one.
- ✓ Refer to the given extract and the play as a whole.
- ✓ Focus on the impact on the audience.
- ✓ Link all performance skills together.

🔗 **Links**   For more about performance skills, turn to pages 5–25.

Worked example

Winston has the lowest status in the play as a whole.

As a director, discuss how the performer playing this role might demonstrate low status to the audience in this extract and the complete play.

You must consider:

- voice
- physicality
- stage directions and stage space. **(12 marks)**

This question is about an extract from the torture scene in *1984*. If this is your performance text and you have the prescribed edition, see pages 73–77.

Sample extract

As a director, I would instruct the performer playing Winston to show the audience that he is both maintaining his status and challenging O'Brien by using a steady but rebellious tone. As the pain of Winston's torture increases, I would direct the performer to show that Winston is breaking down vocally, for example, by stammering as if forcing the words out. I would also direct him to speak with a break in his voice, as if under extreme pressure.

The pain of the torture should also be seen physically. For example, when Winston is strapped into a chair, as the torturers go to remove his fingertips, I would direct him to tense his body, bracing against the pain he knows is coming. This will make the audience empathise with the pain he is feeling.

Indicate how you, as a director, would make decisions relating to characterisation.

This is an extract from a complete student answer. To complete this answer, you would need to demonstrate further how you would work with a performer to develop character and situation, while:

- placing the extract in **context** and showing the character's journey
- considering different aspects of the character, such as status, motivation
- referring to stage directions and use of stage space
- supporting your answer with examples.

Now try this

Choose a character from your performance text and select one scene in which that character appears. Decide which aspect of this character you feel is important.

As a director, discuss how the performer playing this role might demonstrate this to the audience in this extract and the complete play. **(12 marks)**

Question (c): costume

Question (c) asks you about specific choices in the extract for a designer. You need to discuss how you would use a particular **design element** to make the production more appealing to an audience. You will be given a **choice of three** of these design elements: **costume, staging, props/stage furniture, set, lighting** or **sound**. Here, the focus is on **costume**.

 Links   See pages 41–47 for more on costume.

Answering the question

Question (c) is worth **14 marks**, so spend around **23 minutes** on this question.

✓ **Discuss** your ideas **in detail** and consider different options and opinions.

✓ Show how your ideas **enhance** the extract, such as using costume to signify status.

✓ Make the **audience** central – how will your ideas affect the audience?

✓ Make **links** to other design elements and to the play as a whole.

✓ **Justify** your ideas and support them with **evidence** from the extract and the wider play.

✓ Show how your ideas represent or **symbolise** the play's **themes** or ideas

✓ Keep your ideas **practical** for the performer.

Worked example

Discuss how you would use **one** design element to enhance the production of this extract for the audience.

Choose **one** of the following:

- costume
- staging
- props/stage furniture.   **(14 marks)**

This question is about an extract from *Twelfth Night*, from Act 3, Scene 4, lines 1–91. If this is your performance text and you have the prescribed edition, see pages 111–117.

Sample extract

As a costume designer for this extract, I would want to show the audience the status of each of the characters. As head of the household, Olivia holds the highest status. However, she is mourning the death of her brother so I would design a black dress, keeping the design simple and without accessories. This would be full length and have long sleeves, covering her arms and legs, to show that she has rejected men and marriage.

I would then design a second dress to be worn once Olivia meets Cesario. This would have elegant, swirling patterns of grey and silver, which would appear and disappear under the intensity of the lighting. The patterns would represent Olivia's confused emotions and also the storm that brought Cesario to her. They would also represent the confusion of the plot.

Make connections. Here, the student links the characters' status to their costumes, adding context.

Include plenty of detail, for example about style and colours.

Link briefly to other production elements, to show that the costume must be consistent with and complement these.

This is an extract from a complete student answer. To complete this answer, you would need to demonstrate further how the chosen element (in this case, costume) could be used to enhance the production of this extract. Remember to suggest how costume can:
- reference the play's specific situation, era, location or symbolic meaning
- show a performer's status
- indicate the style of the performance.

Now try this

Choose a scene from your performance text.

Discuss how you would use **costume** to enhance the production of this extract for the audience.   **(14 marks)**

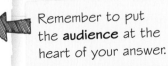 Remember to put the **audience** at the heart of your answer.

Question (c): staging

Question (c) asks you about specific choices in the extract for a designer. Here, the focus is on **staging**.

🔗 **Links**   Turn to pages 58–61 for more on staging.

Worked example

Discuss how you would use **one** design element to enhance the production of this extract for the audience.

Choose **one** of the following:

- costume
- staging
- props/stage furniture.   **(14 marks)**

This question is about an extract from *DNA*, from Act 3 – the scene in the wood where we first see Adam.

Refer clearly to the **audience**, to put it at the heart of your response.

Sample extract

As a designer, I would choose theatre-in-the-round staging to highlight to the audience how the characters are constantly watched within the play. However, I would adapt this so that a small section of the stage is free of the audience. Here, I would raise the staging in a gentle slope that is easy and safe for performers to climb. This would provide clear sightlines. I would cover this area with leaves to represent the woodland, and to make the sightlines clearer I would also include a leaf-patterned gobo in the lighting design for this section of the stage.

I would design the entire performance area to be covered in dirty, patchy, artificial grass and I would add leaves and bits of rubbish. This would provide flexible basic staging for the different locations in the play.

In this scene, several characters leave to go to different locations, so I would design a number of exit routes through the audience. For example, when Brian takes Adam back to the hedge, they would leave upstage, over the raised area, as if he is entering the woods. This supports the text as, earlier in the scene, Cathy says they found Adam up the hill.

Justify each decision you make. This student explains how ensuring that a small section of the stage is clear and raised will support the sightlines of the audience.

Consider the practical and safe use of the staging. Here, the student discusses how the gentle slope is easy and safe for the performers to climb.

Use accurate and appropriate technical vocabulary, such as 'theatre-in-the-round' and 'gobo'.

This is an extract from a complete student answer. To complete this answer, you would need to demonstrate further how the chosen element (in this case, staging) could be used to enhance the production of this extract. Remember to state how the staging may:
- reference the play's situation, era, location or symbolic meaning
- show a performer's status
- indicate the style of the performance.

Now try this

Choose a scene from your performance text.

Discuss how you would use **staging** to enhance the production of this extract for the audience.   **(14 marks)**

Remember to put the **audience** at the heart of your answer. The perspective of the audience will be different to that of the characters on stage, so the audience must be clear about what is going on and why. It is also vital for any subtleties to be clear to the audience, to ensure no one becomes confused.

Question (c): props

Question (c) asks you about specific choices in the extract for a designer. Here, the focus is on **props/stage furniture**.

 Links   You can revise props and stage furniture on page 59.

Worked example

Discuss how you would use **one** design element to enhance the production of this extract for an audience.

Choose **one** of the following:

- costume
- staging
- props/stage furniture.   **(14 marks)**

This question is about an extract from the torture scene in *1984*. If this is your performance text and you have the prescribed edition, see pages 73–77.

Refer clearly to the **audience**, to put it at the heart of your response.

Sample extract

As a designer, I would want the audience to understand that the torture used by the regime is efficient and without emotion. I would design a two-tiered metal trolley, which would hold the tools in a way that the audience can see them clearly. Instead of covering the trolley with blood, I would design it to be spotless to show how impersonal the torture is. I would also add wheels to the trolley to make it portable for the performers, but also to highlight the regime's efficiency.

Like the trolley, I would design the tools to be metal and highly polished. This would reflect the merciless expertise of the regime. Each tool would be large enough for the audience to be able to identify its chilling purpose. For example, a scalpel would have a straight, stainless steel handle for an easy grip, with a curved blade to hint at its efficient slicing power. I would make sure the blade is visible to the audience, so that there is no doubt what is about to happen to Winston – building sudden tension.

The tools would be laid out in a highly organised way, so that they are easy to reach. I would lay them directly on the metal trolley, rather than on a cloth, so that the clang as they are replaced rings through the theatre.

Consider the practical and safe use of the props. In this example, the wheeled trolley enables the performers to enter and exit the stage with the props quickly, safely and fairly quietly.

Justify each decision you make. This student explains how ensuring that the tools are big enough will allow the audience to identify clearly what each one is and its purpose.

This is an extract from a complete student answer. To complete this answer, you would need to demonstrate further how the chosen element (in this case, props/stage furniture) could be used to enhance the production of this extract. Remember to consider how the props/stage furniture may:

- reference the play's situation, era, location or symbolic meaning
- show a performer's status
- indicate the style (such as realistic or symbolic) of the performance.

Now try this

Choose a scene from your performance text.

Discuss how you would use **props** and **stage furniture** to enhance the production of this extract for the audience.   **(14 marks)**

 Remember, your answer will need to include a range of aspects in relation to **both** props and stage furniture.

99

Question (c): set

Question (c) asks you about specific choices in the extract for a designer. Here, the focus is on **set**.

 Links Turn to pages 55–62 for more about set.

Worked example

Discuss how you would use **one** design element to enhance the production of this extract for the audience.

Choose **one** of the following:

* set
* lighting
* sound. **(14 marks)**

This question is about an extract from *An Inspector Calls*, from the beginning of Act 1.

Sample extract

As a designer, I would want to show the audience that the Birlings think they are safely isolated from the poverty and unhappiness of the outside world. To do this, I would build on an end-on stage, a set that feels very enclosed. I would do this by surrounding the dining room with full-height stage flats to represent the walls.

To contrast the strange, almost supernatural, events in the plot, I would design a very naturalistic set. For example, I would cover the flats in early 20th-century wallpaper and I would use furniture from the same period.

There would be one entrance into the dining room: oak-panelled double doors, positioned in the upstage centre flat. This would support the idea that the Birlings are protected from the real world, but would later also highlight how they cannot escape events. Designing the entrance like this would also make it easy for the Inspector to reach any part of the room, preventing other characters from leaving.

I would also design the set to make the family's wealth clear. For example, I would position an elegant dining table side-on to the audience. This would also help give clear sightlines. The table would be laid with expensive items, such as silver candlesticks.

 Refer clearly to the **audience**, to put it at the heart of your response.

 Justify each decision you make. This student explains how full-height flats will create an enclosed and isolated environment, signifying the attitude the Birlings have towards the community in which they live.

 Use accurate and appropriate technical vocabulary, such as 'flats' and 'sightlines'.

 Consider the practical and safe use of the set. In this example, the large double doors through which the Inspector enters become a focal point and allow the Inspector to control the room from that position.

This is an extract from a complete student answer. To complete this answer, you would need to demonstrate further how the chosen element (in this case, set) could be used to enhance the production of this extract. Remember to consider how set could be used to:

* reference the play's specific situation, era, location or symbolic meaning
* show a performer's status
* indicate the style (such as realistic or symbolic) of the performance.

Now try this

Choose a scene from your performance text.

Discuss how you would use **set** to enhance the production of this extract for the audience. **(14 marks)**

Think about how the performers will use the space, as well as what meaning will be conveyed to the audience.

Question (c): lighting

Question (c) asks you about specific choices in the extract for a designer. Here, the focus is on **lighting**.

 Links See pages 48–54 for more about lighting.

Worked example

Discuss how you would use **one** design element to enhance the production of this extract for the audience.

Choose **one** of the following:

- set
- lighting
- sound. **(14 marks)**

This question is about an extract from *The Crucible*, from the beginning of Act 2 to Proctor's words, I think you're sad again. Are you?' If this is your performance text and you have the prescribed edition, see pages 47–49.

Sample extract

As a designer, I would use lighting to make the time of day and the season clear for the audience: Elizabeth says 'It's almost dark.', suggesting it is nearly night-time, while Proctor mentions he was 'planting' and, later, that it is spring. To reflect this in the lighting design, I would cross-fade a white wash with a blue-purple wash, created by coloured gels, to show the change from daylight into an evening sky. This effect would be seen through the open door from which Proctor enters, as indicated in the stage directions.

I would use backlighting at this point to create a shadow, communicating Proctor's approach before he actually appears and introducing a sense of tension. I would repeat this effect later – when Mary Warren, and later Hale and the other visitors arrive. Each new shadow would increase the tension. In addition, the use of shadow would reflect how the Devil is seen in Salem – as dark, threatening, and afraid of the light, which represents God.

The light from the door would remind the audience of the different locations, such as the freedom of the wilderness outside, and the warm safety of the house, which is about to be destroyed. As the scene develops, I would fade to a darker blue-purple wash, to show the passing of time and to symbolise the dark events that will follow.

Refer clearly to the **audience**, to put it at the heart of your response.

Justify each decision you make. Here, taking clues from the text, the student has been able to establish the time of day as well as the season within the year. These points are backed up with evidence from the text.

Use accurate and appropriate technical vocabulary, such as 'gels', 'backlighting' and 'shadow'.

This answer makes symbolic connections to the events that are happening, helping to develop the mood and atmosphere of the extract. For example, the use of lighting to create shadow is linked to the Salem inhabitants' fear of the Devil.

This is an extract from a complete student answer. To complete this answer, you would need to demonstrate further how the chosen element (in this case, lighting) could be used to enhance the production of this extract. Remember to consider how lighting could be used to:

- reference the play's specific situation, era, location or symbolic meaning
- show a performer's status
- indicate the style (such as realistic or symbolic) of the performance.

Now try this

Careful use of colours can powerfully communicate ideas to an audience.

Select a scene from your performance text.

Discuss how you would use **lighting** to enhance the production of this extract for the audience. **(14 marks)**

Links To remind yourself of the **symbolism** of different colours, turn to page 44.

Question (c): sound

Question (c) asks you about specific choices in the extract for a designer. Here, the focus is on **sound**.

 Links For more about sound, turn to pages 63–67.

Worked example

Discuss how you would use **one** design element to enhance the production of this extract for the audience.

Choose **one** of the following:

- set
- lighting
- sound. **(14 marks)**

> This question is about an extract from *100*, from the very beginning of the play when the stage is initially empty to when the Guide begins to speak.

> Refer clearly to the **audience**, to put it at the heart of your response.

Sample extract

As a sound designer, I would want to communicate the other-worldly feeling experienced by the characters in the Void to the audience. This is a feeling of confusion and disorientation. The extract opens with an empty stage and I would underscore this with a faint, recorded sound. The base of the sound would be a mixture of sustained white noise and echoing, jarring music which fades in as the lighting becomes brighter. Alongside this, I would have random sound effects, such as a distant laugh or a sudden metallic clang. Other effects would include a subtle raindrop, a calming sound effect of a gentle breeze through trees and the sound of the sea gently lapping at the shore. I would then contrast these with harsh recorded sounds, such as a dog barking, the sound of glass smashing and a scream. Each specific effect would have a different volume level but all would be echoed to a fade and would then be repeated in a seemingly random pattern. This would convey how the characters are feeling and allow the audience to share their sense of disorientation. The continuity of the white noise would represent the fact that there is an infinite number of sounds all occurring at the same time, symbolising the unique setting that is the Void.

> Justify each decision you make. This student explains how varying the volume helps to disorientate the audience, allowing them to share the characters' feelings.

> Use accurate and appropriate technical vocabulary, such as 'volume' and 'sustained'.

> Think about how aspects such as location and emotion are reflected in the sound effects. For example, this student suggests digitally manipulating recorded sound by adding an echo, and repetition to create the effect of a random pattern.

> This is an extract from a complete student answer. To complete this answer, you would need to demonstrate further how the chosen element (in this case, sound) could be used to enhance the production of this extract. Remember to consider how sound could be used to:
> - reference the play's specific situation, era, location or symbolic meaning
> - show a performer's status
> - indicate the style (such as realistic or symbolic) of the performance.

Now try this

Select a scene from your performance text.

Discuss how you would use **sound** to enhance the production of this extract for the audience. **(14 marks)**

> Remember to consider the **impact** you want the sound to have on the **audience** in your answer.

About Section B

In Section B of the exam, you will have to answer two questions based on a single performance you have seen. Remember, both answers must be about the **same performance**.

Navigating the exam paper

Section B questions will focus on the contributions of **performers** and **designers**.

There are two questions in Section B.

- Question (a), worth **6 marks**, will ask you to **analyse** an aspect of the performance you have seen.
- Question (b), worth **9 marks**, will ask you to **evaluate** a different aspect from the same performance.

> You can take live theatre evaluation notes into the exam, up to a maximum of 500 words.

Planning your time

> The exam lasts for 1 hour 45 minutes (105 minutes) in total. There are 15 marks for Section B, which represents 25% of the total marks. So you should spend about 25% of the exam time – about 25–30 minutes – on Section B questions.

See pages 84–102 for more about Section A.

Analyse and evaluate

The questions in Section B will either ask you to **analyse** or **evaluate** the live performance you have seen. So you need to make sure you understand the difference between analysis and evaluation. In Section B of the exam:

- ✓ **analysis** is picking out key skills or ideas and being able to say how the performer or designers explored these
- ✓ **evaluation** is when you form a judgement about whether an idea or performance element has worked or not, giving effective supporting evidence.

Live performance

On these pages about Section B of the exam, all sample answers and student notes will be based on the National Theatre's 2011 production of *Frankenstein* by Nick Dear, with Benedict Cumberbatch as Frankenstein and Jonny Lee Miller as The Creature.

> A recording of this performance is available from the National Theatre's On Demand streaming service for schools.

> This is what a student analysing and evaluating the moment from *Frankenstein* shown below might write.

Worked example

An example of analysis.

Jonny Lee Miller as The Creature sucessfully used performance skills, including animated facial expressions and a twisted physicality, to show the creature's animal characteristics. The lighting used at this moment was particularly strong, as it used a powerful LED spotlight above the performers to highlight the struggle between Frankenstein and The Creature effectively.

Benedict Cumberbatch as Frankenstein and Jonny Lee Miller as The Creature in the National Theatre's 2011 production of *Frankenstein*.

The beginnings of evaluation.

Now try this

Using the definitions of analysis and evaluation above, take **one** key moment from a live theatre performance you have seen. Make notes that both analyse and evaluate this moment.

> For Section B your answer **must** be based on a live theatre performance and **not** a recording of a performance. You **cannot** base your answers on the production of *Frankenstein* used in these pages, or any other recorded performance.

Section B questions

It is important that you are familiar with the type and style of the questions you will face in Section B, and that you think carefully about how to prepare for this part of the exam.

Planning checklist

To prepare well for the exam, make sure you:

- ✓ build up a good bank of **relevant** drama vocabulary and terminology that you can draw on in the exam
- ✓ understand the difference between answering an 'analyse' question and answering an 'evaluate' question
- ✓ research the play you have seen; take careful notes of the style of performance or design approach used
- ✓ prepare detailed and relevant notes to take into the final exam.

See page 109 for more on what is allowed in the exam. For more on effective note-taking, turn to page 110.

This student has seen the National Theatre's 2011 performance of *Frankenstein*. They have started to prepare notes, guided by the checklist opposite.

1. Drama vocabulary and terminology for *Frankenstein*: gothic drama, physical theatre, end-on staging, stage make-up effects
2. Performance elements and skills for analysis: movement, gesture, facial expression, physicality
3. Evaluation of these skills: Jonny Lee Miller's movement is superb, with a menacing gait and strong eye contact
4. Details of the design style: the sound design uses a mix of electronic and emphatic music from the group 'Underworld'

Tackling Section B questions

When answering both Section B questions:

- provide a **balanced answer** for both evaluation and analysis
- respond to the **elements** mentioned in the question (for example, in the sample questions below the elements are stage space and lighting)
- provide **supporting examples** that are **detailed** and **well developed** (this is when your notes come in handy!)
- use the **drama vocabulary and terminology** that you have learned throughout the course.

The image below gives an example of Miller's 'menacing gait and strong eye contact' noted by the student above.

Jonny Lee Miller as The Creature and Naomie Harris as Elizabeth in the National Theatre's 2011 production of *Frankenstein*.

Worked example

Analyse how stage space was used to engage the audience during the closing moments of the performance. **(6 marks)**

An 'analyse' question

This example refers specifically to **stage space** and how it was used at the **end of the performance**. The key word in the question is **engage**. You need to analyse **how** the performers used stage space to catch the attention of the audience.

Worked example

Evaluate how lighting was used at different moments of the performance to create impact for the audience.

(9 marks)

An 'evaluation' question

This example is about **lighting**. No section of the performance is specified, so you can write about the one you feel is most relevant. You need to **analyse** the way that lighting was used and **evaluate** the impact of the lighting choices on the audience.

Now try this

Apply one of the questions above to a live performance you have seen. Use the checklist at the top of the page to create a plan of how you might answer this question.

In Section B of the exam, the analysis question asks you **how** something was achieved and the evaluate question asks you both **how** and **whether** it was achieved.

Question 9 (a): performance

In Section B of your exam you will have to answer questions about the **live performance** you have seen. Question 9 (a) will ask you to **analyse** how an element of the **performance or design** was used to engage the audience. On this page, the focus is on **performance**. See page 106 for a focus on design.

Answering the question

Question 9 (a) is worth **6 marks**, so you should aim to spend about 10 minutes on this question. This allows you about 15 minutes for Question 9 (b), which is worth 9 marks.

In your answer to this question, you will need to **analyse** an element of performance. When **analysing** a performance:

- ✓ pick out different elements used by the performer to **engage** the audience
- ✓ give **specific examples** of the **effect** these elements have on the audience
- ✓ use **appropriate vocabulary** and **drama terminology**.

Worked example

Analyse how movement was used to engage the audience during the opening moments of the performance.

(6 marks)

This question focuses on **movement**, so you need to outline how and where movement has been used, and the **effect** of this on the **audience**.

This question specifies the **opening** of the performance, so you should only focus your answer on this section. Notice the word '**engage**' – you need to think about the response of the audience.

This question asks you to **analyse**. Analysis will include identifying the different skills used to contribute towards the performance.

Sample extract

The opening scene of the National Theatre's 2011 production of *Frankenstein* showed the birth of Frankenstein's Creature. In his role as The Creature, Jonny Lee Miller used striking body language and large, exaggerated gestures, as he crawled out of the womb-like structure. The movement was uncontrolled and quick, which immediately engaged the audience in the action. Miller's facial expressions helped to show The Creature's animal-like nature: The Creature's expressions were larger than life and almost unnatural, which meant that the audience was fully engaged with the character and keen to see what might happen next. At this point, The Creature's movements were more focused and more carefully controlled, and required strong physical skills from the performer. When Miller looked out towards the audience, The Creature's facial expressions were very clear, bringing the character to life for the audience.

This answer is about the National Theatre's 2011 production of *Frankenstein*, in which Benedict Cumberbatch played Frankenstein and Jonny Lee Miller played The Creature.

Keep your analysis focused on the performance element specified in the question – in this case, movement – and use technical vocabulary to demonstrate your knowledge.

Comment on how the performance helped to engage the audience.

Performance questions may focus on a number of areas – these may include performance style or stage space as well as movement.

 Links   See pages 12–15 for a reminder about the use of movement in performance.

Now try this

Think of a live performance you have seen.
Analyse how physical skills were used to engage the audience at a key moment during the performance.   **(6 marks)**

Remember to pick out different physical skills used by the performers to **engage** the audience and to give **specific examples** of the **effect** these skills have on the audience.

Question 9 (a): design

Question 9 (a) will ask you to **analyse** how an element of the **performance or design** was used to engage the audience. Here, the focus is on **design**. See page 105 for a focus on performance.

Answering the question

Question 9 (a) is worth **6 marks**, so you should aim to spend about 10 minutes on this question. This allows you about 15 minutes for Question 9 (b), which is worth 9 marks.

In your answer to this question, you will need to **analyse** an element of design. When you are analysing a performance:

✓ pick out different elements used by the designer to **engage** the audience

✓ give **specific examples** of the **effect** these elements have on the audience

✓ use **appropriate vocabulary** and **drama terminology**.

> This question focuses on lighting, so you need to comment on how lighting **effects** (such as colour) or **techniques** were used, and what the effect was on the **audience**.

Worked example

Analyse how lighting was used to engage the audience during a key moment of the performance.

(6 marks)

> This question specifies 'a key moment of the performance', so here you need to choose an **appropriate key moment** to focus on in your answer. Notice the word '**engage**' – you need to think about the response of the audience.

Sample extract

A key moment where lighting was used by Bruno Poet, the lighting designer, was when Frankenstein and The Creature came face to face. Here, the designer used various different types of lamp and a range of lighting effects to create atmosphere and engage the attention of the audience. The LED strip-lighting used at this moment blended with the smoke on stage to give a sense of depth to the space, making the space seem larger than it actually was. Side lighting was used to throw a shadow off both Frankenstein and The Creature. This added to the mysterious and dark tone and style of the production as a whole and highlighted this important moment, where the audience is unsure what might happen next. The use of harsh white lighting , combined with the cold way in which Frankenstein examined The Creature's body, added another level to the scene.

> This answer is about the National Theatre's 2011 production of *Frankenstein*, in which Benedict Cumberbatch played Frankenstein and Jonny Lee Miller played The Creature.

> Make it clear which moment in the play you are analysing and comment on a range of the lighting effects and techniques used at that point in the performance.

> Keep your analysis focused on the design element specified in the question (here, lighting) and use technical vocabulary to demonstrate your knowledge.

> Design questions may focus on a number of areas, including set, costume, sound and lighting.

> Comment on how the design has helped to engage the audience. Here, the student gives details of the atmosphere created by the lighting.

 Links Turn to pages 41–67 for a reminder about the different design roles and what they involve.

 Links See pages 48–54 for more about lighting.

Now try this

Think of a live performance you have seen.

Analyse how sound was used to engage the audience during a key moment of the performance.

(6 marks)

> Remember to use appropriate vocabulary and drama terminology in your answer.

Question 9 (b): performance

Question 9 (b) will ask you to **evaluate** how an element of the **performance or design** was used to create impact for the audience. On this page, the focus is on **performance**. See page 108 for a focus on design.

Answering the question

Question 9 (b) is worth **9 marks**, so you should aim to spend about 15 minutes on this question. In your answer to this question, you need to **evaluate** an element of performance.

- ✓ pick out different elements used by the performer to create **impact** for the audience
- ✓ analyse **how** these elements were used by the performer
- ✓ give **specific examples** of the **effect** these elements have on the audience
- ✓ make sure your **evaluations** are well **balanced** and **justified**
- ✓ use **appropriate vocabulary** and **drama terminology**.

This question focuses on the use of **space**, so you need to **analyse how** and where space has been used **effectively**, and give fully justified conclusions.

Worked example

Evaluate how performers used space to create impact for the audience. **(9 marks)**

This question asks you to **evaluate**. You need to make **personal judgements** about the performance that focus on the element in the question (in this case, space). The question does not specify any particular moment, so choose the moments from the performance you feel are most relevant.

Performance questions may focus on a number of areas – these may include performance style or stage space as well as movement.

Sample extract

The use of stage space was particularly effective in the moment from *Frankenstein* where The Creature discovers nature. Here, Jonny Lee Miller as The Creature started on the floor, using low levels and displaying the baby-like side of the character. This worked well, as it showed The Creature experiencing something for the first time.

The moment when The Creature got to his feet and staggered towards the rising sun was enhanced with uplifting music and birdsong. The use of space combined with sound in this moment was powerful, as it showed The Creature's fascination with these new experiences. As the rain effect started, the performer stopped still, as if The Creature was dazed, before rolling joyfully in the grass. This was a successful moment, as the performer was able to use space to show the character's sense of amazement and delight at his discoveries

This answer is about the National Theatre's 2011 production of *Frankenstein*, in which Benedict Cumberbatch played Frankenstein and Jonny Lee Miller played The Creature.

Notice the word '**impact**' in the question. You need to **analyse how** space was used to create impact for the audience and then **evaluate** how well this was done. You can reflect negatively or positively in an evaluation question, as long as your points are well justified and supported with specific examples from the performance.

Make your evaluation detailed and take care to support your judgements with specific examples. Remember to use technical vocabulary to demonstrate your knowledge. Here, the student connects the use of space with the development of the character, showing a wider knowledge of the play overall.

When answering Section B questions, try to demonstrate a real engagement with the live performance and offer a personal view on it.

🔗 **Links** See pages 5–25 for a reminder about which skills can contribute to the use of space.

Now try this

Think of a live performance you have seen.

Evaluate how the performers communicated the style of the performance to create impact for the audience. **(9 marks)**

Remember to make sure that your evaluations are well justified and supported with examples from the performance.

Question 9 (b): design

Question 9 (b) will ask you to **evaluate** how an element of the **performance or design** was used to create impact for the audience. On this page, the focus is on **design**. See page 107 for a focus on performance.

Answering the question

Question 9 (b) is worth **9 marks**, so spend about 15 minutes on this question.

✓ Pick out key elements, such as effects and materials, used by the designer.

✓ Analyse **how** these elements were used by the designer.

✓ Give **specific examples** of the **effect** these elements have on the audience.

✓ Make sure your **evaluations** are well **balanced** and **justified**.

✓ Use **appropriate vocabulary** and **drama terminology**.

Worked example

Evaluate how set design was used to create impact for the audience. **(9 marks)**

Design questions may focus on a number of areas, including set, costume, sound and lighting.

This question focuses on the use of **set design**, so you need to **analyse how** and where set design has been used **effectively**, and give fully justified conclusions.

This question asks you to **evaluate**. You need to make **personal judgements** about the performance that focus on the element in the question (in this case, set design). The question does not specify any particular moment, so choose the moments from the performance you feel are most relevant to answering the question.

Sample extract

The use of set in *Frankenstein* was very successful in the powerful opening of the performance. Here, Mark Tildesley, the set designer, created a womb-like structure out of canvas and wood. This worked well, as it added to the production's historical setting. In addition, the materials chosen suggested a return to nature, which is a strong theme in this production. The set was designed so that the canvas structure had a constant beat, like a heartbeat. This symbolised the birth of The Creature, as he crawled out onto the stage. This was a brilliant moment and it had an impressive impact on the audience. Not only was this our first introduction to The Creature but it was also the start of the performance, and the audience was fascinated to see what might come next.

The stage itself was made from wooden line slats – a hard surface, symbolising The Creature's harsh birth. The womb-like structure was positioned centre stage, which engaged audience's attention completely.

Notice the word '**impact**' in the question. You need to **analyse how** the set design was used to create impact for the audience and then **evaluate** how well this was done. You can reflect negatively or positively in an evaluation question, as long as your points are detailed, well justified and supported with specific examples from the performance.

Use technical vocabulary to demonstrate your knowledge.

🔗 **Links** See pages 55–62 for a reminder about set design.

This answer is about the National Theatre's 2011 production of *Frankenstein*, in which Benedict Cumberbatch played Frankenstein and Jonny Lee Miller played The Creature.

When answering Section B questions, try to demonstrate a real engagement with the live performance and offer a personal view on it. This approach is particularly relevant when answering Section B questions.

Now try this

Think of a live performance you have seen.

Evaluate how sound was used to create impact for the audience. **(9 marks)**

Remember to make sure that your evaluations are well justified and supported with examples from the performance.

Preparing for Section B

You need to know what you are allowed to take into the exam, as well as how to prepare for Section B.

Exam materials

For Section B of the exam you will be able to take up to 500 words of notes in with you. These notes:

- can be handwritten or word-processed
- must not exceed the **500-word limit**
- must not include pre-published material.

Pre-published materials include programmes and photographs. This means you cannot take extracts from books or articles into the exam. It is also unnecessary to do so, as Section B is examining your ability to **respond personally** to the live performance.

Performer's use of voice, movement, performance style and space/staging, including notes on performers in specific roles

Sketches, drawings and diagrams

How ideas were communicated during the performance

Use of the theatre space

What live performance evaluation notes may include

Design considerations, including the use of costume, set, lighting and sound

Director's concept/interpretation and the chosen performance style

Impact on the audience, including, specifically, on the student, and how this was achieved

How to prepare for Section B

- **Watch** the performance closely and prepare effective notes on what you have seen.
- **Practise exam-style questions** based on the performance you have seen. While Section B of the exam will ask you to analyse and evaluate the performance, you won't know which question (6 or 9 marks) will be based on performance and which on design. So practise with a combination of analysis and evaluation for both performance and design elements, and also vary the elements of design and performance you use in your exam-style practice.
- **Research and learn about areas you know less about.** For example, if you are unsure about the techniques, equipment or materials used in the lighting design, increase your knowledge so you can confidently refer to these areas in the exam.
- **Read around the performance you have seen** (for example, reviews). This will help you understand the background or style of the piece (though remain clear about your own views of the performance).

Top preparation tips for Section B

☑ Prepare detailed and well-structured notes you can access easily in the exam.

☑ Build up a bank of appropriate vocabulary and drama terminology over the course of your GCSE.

☑ Be clear about the difference between analysis and evaluation.

See page 104 for more on the difference between analysis and evaluation questions. See page 110 for more on preparing useful evaluation notes.

Now try this

Start a technical vocabulary bank. This will help you see where your knowledge of drama-related terminology is good and where you have gaps in your learning. Use 'Performance' and 'Design' as your headings.

Preparing useful evaluation notes

You are allowed to take live performance evaluation notes into the exam with you. You can only take a maximum of 500 words into the exam, so make sure you prepare your notes carefully.

Dos and don'ts when writing live performance evaluation notes

👍 DO keep your notes **brief** and make them **useful** – avoid whole sentences. These are notes you should be able to draw on quickly. They should not be prepared answers.

👍 DO use key words as 'triggers' for what you saw in performance.

👍 DO use diagrams, sketches and drawings, as they will not take up any of your total word count and they will help you to remember key moments from the performance.

👎 DON'T use published materials – your notes should be all your own work.

👎 DON'T create notes based on guessing what the question might be. You should be prepared to respond to any question on the live performance.

👎 DON'T focus your notes too heavily on answering either the performance or the design questions. Aim to write balanced notes, with around 250 words on performance and 250 words on design.

👎 DON'T focus too heavily on one or two elements of the production: aim for balanced notes that cover the full range of elements.

Structuring your notes

Your time is limited in the Section B exam, so have your notes easily accessible.

Sub-headings can be used to:
• identify different elements, such as voice and movement
• identify key moments from the production.

You could also use two different **colours** to separate out design and performance aspects, so you can quickly see which notes to use for the right question in the exam.

Avoid following a structure that doesn't work for you – it is vital that the layout of your notes allows you to access the information quickly.

This student has structured their notes to explore a key moment, using just 31 words to cover both performance and design elements.

These notes are **trigger words**, to help the student draw on their memory of the opening scene from *Frankenstein*.

Lighting – colourful, side and downlighting, LED batons, sudden flashes, hanging light structure in opening (multiple bulbs).

Use of voice – clearly articulated diction from Dr, guttural screams, unformed words, loud, well projected, no specific accent

This student has used red for design notes and blue for performance notes. See how a lot of information is contained in only a few (34) words.

Opening scene – birth of Creature, twisted and extreme physicality, low levels, loud and animal-like noises, little costume, red wash of lighting, dramatic percussion and strings recorded music. Audience engaged from start.

Birth, red wash, womb-like set, dramatic music, audience engaged, Underworld music, bulb-like structure above stage, Creature movement, heartbeat, appears suddenly, elements of surprise, physicality and gesture.

This student has drawn a basic sketch to help them recall a key moment from the National Theatre's 2011 production of *Frankenstein*: the 'birth' of The Creature.

Now try this

Use the suggestions on this page to create a first draft of your **500-word** evaluation notes on the live performance you have seen. Use a structure that works for you.

Answers

Where an example answer is given, this is not necessarily the only correct response. In most cases there is a range of responses that can gain full marks. Example answers are often based on one of the eight possible performance texts for Edexcel GCSE Drama.

THEATRE MAKERS

1. Key roles in the theatre

Answers should:

- clearly identify which role (performer, director or designer) is being discussed

- include specific details and examples to explain why each role made a lasting impression

- consider which skills and/or production elements were used and exactly what made them effective.

For example, if you were writing about the National Theatre's 2011 production of *Frankenstein*, you might discuss the way in which Jonny Lee Miller, playing The Creature, used child-like body language and physical skills to represent the innocent nature of the character, which was unexpected as The Creature is traditionally presented as a monster. In terms of direction, you might consider the effective use of ensemble sections of the production to highlight the isolation of The Creature in contrast to the rest of society. Finally, in terms of design, you might feel that the large collection of light bulbs hanging from the ceiling over the audience was an effective way of showing the power used to bring the creature to life, as well as suggesting the influence of science.

2. The audience

For example:

For my production of *100*, the target audience would be young people aged between 14 and 18 years. The main reasons for my choice are that I would want this age group to think carefully about what is important in life. I believe that many young people find their lives controlled by social media, their smartphones and other modern technology and often are missing out on what is really important. I think the character of Sophie would be particularly interesting as she spends her life working hard, only to have that life cut short by a serious illness. This may help young people to realise that it is important to find a balance in life before it is too late, and encourage them to engage with this key message of the play.

3. Theatrical concepts

For example:

The overall concept I have for my production of *Twelfth Night* sets the play in the future and uses the sci-fi genre. Rather than a traditional shipwreck, I would have a spaceship crash-land on the planet of Illyria. This would give the costume, set, sound and lighting designers many opportunities to develop a futuristic style. As the play is a comedy with a plot that already asks the audience members to suspend their ideas of what is likely, this style would work well. It would enhance the comedic nature of the piece, highlighting the already slightly ridiculous story.

4. Conventions and terminology

- Cross fade – designer; gradually taking out one lighting or sound cue and replacing it with another at the same time

- Cue – performer, designer; a signal for something to happen (for example, where a specific line is the cue for a blackout)

- Cyclorama – designer; a large curtain or cloth placed upstage and used to depict the background of the scene

- Flats – designer; a flat piece of scenery, which can be painted and positioned on stage

- Fresnel – designer; a specific type of lantern using a specially designed lens that can produce a lot of light

- Gobo – designer; a shaped plate that is placed in front of a lamp to produce a shadowed pattern (for example, prison bars)

- Lanterns – designer; the general technical term for a range of lights

- Proxemics: performer, director; the physical space between the performers, set and audience

- Semiotics – performer, director, designer; what someone or something symbolises

- Soundscape – designer; a sound effect designed to portray the events or emotions of a scene

- Stage left – performer, director, designer; the area of the stage that is on the performer's left-hand side

- Stage right – performer, director, designer; the area of the stage that is on the performer's right-hand side

Performer

5. The performer

Note: example answers are given in brackets.

- What is my character's age? (The Guide from *100* is in his 50s.)

- Where is my character from? (Arthur Birling from *An Inspector Calls* is from a fictional area of the North Midlands.)

- What does my character want to achieve in the play? (The character of Reverend Hale in *The Crucible* wants to achieve justice and find out the truth about the strange events in Salem.)

- What status does my character have? (Dr Maudsley from *Blue Stockings* is a well-known psychiatrist and well-respected doctor and so is likely to be of a higher status.)

- How does my character feel about other characters in the play? (In *1984*, Winston is in love with Julia, but he feels anxious when approaching O'Brien.)

6. Tone and intonation

For example, an answer might focus on the character of the Inspector from *An Inspector Calls,* in his first scene in Act 1:

If I was playing the role of the Inspector in this scene, I would use a harsh and clipped tone to interrupt Birling. This would show how the Inspector feels about the suicide of Eva Smith. It would also express his intention to be clear with the Birlings that this is a tragic case and that they are all involved in Eva's downfall in some way. I would also use clarity, as the Inspector is stating the facts of the case.

7. Pause and pitch

For example, an answer might focus on the character of Nia in *100*, in the Void scene, near the end of the play:

In this scene, there is an exchange between Nia, Alex and the Guide, where the Guide is anxiously encouraging Nia and Alex to choose a memory. If I was playing Nia, I would use a low pitch at the start of the scene to indicate that Nia feels disappointed and unable to compete with the achievements of Ketu, which were the focus of the previous scene. However, when Nia says 'That's right!', realising that her memory could be something deeply personal, I would use a higher pitch to convey her sense of hope and excitement. I would increase the pace throughout the scene as Nia's thoughts spill out, only pausing before Nia says 'after the carnival'. This pause would emphasise Nia's final decision about which memory to choose.

8. Clarity and pace

For example, an answer might focus on the character of Mrs Welsh in *Blue Stockings*, at the start of Act 1, Scene 13:

At this point in *Blue Stockings*, the character of Mrs Welsh makes an educated and passionate speech about giving women full membership at the university. This is almost a political speech and needs to be persuasive. If I was playing Mrs Welsh, I would use pace, with a slow and clear voice, to help express the character's intentions. As the speech is very 'wordy', I would use clarity to make sure that each word is delivered effectively. On the line 'Consider the possibility of an optical illusion', I would make sure that each word is spoken with the correct pace, so that the words are delivered separately and clearly.

9. Accent and inflection

For example:

Viola is a lady of Messaline. As she is a privileged young woman, a performer playing this character should use an accent that reflects her relatively high-status background. However, in order to protect herself, Viola disguises herself as a man – Cesario – and becomes a page in the household of Duke Orsino. In her role as Cesario, Viola has changed both her gender and her status, and a performer playing the character should reflect these changes by using different accents for Viola and Cesario. This will also help the audience to keep up with the action.

10. Emphasis and volume

For example:

In Act 3 of *The Crucible*, emphasis might be put on the lines spoken by the girls as they accuse Mary Warren of sending spirits to harm them. The lines might be spoken with more of a blaming tone, to sound aggressive and attacking.

11. Diction and nuance

For example:

In the final scene of *An Inspector Calls*, Mr Birling picks up the telephone receiver and takes a call. The stage directions tell us that when he replaces the receiver, he does it slowly, and also that he seems to be panicking. Nuance and diction could be used to show Mr Birling's feelings of anxiety and confusion as he delivers the news that a police inspector is on his way. The use of nuance in particular would help the audience to hear the fear in Mr Birling's voice about what has just happened and what will happen next. Diction would help to make sure each word is delivered clearly and allow the performer to show Mr Birling is thinking carefully about every word he says.

12. Facial expression and body language

For example:

An answer might focus on the moment in Act 3 in *DNA* where the gang discover Adam. Adam's facial expression and body language might come across as confused and a little frightened. His body language might be closed, to show he is guarding himself in a protective way, particularly in the way he responds to the others on stage (as they were behind his initial attack). As Adam has been living in the woodland for a great deal of time, his body language might also be quite animal-like, moving close to the ground, with twisted limbs and a screwed-up facial expression. This would help show how the rough treatment has destroyed his character's human dignity as well as the physical impact it has had.

13. Gesture and proxemics

For example, these are two key moments from *1984*.

(a) When Winston has a terrible nightmare towards the end of the play, Julia (his lover) comforts him. The way in which Julia calms Winston down by putting her arms around him is a caring and loving gesture.

(b) When O'Brien takes Winston for questioning, Winston finds himself surrounded by torturers; they stand near a trolley that has various tools on it. The use of proxemics is important here: where the torturers stand in relation to where Winston is strapped to a chair will show how dangerous they are and how scared Winston is. This will be emphasised as the torturers move towards Winston, closing the gap of 'safety' between Winston and those who are looking to hurt him.

14. Stance and stillness

For example, in the play *Twelfth Night*:

- Act 1, Scene 3: Sir Toby's stance should show that he has been drinking with Sir Andrew. He may be a little uneasy on his feet, showing that he has alcohol in his bloodstream. His stance could also suggest that his status is higher than Sir Andrew's and that he is taking the lead; this is shown in the way Sir Toby corrects Sir Andrew in 'You mistake, knight'.

- Act 2, Scene 4: In this scene Viola (as Cesario) is talking to the duke. The performer playing Viola might use a stance that shows she is pretending to be a male character having a 'man-to-man' discussion. For example, the performer could stand with legs apart or hands on hips in fists, to appear masculine. However, there are moments where Viola's true identity might come through. Here, stance could be used to reveal what the audience already knows: that Viola is in love with the duke. For example, the performer could soften their stance, perhaps leaning towards the duke to show Viola's interest in him.

- Act 1, Scene 5: This is the first time that we meet Malvolio, Olivia's steward. The character is very pompous and his behaviour often shows that he feels that others are beneath him. As Malvolio enters with Olivia, the performer playing this character could use stance to establish Malvolio's idea of his own status. This might include the performer playing Malvolio standing in an upright way with his chin slightly raised, as though he is looking down his nose at others.

15. Movement and spatial awareness

For example:

During Sophie's memory in the play *100*, Sophie remembers being 12 and putting on make-up. The stage directions indicate another performer should play Sophie's 'mirror image'. Here, the performer playing Sophie could use slow and deliberate movements to suggest she is not used to putting on make-up and wants to do the best job she can, and so is concentrating hard. The performer might lean towards the 'mirror' to emphasise this idea. The performer playing Sophie's mirror image needs to make very precise movements to be effective, matching Sophie's facial expressions as well as her body language in close detail.

16. Personality and purpose

For example:

The character of Mrs Welsh from *Blue Stockings* is the mistress of Girton College, Cambridge. Her high status as an academic leader and her academic learning are shown in the way that she lectures and advises Tess in Act 1, Scene 6. As a leader, Mrs Welsh is passionate about allowing female students the opportunity to graduate. This comes across in the speeches that she makes, which are intended to inspire others. For example, in Act 1, Scene 13, Mrs Welsh makes a persuasive speech about why women should be allowed to graduate, in which she says: 'giving our girls an education won't only mean better nurses and teachers. It'll brighten the world for our sons and daughters for generations to come.'

17. Motives, aims and objectives

For example:

Line: The Mayor's first line in Scene 1 of Nikolai Gogol's *Government Inspector*: 'It's not good, gentleman. That's why I've gathered you all here.'

Objectives:

(a) I want to scare the others.

(b) I want to show that I am scared.

(c) I want to sort out this problem.

Outcomes of line:

(a) The mayor wishes to use fear as a way of inspiring the others to take action.

(b) The Mayor as comes across very nervous and anxious.

(c) The Mayor appears very focused and in control of the situation, raising his status in the scene.

18. Development and relationships

For example:

In *The Crucible*, John Proctor's relationship with his wife, Elizabeth, is central to the play. At the start of Act 2, there is an obvious tension in John and Elizabeth's relationship because of Proctor's past affair with Abigail. This is shown when Elizabeth wants to know where John has been; also, both characters struggle to hold a conversation with each other. This tension builds up as the scene progresses, and ends with Proctor failing to remember the commandment based on 'adultery' in front of Elizabeth. This relationship is key to the plot as well as to how Proctor develops as a character. It shows, for instance, why he is so reluctant to shame Elizabeth by announcing his affair, and how sorry he is towards the end of the play when it seems certain he will hang. Without this relationship, Proctor's intense response to Abigail's accusations of witchcraft would not make sense, and this adds depth to Proctor's character.

19. Research and impact

For example:

Dr Maudsley from the play *Blue Stockings* provides an important voice in the debate about whether women should be able to graduate with degrees from Girton College, Cambridge. A performer playing this role might look into the life of the real Dr Maudsley: what he did, the way he lectured, his relationships with other academics, perhaps how his students saw him. Research might focus on Maudsley's writings, which reveal his opinions on female education, as well as the wider social and historical context, which would show that Dr Maudsley's views were not uncommon among men of his time. As Jessica Swales says in her introduction to the play, 'it would be easy to assume that those who condemn women's education with as much vitriol as Maudsley or Lloyd are heartless misogynists. That's simply not the case.' Therefore a performer might research the playwright's intentions and ideas, as well as the social, historical and political context in which the play was written.

20. Still images and asides

For example:

At the end of Ketu's memory in the play *100*, we learn that Ketu cannot live with the lie of pretending that the Earth is flat. Because of this, he decides to end his life and this important moment could use still image to support the message to the audience. The stage directions indicate that the other performers should 'create a tree'. Using physical theatre, the other cast members could shape their bodies into the form of a tree, making use of levels, as well as bamboo sticks to represent the branches. This stark still image, built and then held behind Ketu as the narration continues, would foreshadow the events which are to come. Then, when the narration ends and just before he hangs himself, Ketu could become part of the still image, which now freezes again. The performer playing Ketu could show the character's final realisation that the Earth is round using a strong facial expression of wonder. This would be a powerful way of emphasising Ketu's discovery in the moments before he takes his own life.

21. Monologue and physical theatre

For example:

In Act 1, Scene 6 of *Blue Stockings,* Mrs Welsh delivers a monologue about the freedoms felt by women at the time, that begins 'Oh, the world? The world makes little sense to me.' This scene takes place in Mrs Welsh's office, as she gives a one-to-one tutorial to Tess and tries to find out about what happened earlier with Dr Maudsley. A performer approaching this speech might use this context as a way of approaching the style of the speech. For example, the monologue could be delivered in the style of someone who is teaching or lecturing. At the same time, it could show that Mrs Welsh understands this battle the women face to graduate, but that she also realises that how they approach the battle is vital. Therefore, I would try to communicate a persuasive style through the use of direct eye contact between Mrs Welsh and Tess throughout the speech. I would place vocal emphasis on the line 'Patience is vital', and use careful intonation in order to underline the serious message of the monologue.

22. Narration and multi-role

For example:

In *The Crucible*, the playwright Arthur Miller gives very detailed stage directions at the start of each scene to outline exactly what is happening. These directions are normally about the setting of the scene or they provide details about the characters on stage. Although these directions would usually be used by performers as a guide to the scene, one approach could be to speak the stage directions aloud, as narration. This would help an audience to understand the precise way in which Miller imagines his scenes and would also allow the spectator to 'see' what the reader 'sees'. This would also enable the director and performers to add interest to the performance and create contrasts for the audience. For example, the scene could change from Proctor's house to the court, to show the connection between the trial and the accusation of Elizabeth – the set could even be changed in front of the audience, during the narration of the stage directions. Though speaking the stage directions is often considered a Brechtian technique, this approach could create a fresh interpretation of this well-known text.

23. Mime, flashback and flash forward

For example:

Throughout the play *DNA* by Dennis Kelly, the characters of Phil and Leah spend lots of time on stage together. In these scenes, Leah mostly speaks non-stop and Phil says very little – he is often eating rather than speaking. Mimed sequences could be used for many of these scenes between them. One example is at the end of Act 3, when Leah finally loses her temper with Phil. The scene is the end of the story between Phil and Leah, and is a result of all the scenes that have gone before – in which Phil has not responded to Leah. This moment is almost entirely written in stage directions and shows both characters sitting in silence and sharing sweets. It ends with Leah storming out, leaving Phil alone on stage. Mime and non-verbal communication could be used to build up tension in the scene, so that Leah's sudden exit makes sense and captures the end of the relationship between them. This would be particularly clear in the way that Leah takes the sweet that Phil offers, chews it and then spits it out. Leah could show that she is frustrated and angry through the use of a mimed gesture, such as a stamped foot or a look of disgust at Phil. Her fists could be held tight and her walk could be heavy as she stamps off, leaving Phil behind.

24. Symbolism and split scene

For example:

In the play *1984*, Room 101 is mentioned regularly throughout the play, as a threat to characters such as Winston. The idea of Room 101 becomes symbolic of the fear felt by characters such as Winston and Julia, who wish to escape Oceania and the control of Big Brother. This symbolism is reinforced at the end of the play, when Winston's fear of rats is used against him during his interrogation in Room 101, and a cage of rats is put close to his face. The reactions of Winston and Julia to the mention of Room 101, as well as the way in which those representing Big Brother mention it, could reflect both the control Oceania has over its citizens and the terrible fear under which the citizens of Oceania live. This would be an interesting way of symbolically representing Big Brother's control over characters like Winston.

25. Caricature and choral speaking

For example:

There are many moments in the text of Arthur Miller's *The Crucible* where characters speak together, so choral speech could be very effective in this play. For example, choral speech could be used to highlight the girls' hysteria, which they are using to convince the townspeople that there is witchcraft in Salem. Choral speech could also be used to show how Abigail and the other young girls work together to persuade the court that Mary Warren is bringing bad spirits upon them. At this point in the play the girls act as though they have been taken over by an outside force and they speak in exact unison. Choral speech would be an effective way of bringing the many voices together. This would also show the power multiple, united voices can have over the innocent, as they drown out any other protesting voices.

Director

26. The director

Answers should include reference to the following skills and reasons:

- An understanding the text, style and genre of the play; to be able to form a consistent overall vision
- The ability to work in a team; to be able to use every team member's strengths
- Strong communication skills; to pass on the vision and ideas to the other team members
- The ability to interpret a performance text; to be able to understand the playwright's intentions clearly
- The ability to turn ideas into reality; to be able to take the ideas from the page to the stage
- Creativity; to be able to create an interesting interpretation that will entertain an audience
- Leadership and management; to keep the project under control and to make sure that team members are doing their jobs properly
- Problem-solving skills; to remove any issues that are stopping progress being made
- A strong understanding of both performance and design techniques; to develop an overall understanding of the whole team
- An understanding of health and safety issues; to ensure that the project can be completed safely.

27. Messages and subtext

In your answer, you could consider techniques such as visual asides and vocal effects. For example:

In Act 2, Scene 8 of *Blue Stockings*, Will tries to speak to Ralph about Tess. However, he is dragged into a game of cards with the men, which starts to get very noisy. A performer playing Will could show that the character is not really having fun by looking towards the audience and forcing a smile while he is playing the game. A slight hesitation in his voice at the start of each line would also suggest that the character is not focused on the game and has other things on his mind.

28. Genre and style

When discussing the play's main themes and issues, answers should consider:

- the overall message of the play
- the main interests of individual characters or small groups of characters
- characters' overall objectives or what motivates them to act in particular ways
- what the playwright is trying to communicate – for example, is the play a metaphor for something else? What is the wider context of the piece?

For example:

A key theme in *1984* is power, which leads to Winston's torture. As a director, I would use physical theatre, at this would help to convey the brutal violence experienced by Winston. If Winston was lifted and carried by the other members of the cast, it would also allow the audience to understand Winston's helplessness.

29. Types of staging

Answers should consider:

- the different types of staging – their pros and cons
- the position of performers on stage and how they interact with the set and stage furniture

- entrances and exits
- audience awareness (such as sightlines and levels)
- the context in which the play was originally created.

For example:

When staging Act 1 in *DNA*, I would choose promenade theatre. The structure of the play is cyclical – so the audience would move from location to location in a repeated order. In this way, the audience would make the same journey as the characters. This would allow the audience to share the characters' experience of changing location, keeping them on their toes and not allowing them to rest or relax for any period of time – in the same way that the characters are unable to rest.

30. Consistency and communication

Key information might include points such as:

- who the characters are
- where and when the scene is set
- what the situation is
- what themes or key messages need to be communicated
- what each character's motives are.

For example, to understand the narrative and themes in Act 3, Scene 3 of *Twelfth Night*, the audience would need to know this information:

- Sebastian is alive.
- Antonio rescued Sebastian from the storm.
- Antonio is a wanted man in Illyria, as he fought against the city and stole from the people.
- Antonio lends Sebastian his money and arranges to meet him later at their lodgings.

31. Purpose

For example:

The central purpose of *Government Inspector* is to highlight political corruption. To get this across to the audience, I would make careful choices about staging. For example, I would place the performance 'in the round', which would allow the audience to have a wider perspective of the whole situation. This way, the audience would be able to see that corruption is blinding the officials and creating confusion, and that the characters on stage see only a small part of the truth.

32. Managing the audience

For example:

A key moment in *100* is at the very end of the play when Alex, who has not thought of a suitable memory, is left alone on stage. I want the audience to feel shocked and sad for Alex, but I also want them to be left wondering what will happen to him. I would achieve this reaction using the tone of the Guide's final lines to increase the tension. As the Guide continues to count to 100, I would direct the performer to increase their volume and raise their pitch to emphasise to the audience how time is running out. As Alex scrambles for a memory to cling to, he should become more desperate, with the performer using a tense body language and panicking vocal tone to shock the audience. When the Guide leaves the stage, Alex is left completely isolated and the audience, like Alex, would be left in suspense.

33. Choosing location and time

Answers should consider:

- the overall vision for the production
- the central message to be conveyed
- more than one possible location
- consistency of vision throughout the performance.

For example:

As a director, my vision for *An Inspector Calls* involves setting the play in London, against the backdrop of the financial crisis that began in 2008. The central message I want to convey is that there is still a significant difference between those who have money and those who do not. The production would emphasise the idea that people still have a responsibility to each other and that our actions have consequences for others. Although the action only takes place in one location, others are mentioned in the text. The setting of London in 2008 would work well and support the consistency of the production as a whole. For example, it would still be possible for Eva Smith to have worked in a factory (manufacturing was one of the first industries to suffer in the crisis) and then in a shop, and then to have met Gerald and Eric at a bar that has a bad reputation.

34. Contexts

For example:

The original performance of the play *1984* focused heavily on the impact of technology on individual freedom. This reflects a social context in which the authorities use modern technology (such as the internet, mobile phones and GPS) to track individuals and gather information about them. As a director, my interpretation of *1984* would highlight the way our society relies on mobile and connected technology. I would make sure technology plays a central role in the production, with the audience constantly surrounded by screens. The screens would be able to show the action from different perspectives, suggesting there is no escape from the constant surveillance. I would also have the screens on at all times, showing images from before the start of the play and even from outside the auditorium during the interval. This would constantly remind the audience that we are always being watched and monitored.

35. Mood and atmosphere

1 For example:

   In Act 3 of *The Crucible*, I would want to convey a dark and serious mood. To do this, I would first use the sound of a thunderstorm to underscore the action. Here, the thunder, which is often thought of as frightening or threatening, would symbolise the voice of God, which is being ignored. I would also use cold, stark lighting and a simple set design, made of only bare wood. The performers would be dressed in dull, plain colours, with the judges in black, highlighting the serious nature of the issues being discussed and reflecting the heavy mood. The lack of brighter colours would suggest there is no joy or happiness.

2 For example (based on the sample answer for question 1 above):

   I would expect that an audience might react to this mood with tension and a growing sense of fear about what might happen next. The judges do not intend to listen to John Proctor, Giles Corey or Francis Nurse: they believe the girls are telling the truth and they are blinded by their own points of view. As this becomes clearer, an atmosphere of frustration and looming disaster would be created.

36. Style

Answers should:

- be very clear about the specific style chosen and why
- give clear examples of how that style can be reflected in a range of performance elements, including the set, costume and lighting.

For example:

For my production of *100*, I would choose an abstract, minimalist style because of the abstract nature of the piece. Designers could help to achieve this style by considering where each of the four boxes should be positioned be on stage. They must be visible to the audience, but also able to create a distance between the Guide and the other characters. I would also want the boxes to somehow represent each of the characters – to suggest they are all expected. Therefore, I would have Ketu and Sophie's boxes each separated and alone, while Alex and Nia's boxes would be closer together, indicating they have some connection. The set designers could also help with the appearance of the boxes. I would have plain black boxes, each featuring a symbol to represent one of the characters. For example, on Ketu's box, I would paint images of the Earth and the Sun, while Sophie's box could have images of make-up and an office block. For Alex, I would include an image of a motorcycle and for Nia, I would include an image of a bed.

37. Presenting location and time

For example:

In *Blue Stockings*, important locations are the Girton College dormitory rooms, the library, a classroom, and the orchard. The time period is late Victorian (1896). The location could be represented by furniture, such as bookcases for the library, a desk for the classroom, and a single apple tree for the orchard, which would be kept on stage at all times. The time period could be reflected in period costume, as well as in the style of the bicycle, types of books, pens and writing paper, and the style of bags carried.

38. Blocking

Answers should:

- consider the status of the characters on stage
- consider the relationships between the characters on stage
- use appropriate technical vocabulary when referring to areas of the stage.

For example:

Performance text: *DNA*. Scene: Act 3, Scene 3 – A wood.

Characters on stage and their status:

Phil	High status	He takes the initiative by talking directly to Adam and then further shows his high status by giving the others instructions.
Cathy	High status	She has a lot of information and is still in control of herself.
Brian	Low status	His low status is due to the heavy stress he has been under since Adam's disappearance.
Leah	Medium status	She is happy to let others take control, but she cares and is the first to speak to Adam.
Mark	Medium status	He is keeping fairly quiet but recognises that Brian needs some psychiatric help.
Lou	Medium/ low status	She is terrified about the consequences and can only see the problem – not a solution. She begins to panic, lowering her status further.
Jan	Medium status	She remains very quiet for the majority of the scene but she is listening, gathering information and considering the situation.
Adam	Low status rising to high status	His low status at the start is due to his physical injuries and the state of his mental health. His status grows as he tells his story and the characters learn of his determination to survive.

Position of characters on stage:

Phil	Centre stage, between Cathy and Adam, to reflect his status. He is slightly isolated from the others and has his back to the group, but all except Adam can look at him.
Cathy	Upstage centre. Controlling the rest of the group and able to see everyone at all times.
Brian	Next to Cathy, but slightly to stage right and lower downstage. This shows he is led by Cathy, who has him under control.
Leah	Stage left. Slightly away from the others but able to witness everything that is going on.
Mark	Stage right, quite close to Brian. He is closer to the group than Lou, to show that he is not frightened, but that he is still wary and trying to work the situation out.
Lou	Stage left, between the group and Leah. She is more isolated than Mark and can move downstage as she becomes more frightened, therefore lowering her status.
Jan	Stage right, next to Mark. This shows she has a stronger relationship with Mark than with the others. It also indicates that she is considering the problem in a similar way to Mark.
Adam	Downstage centre. Adam has low status and is the centre of everyone's attention. He is isolated but also surrounded by the group, to stop him from escaping.

39. Stage business, relationships and proxemics

For example:

Performance text: *Twelfth Night*. Key scene: Act 2, Scene 4. Character: Duke Orsino

One of the key messages of the play is Olivia's rejection of Orsino, which has left him depressed and upset. He calls for Feste to sing to him, as he believes this will make him feel better.

Stage business:

- Orsino is sitting at a chessboard, moving the pieces around, as he tries to distract himself by playing a game. He does this slowly and with great effort, indicating his mind is somewhere else (thinking about Olivia and trying to work out why she constantly rejects him).
- He picks up chess pieces and fiddles with them in his hand.
- He rubs the chessboard with a handkerchief, as if polishing it to clean it.

40. Characterisation and style

For example:

Performance text: *1984*. Character: O'Brien. Scene: The torture scene

Options for playing the role:

(1) O'Brien is angry and violent, shouting and appearing to be out of control emotionally. O'Brien could be screaming in Winston's face, trying to frighten him and bully him into giving in.

(2) O'Brien is calm, cold and calculating. He appears to have considered every move and torture technique he uses on Winston.

In this scene, I would direct the performer playing O'Brien to make the character cold-hearted and calculating. This is far more terrifying than someone who is out of control, as it shows that they are thinking carefully about how to cause the pain and are almost enjoying their power. It would also demonstrate that O'Brien does not care about the pain of others and will therefore let the torture continue as long as necessary. Finally, the contrast of O'Brien's calm approach against the violence experienced by Winston would highlight the cruelty and efficiency of the torture.

Designer: costume

41. The costume designer

Required skills and reasons why they are important for a costume designer include:

- understanding the text, style and genre of the play; to be able to represent accurately the requirements of the text, style and genre consistently through the costume design
- the ability to work in a team; as costume is only one part of a production, the costume designer must work with others to ensure consistency
- strong communication skills; to be able to work with others and indicate how costume ideas can be incorporated into the production
- the ability to interpret a text; to be able to understand the requirements of the narrative
- the ability to translate ideas into costumes and accessories; to design costume that is consistent with the other production elements and communicates a range of information to an audience
- creativity; to provide entertainment and interest for an audience
- problem-solving skills; to be able to resolve any technical or creative problems with the costume
- a strong understanding of costume techniques and equipment, including materials, colours and construction techniques; to ensure that the costume design uses the most appropriate and effective techniques and equipment
- an understanding of health and safety issues; to ensure costumes do not put the audience, the performers or anyone else involved in the production in danger.

42. Costume and context

You answer should:

- refer to key information about the character or characters selected
- indicate how this information can be represented in the costume (remember that costumes can change or be enhanced)

- consider the colour and style of the clothes as well as the style of the production.

For example, in *1984*, the character of Julia:

- pretends to be a loyal member of the Party. To show this, she could wear a uniform of dull and shapeless beige coveralls
- is passionate. This could be symbolised by a red hair band, which she wears to hold her hair in place
- is rebellious and brave. To show this, Julia could wear, under her coveralls, a brightly coloured t-shirt with the word 'Rebel' written on it.

43. Aspects of costume

When answering this question you need to:

- consider the context of the scene and what has happened to the character before your chosen moment
- think about the style of the production as well as the key elements of time, location and genre.

For example:

In *Twelfth Night*, Act 1 Scene 3, we first meet Sir Toby Belch, a notorious drunkard. Sir Toby could carry a hip flask, which could be attached to his belt by a chain. This would show that it is constantly with him and that he is afraid of losing it. As a member of the gentry, Sir Toby would also carry a sword. This would be highly decorated with jewels, showing his social status rather than any combat skills. Sir Toby's hair would be generally untidy, to indicate his constant drunkenness. He could also carry a handkerchief which he uses constantly to mop his forehead, suggesting that he is unfit from leading a very unhealthy lifestyle. Make-up could be used to give Sir Toby a red nose and cheeks, which are common signs of drunkenness.

44. Materials and colours

In your answer you will need to refer to any symbolic colours that will help the audience understand the character.

For example:

In *Twelfth Night*, Malvolio is a famously gloomy character. To show this, he would first be dressed in formal robes to indicate his status as the steward of the household. The robes would be in blacks and greys, reflecting his serious mood and the fact that he is quite a dull, boring person. Malvolio then receives what he believes is a letter from Olivia declaring her love for him and asking him to wear bright yellow stockings. This is actually a trick being played on Malvolio by other characters, but he falls for it. As a result, during Act 3, Scene 4, his status is quickly lowered, and he is made too look like a fool. The strong visual contrast between the formal black and grey robes and the ridiculous bright yellow stockings would symbolise this drop in status.

45. Accessories and masks

When answering this question, you will need to consider:

- what the character needs to communicate to the audience at your selected point in the play
- the style and genre of the piece
- the costume the character will be wearing
- how the costume can be enhanced and what impact this will have on an audience.

For example, in Act 2, Scene 1 of *Blue Stockings*, Mr Banks has just entered the staffroom at Trinity College. He is met by three men, who offer him a promotion.

The key information the audience needs is:
- Mr Banks has been teaching
- he is dedicated to his work
- he has been offered a promotion.

To help convey this information to the audience through Mr Banks's accessories, I would give Mr Banks a leather briefcase, which is well worn but cared for, to carry. This would suggest he has been teaching for some years and is hard-working. Mr Banks should also carry an umbrella and have a handkerchief in his breast pocket. These would give him an air of someone who cares for his appearance but who is not extravagant. As these items are also practical ones, they would suggest that Mr Banks is a man who works hard and has a practical approach to life.

46. Make-up and hair

When answering this question:
- consider the situation your character is in. For example, is the situation stressful or has there been a lot of physical activity?
- consider the time period in which the play is set and whether the character would feel that a particular hairstyle is important or not.

For example:

In Act 4 of *The Crucible*, after months of being locked in a dirty prison cell, John Proctor is brought out to meet Elizabeth on the day of his execution. As he has been kept in damp and filthy conditions, his make-up should show that he was is and unkempt. For example, teeth should be yellowed and there should be bruises on his wrists and ankles to suggest he has been chained. His hair would have grown so a wig would be needed to show hair that is long, knotted and dirty. These details would help to communicate Proctor's desperate situation visually to an audience

47. Practicality and safety

In your answer you will need to:
- refer to the weight, material, colours, flexibility and noise levels of the costume
- consider what the costume will look like and what this will communicate to the audience
- give clear reasons for your responses and ideas.

For example:

In the stage directions for Act 1 of *An Inspector Calls*, we are told that Goole should wear a simple suit typical of the era, and that the suit is dark in colour. At the time, this kind of suit would have been made of wool, which is quite heavy and very hot under stage lighting. Therefore, the costume should be made out of cotton, which is lighter and cooler for the performer to wear on stage. Using a dark suit with a faint pattern will disguise the fact that the suit is made of cotton while still reflecting the stage directions. Additionally, a dark colour will not reflect the light as much, so will be less distracting for the audience. Finally, Goole's shoes should be made of black leather, but with a softer rubber sole. This will stop the sound of the Inspector's footsteps becoming distracting, which is especially important as he moves around the stage a lot.

Designer: lighting
48. The lighting designer

Required skills and reasons why they are important for a lighting designer include:
- understanding the text, style and genre of the play; to be able to accurately represent the requirements of the text, style and genre consistently through the lighting design
- the ability to work in a team; as lighting is only one part of a production, the lighting designer must work with others to ensure consistency
- strong communication skills; to be able to work with others and indicate how lighting ideas can be incorporated into the production
- the ability to interpret a text; to be able to understand the requirements of the narrative
- the ability to translate ideas into practical lighting states; to design lighting that complements the production and communicates a range of information to an audience
- creativity; to provide entertainment and interest for an audience
- problem-solving skills; to be able to resolve any technical or creative problems with the lighting
- a strong understanding of lighting techniques and equipment, including lanterns, lamps, colours, gobos and other special effects; to ensure the lighting design uses the most appropriate and effective techniques and equipment
- an understanding of lighting angles; to ensure the lighting can have a strong impact on the performance, creating interesting effects without blinding the audience or performers
- an understanding of health and safety issues; to ensure lights do not put the audience, the performers or anyone else involved in the production in danger.

49. Colour, symbolism, mood and atmosphere

For example:

During the opening of Act 1 of *An Inspector Calls*, when the family sits together around the table, I would want to create a bright, warm atmosphere. I would therefore use very warm, comfortable colours, such as yellow and orange, which suggest candlelight and an open fire. The lighting levels would need to be high, to indicate this warmth but also to show that the family can afford to be comfortable. At the same time, I would contrast this scene with the Inspector waiting outside the house, in the cold and dark, to make his entrance. To do this, I would place the Inspector in a wash of pale blue lighting. The lighting angle would be very steep, so as to create shadows on the Inspector's face. This would add to our mysterious impression of him. I would enhance this effect with a low level of lighting to make the shadows obvious.

50. Style, location and era

When answering this question, you need to be very clear about where and when your selected scene is taking place. For example:
- Is the scene set inside or outdoors?
- Is it well lit or dark?
- What time of day is it?
- What forms of lighting would be in the location (such as sunshine or moonlight if the scene is set outdoors)?

Make sure your ideas are consistent with the style of your piece.

For example:

In *DNA*, the location of a wood is used several times. To make this location clear to the audience, I would use a green wash to represent the leaves on the trees. In addition, I would use a 'leaf' gobo to project a speckled effect across the whole of the stage area. This would allow the audience to see instantly that the location is surrounded by trees – that it is a wood. To complete the effect, I would have a small area of the stage lit by a small, yellow light. This would represent the sunlight coming through in one place. All of the colours would then be enhanced with subtle white lighting – bright enough to ensure the audience can see the performers, but without hiding the effects created by the gobo and gels.

51. Types of lantern

When answering this question, remember to consider:

- the impact the techniques will have on your audience
- how they will enhance the performance.

For example:

In a production of *1984*, just before Winston and Julia are arrested, they stand together on stage. At this point, they could be lit by a narrow profile spotlight, which would be helpful because it would leave the rest of the stage in darkness. At the moment they spring apart, standing away from each other, the single spotlight could snap out and be replaced by two hard-edged profile spotlights. These would illuminate both performers but still keep the rest of the stage in darkness. Finally, as there is a loud crash and the stage becomes filled with uniformed men, the lighting state could suddenly snap to a full flood of bright, white lights, washing the stage with light and offering no hiding place for either Julia or Winston. This is helpful, as it directs the focus of the audience towards Winston and Julia until the uniformed men come in.

52. Lighting angles

For example:

In Act 3 of *The Crucible*, Elizabeth Proctor is questioned in court about why Abigail Williams was sacked from her role as the Proctor's servant. Both Abigail and John Proctor are in the room, but have been told by Judge Danforth to turn their backs so as not to influence Elizabeth's answer. As a result, Elizabeth is feeling isolated. To show this, I would use a profile spotlight angled as a downlight. This would highlight Elizabeth's isolation and also place a strong light on her face, so the audience would be able to see her reactions clearly. I would then use up-lighting on both John Proctor and Abigail, to create a more mysterious, tense mood that suggests they feel awkward about the difficult questions that Elizabeth is being asked.

53. Gels, barn doors and gobos

In your answer, you need to consider:

- where the selected scene is located
- whether you could use a gobo to indicate that place.

If the style of your piece is non-naturalistic, you could also consider using shapes or shadows to represent characters or events, rather than physical locations.

For example:

During Nia's memory in *100*, a gobo could be used to indicate she has selected an appropriate memory. As she is reliving the flashback, the lighting could slowly crossfade from general lights to a sepia-coloured wash. Outlining this could be a gobo representing a picture frame, which becomes fully formed just before the 'camera flashes' and the scene ends with a blackout. Using lighting and a gobo for each successful memory repeatedly in this way will help to guide the audience through the process in the Void.

54. Structure and focus

In your answer to this question, you need to consider:

- the layout of the stage
- what is happening before and after the scene (for example, do you want to be able to change set or bring on performers without them being seen?)

- what the main focus should be (for example, do you want the audience to focus on specific aspects of the set, or on a specific character?)
- the levels of light you require, and which colours you will need
- any areas of shadow or darkness you would like on the performance area.

For example:

In Act 2, Scene 11 of *Blue Stockings*, the scene opens with the women in high spirits; they are hopeful they will win the vote to allow them to graduate. However, at the same time, groups of men are involved in a violent protest against allowing women to graduate, and they approach the women quickly. To show this growing threat, I would have the front of the stage lit up, to focus the audience's attention on the women and Will. During this opening exchange, I would then fade up the lights at the back of the stage, to show the group of men getting closer. As the light gets stronger, this would then focus the attention of the audience and make it clear that the threat provided by the group of men is very real. The moment a stone is thrown through the window, the lights would be equally bright, to indicate that the men are now in the same location and that the protest has arrived at Girton.

Designer: set

55. The set designer

Required skills for a set designer include:

- understanding the text, style and genre of the play
- the ability to work in a team
- strong communication skills
- the ability to interpret a text
- the ability to turn ideas into practical set construction
- creativity
- problem-solving skills
- understanding set design and construction techniques and equipment
- understanding different performance spaces and staging
- understanding audience perspective angles
- understanding health and safety issues.

All of the above skills are important, as they enable a set designer to plan a design that is appropriate to the style, genre and period of the performance, and to make sure the set design is consistent. They also help the set designer to work as part of a team to create a shared vision for the production. Finally, being able to combine creative and practical approaches with a good understanding of performance spaces, construction challenges and sightlines helps to create a much smoother process. It also helps the set designer to predict and avoid problems.

56. Style and genre

For example:

The play *DNA* provides some interesting challenges for the set designer. I would use a non-naturalistic style for this production because the play uses three different locations in rotation – a street, a field and a wood. Additionally, each scene is relatively short and therefore the scene changes need to be quite quick and very smooth. I would divide the space into three areas. I would use appropriate colours for each area and a symbolic set–for example leaves, grass or street furniture – to represent each location. This would help the audience to understand the setting for each location and would support the non-naturalistic style of the play. It would also allow scenes to be changed quickly, helping the flow and pace of the performance.

57. Colours, location and time

When answering this question:
- First, decide on the key themes and issues within your chosen scene.
- Then consider what you want your audience to feel about the scene and what you want to communicate to the audience.
- Next, consider which colours will support your ideas.
- Finally, consider how you can use those colours in the set; for example, through the flooring, furnishings, walls, drapes or other stage properties.

For example:

At the end of Ketu's memory in *100*, Ketu becomes more comfortable with his decision to end his life and, at the moment of his death, he claims he can see everything so clearly – the Earth and stretching out beyond that, the universe. To help to represent this moment of peacefulness, I would have each of the four boxes change colour. To achieve this, I would make the boxes out of strong Perspex with a black board set slightly back from each face. This would give the impression that the boxes are plain black. However, I would have small colour-changing LED lighting between the Perspex and the fascia, which could be operated remotely. Just before Ketu dies, when he 'sees' clearly that the Earth is round, the LEDs could light up, changing the colour of the boxes, using green and blue to represent the Earth, then yellow for the sun, and finally a gentle white to symbolise his sense of peace.

58. Practicality, health and safety

A set designer for a touring production must consider how the set:
- can be portable and still communicate the production's main messages effectively
- can make use of flats and other easy-to-move stage properties, such as furniture
- can be used in multiple ways.

For example:

My set would be used for a touring production of *Twelfth Night*. I would want to make it as portable as possible. The style of the production would be quite traditional. Therefore, I would use two collapsible flats (for ease of transportation) to represent 16th-century Mediterranean palaces, showing paintings of marble columns and portraits of previous dukes. The main colours would be burgundy and terracotta, to reflect the colours and building materials of the time. As key moments take place outside, I would have traditional busts on Greek-style column plinths, as well as a variety of green plants I would have the box tree on stage throughout the performance; this could be part of a pair of carefully shaped bushes, representing the high status of Olivia's household. If the box tree was placed on wheels, it could be turned to show a different type of plant on the other side, helping to represent Orsino's household as well, which is also of high status. Finally, the box tree would be hollow, allowing performers to climb inside and peer out at Malvolio as he opens the letter he believes has been written by Olivia.

59. Props and stage furniture

Your answer could include:
- reference to the small, detailed personal props the character may use and which reflect their character traits or status

- ideas about any patterns, detail, colours and materials used in the design of the props
- reference to the location and time period in which the production is set
- ideas linked to the themes and issues of the play.

For example:

In *An Inspector Calls*, Inspector Goole would have a notebook and pencil. Both items should reflect the year in which the play is set: 1912. Therefore, the notebook will be hard-backed and have a spine, rather than being spiral bound, which is a much later invention). The pencil would be solid-looking and a dark colour; it should not have an eraser at the end as this is also a later invention. The notebook and pencil would have a specific meaning for the character, indicating to the audience that Goole is an inspector who keeps detailed notes about the case he is investigating and of the interviews he conducts. This will have an unsettling impact on the other characters, as they will be unable to see what Goole is writing about them. Additionally, Goole would wear a pair of round spectacles, with a narrow metal frame – a fashion that suits the period of the play. This would symbolise the fact that the Inspector can see things the other characters do not.

60. Levels, entrances and exits

When answering this question, remember that a set designer needs to:
- consider where the action takes place
- consider where the characters are coming from/going to
- ensure the performers are able to access the stage quickly and easily.

For example:

In Act 1, Scene 4 of *Government Inspector*, the Mayor runs across the stage in a panic while his wife, Anna, and daughter, Maria, speak with him. As the style of the piece is comedy, the use of several entrances and exits could add to the humour of this scene. In this case, I would have four entrance/exit points on stage left, four on stage right and one from upstage centre. This would also give the performers the flexibility to choose the most effective entrances and exits. For example, humour could be created by keeping Anna and Maria in one location downstage centre, and allowing the Mayor to enter and exit on opposite sides of the stage. If the Mayor first enters the stage downstage left and exits upstage right, he could then re-enter the stage upstage right and exit downstage left. If space is used carefully, the Mayor could also exit one side of the stage and re-enter on the other, an old but effective way of confusing the audience. Repeating this sequence would increase the humour – especially if Anna and Maria are looking in the wrong place for the Mayor to appear.

61. Types of staging and terminology

For example:

For a production of *The Crucible*, I would use theatre-in-the-round. This would be effective because in this style of staging the audience surrounds the action. This would give the production a very enclosed and intense feeling, which is how many of the characters in the play feel. It would also create the feeling that the audience is closely examining events, which would relect the way the Church and court do this in Act 3. In addition, as members of the audience can see each other, there is a constant reminder that this is a play. This means they can distance themselves and examine the plays themes and issues – such as power, status and the impact of the state vs the individual – with a clearer perspective. The production would use only simple props to represent key areas for example, a bed for Act 1, a table and chairs for Act 2, and benches for Acts 3 and 4. This would keep audience sightlines clear. Finally, the performers would have to leave and enter the space through the audience, again adding to the intense and intimate atmosphere of the production.

62. Symbolism, semiotics, spatial consideration and depth

In your answer, you need to consider:

- how the stage can be used in all three dimensions
- the style of the performance and whether the space could be used to symbolise or represent key ideas or themes in the scene/production
- levels, type of staging, practicality, and health and safety of performers and crew.

For example:

In a production of *An Inspector Calls*, if the performance space were an end-on proscenium arch, the Birlings' dining room could be raised from the ground and sloped forward. This would symbolise the Birlings' wealth and relatively high status in their local community, as well as aiding the sightlines for the audience. The Inspector could then enter from the audience, signalling that he represents the general, everyday people who make up the audience and majority of society. As the play progresses and the Inspector's power and status grow, he could move further upstage, whereas the other characters could move towards the downstage area. The slope of the dining room would need to be relatively gentle, so as not to cause a slip or trip hazard for the performers.

Designer: sound

63. The sound designer

Required skills for a sound designer will include:

- understanding the text, style and genre of the play
- the ability to work as part of a team
- strong communication skills
- the ability to interpret a text
- the ability to turn ideas into sound and identify moments where sound can enhance the performance
- creativity
- problem-solving skills
- a strong understanding of sound production techniques and equipment, including recording and editing software
- an understanding of how space and materials can affect the production sound and have an impact on the performance and audience
- an understanding of health and safety issues (such as volume levels).

All of the above skills are important, as they enable a sound designer to plan a sound design that is appropriate to and consistent with the style, genre and era of the performance. They also help the sound designer to work as part of a team to create a shared vision for the production. Finally, being able to plan and develop the sound design, as well as predict and avoid problems, helps to create a smooth production process.

64. Music and sound effects

For example:

In *100*, during Alex's memory, Alex and two of the other performers re-enact a tense motorcycle race with the other cast members. I would want the recorded sound effect of several high-powered motorcycles, first revving their engines as if getting ready to start the race, which would build tension, and then a longer sound of them accelerating as the race begins. This sound could be faded in to underscore the sequence. In order to increase the tension further, I would also blend in some frantic, fast-paced music with a heavy bass and drum line. This would also convey the speed and risk involved as the riders race through the streets. However, it would also be important to ensure that the speech in the scene can still be heard above the music and sound effects.

65. Atmosphere and time

For example:

In *1984*, Winston and Julia make a decision to keep seeing each other, even though they know there will probably be dreadful consequences. A stage direction describes how they look into each other's eyes in silence as they make their decision. In order to give the silence the greatest impact, I would use tension-filled music to underscore the dialogue between Winston and Julia leading up to the moment of silence. A slight crescendo could be used to suggest the building of tension, and then the music could suddenly snap out, leaving complete silence between the two performers.

66. Location and genre

For example:

In *Twelfth Night*, when Viola first arrives in Illyria, I would include the sound effect of the sea under a dying storm to represent the sea coast. Additionally, Duke Orsino would have a personal ensemble of musicians playing sad, gloomy music to entertain him in his palace. This would demonstrate not only his wealth and status, but also set the tone and atmosphere for the opening of the play. These musicians would be physically on stage and playing live music within the performance and could also be present every time a scene is set in Orsino's palace, as a signal to the audience about the location.

67. Sound equipment and levels

Your answer here may depend on the style of staging you have selected for the production (such as proscenium arch or theatre-in-the-round).

For example:

In Act 2, Scene 11 of *Blue Stockings*, as the demonstration against women receiving degrees approaches the performance area, it may be effective to use sound effects that suggest a large, violent mob of men. These may include things such as the chanting of (anti-women) slogans shouting, and the smashing of windows. Using a crescendo would indicate that the group of men is getting closer and closer. If the speakers are placed behind the audience as well as in front, this would give the impression that the audience is surrounded and very much a part of the action. While this sound effect could be unnerving for the audience members, it would also give them a powerful experience, encouraging them to engage with the strong feelings and to think about the themes and issues of the play.

PERFORMANCE TEXTS

68. *1984*: overview

Examples may include (in addition to those listed on page 68):

- **State vs individual** – Winston is tortured by the State to ensure he does what the Party wants.
- **Reality or fiction** – The torture Winston experiences is so brutal, he cannot answer a simple addition question. This raises questions about the nature of information given to the public.
- **Fact or interpretation** – O'Brien tells Winston that he is suffering from a defective memory, but that he is able to save him.

- **Power** – The development of 'Newspeak' is an attempt by the Party to control the people by forcing a new language on them. This reflects a tactic used by conquering nations over thousands of years.
- **Love** – Winston risks his life by meeting with Julia in the countryside.
- **Trust** – Parsons trusts that, if he does what the Party wants, he will be safe. However, his own daughter informs on him, leading to his execution.
- **Sanity/psychology** – Even though Winston firmly believes in challenging the regime, the torture he experiences is not only physical but psychological, leading him to the conclusion that he was wrong in the first place.

69. *1984*: plot

For example:

Personal data is collected via cookies – small packets of information that leave a digital trace when we visit a website. Cookies can provide all sorts of information, including the machine used, the time and date, and what was looked at. This information can be used to target specific advertising and provide evidence of the websites visited.

Today, our culture is very dependent on devices with screens. This had an impact on the design of the first performance of *1984* in Nottingham in 2013, when many screens were included in the set design.

70. *An Inspector Calls*: overview

Examples may include (in addition to those listed on page 70):
- **Social status** – Mr Birling tells Gerald that he may be in line for a knighthood.
- **Money** – Eric steals to help Eva, believing that money is the solution to his problems.
- **Responsibility** – Mrs Birling sacks Eva when she comes to her for help, as she does not feel she has any responsibility for the situation in which Eva has found herself. While this may be true, Mrs Birling fails to see that she will have some responsibility for what happens in Eva's future.
- **Morality** – Sheila is disgusted by the attitude of her parents and fiancé when they discover the Inspector was not real and that no young woman has committed suicide.
- **Prejudice** – Gerald, on hearing how Eva was a leading figure in the strike at the factory, comments that Mr Birling dealt with the strikers correctly, judging Eva with only limited information.
- **Higher power** – The Birlings think money brings them power, but the Inspector shows them that knowledge and information are more powerful.
- **Generation and gender** – Gerald takes advantage of Eva/Daisy, seeing her as something he can use and believing himself to be superior.

71. *An Inspector Calls*: plot

For example:

Many theatres in London had been bombed and destroyed during the Second World War (1939–45). In 1946, rationing was still in use and it was difficult to find the money to stage plays. The simple structure of *An Inspector Calls* – which uses only one set and no costume changes – means that it could have been staged less expensively than other plays. However, it was still a very challenging environment, which is why the first performances of *An Inspector Calls* actually took place in Moscow and Leningrad (now St Petersburg).

72. *Blue Stockings*: overview

Examples may include (in addition to those listed on page 72):
- **Gender** – Men and women are educated separately, as the College does not believe in combined education.
- **Sacrifice** – Maeve has to sacrifice her education to look after her younger siblings following her mother's death.
- **Protest** – There is a violent protest at the time the vote takes place, which includes the burning of a model of a woman in blue stockings.
- **Education** – The women have to fight for the right to be educated. They have to challenge the prejudice of male students and academics, such as Dr Maudsley and the Senate, which runs Cambridge University. They also struggle to find tutors who are willing to risk their own careers in order to teach them.
- **Balance** – Tess works hard to balance her personal and professional lives. While committed to her studies, she has fallen in love with Ralph. This is further complicated when Will admits he is in love with her. It is a balancing act she does not get right, as she fails her exams.
- **Choice** – The graduates have to make a choice: whether to vote for or against graduation rights for women. The women also face a choice: whether to fight for those rights or to accept the situation as it is.

73. *Blue Stockings*: plot

For example:

There are still many places around the world where there is inequality in education. Often, the inequality is based on gender; however, other factors, such as poverty, can also have an impact. The story of Malala Yousafzai, who was shot by the Taliban at the age of 15 for attending school in Pakistan, was in the news at the time of the first performance of *Blue Stockings* in London in 2013. This helped to highlight the play's a very modern message, in spite of its historical context.

74. *The Crucible*: overview

Examples may include (in addition to those listed on page 74):
- **Guilt** – At the end of the play, Elizabeth feels guilty about the way she has treated Proctor. She realises that she has punished him severely for his affair and that he genuinely was trying to make up for his mistake.
- **Responsibility** – Reverend Hale feels his initial reaction (he was convinced that witchcraft was the cause of the problems) makes him at least partly responsible for what is happening.
- **Revenge** – Abigail uses the situation to get revenge on Elizabeth, who she sees as an obstacle to her relationship with Proctor.
- **Morality** – Although she is afraid, Mary Warren understands she has a moral responsibility to try to stop what is happening when she tells Proctor that people have been condemned to hang.
- **Gender** – For the first time, the girls have a higher status and are listened to by the men.
- **Race** – Tituba, while being questioned and under extreme pressure, shocks the village by claiming the Devil told her that white people are under his control. This shocks the white villagers, who find it hard to believe that white Christians could be swayed by the power of the Devil.
- **Status and power** – The rigid social structure of the community is turned upside down by the events in Salem,

as those at the lowest end of the social structure (such as slaves and unmarried girls) come to hold power. This means they can challenge those who traditionally held the most power (such as the minister and rich landowners).

- **Individuality vs society/the system** – Mary Warren tries to stand up to the group of girls by telling the court they are lying. This is a big personal risk, as she knows that anyone who challenges the girls will probably be accused of witchcraft and face the death penalty.

75. *The Crucible*: plot

For example:

In the 1950s, US Senator Joseph McCarthy claimed that communists and Soviet spies and sympathisers had accessed the United States, and he started a campaign to discover them. While there were some spies in the United States at the time, thousands of people – who were guilty simply of having politically 'left wing' ideas – were accused of being communists. They faced high-profile trials, often without enough evidence. Many innocent people lost their jobs and went to prison. The trials caused a lot of fear in the United States.

Arthur Miller saw similarities between McCarthyism (often referred to as a 'witch hunt') and the Salem witch trials, and wrote *The Crucible* as a metaphor for what was happening at the time. Audiences would have been very aware of the McCarthy trials and would have quickly understood that the play was an attack on the US government and the Establishment.

76. *DNA*: overview

Examples may include (in addition to those listed on page 76):

- **Responsibility** – Phil takes responsibility for trying to solve the problem by faking evidence.
- **Status** – Cathy becomes the leader of the group at the end of the play, taking control from John Tate and Phil, who give up their leadership.
- **Bullying** – John Tate threatens Richard with violence when Richard challenges his leadership of the group. The rest of the group are frightened of John and always do as he says.
- **Truth** – When it becomes clear that Adam is not dead, Phil starts manipulating the situation to ensure the story they have created becomes the truth.
- **Peer pressure** – When Leah expresses her horror at the solution Phil suggests, Phil re-establishes his position by asking a rhetorical question, in this way reminding Leah that the group is more important than an individual.
- **Consequences** – Brian suffers a severe breakdown, which enables Phil to take control of him. As a result, Phil manipulates Brian into killing Adam, causing further damage to Brian's mind and leading him to take stronger medication.

77. *DNA*: plot

For example:

Peer pressure is a key cause of bullying, as members of a group work together to ensure they are not the ones who become the victim of the bullying. Because they are afraid of the combined power of the group, individuals within that group are less likely to stand up to/disagree with decisions made. Recently, there has been an increase in cyber bullying (using technology to bully victims from a distance). Fear of embarrassment, humiliation and exclusion causes some people to send bullying texts and messages on social media. The consequences can be extremely serious. For example, bullying has led people to hurt themselves or even take their own lives.

The first performance of *DNA* was part of the National Theatre Connections programme, which aimed to engage young people with theatre. Therefore, large groups of young people were able to see the performance and connect with the characters in the play, who looked and sounded like them. This meant the young audience was able to understand the relevance of the play's anti-bullying messages.

78. *100*: overview

Examples may include (in addition to those listed on page 78):

- **Priorities** – As Alex becomes more desperate to find that one memory which will allow him to pass into the afterlife, he cries out to the Guide, saying he 'had a lot of good moments!' and asking why these memories are not good enough for the Guide. The Guide points out that the camera doesn't flash because these memories are not good enough for Alex. This makes Alex think about what he really wanted to do in life – 'to race bikes'.
- **Time** – The count to 100 occurs several times during the play, emphasising how short time in the Void is. At the end of the play, as Alex struggles to find a memory that will help him pass into the afterlife, the Guide punctuates each line with the next count, from 96 to when he tells Alex that there is no more time to decide.
- **Truth** – After Ketu appears to give up his theory that the Earth is round, admitting that it is flat, his village celebrates. However, Ketu finds it impossible to ignore the truth he has discovered. Eventually, he takes his own life rather than continue to live with such a lie.
- **Consequences** – Sophie recalls being ill and bedridden. She reflects that her 'so-called friends' initially came to visit her, but only because they thought she might be of use to them professionally. When they noticed this is not the case, the visits stopped. Sophie realises that her determination to succeed in her career has left her personally lonely and isolated.
- **Belief** – The Guide introduces himself by welcoming Ketu, Sophie and Alex to 'death'. They ask him if he is 'Death' or God or the devil. The Guide rejects these ideas but the discussion opens up the idea that there is some kind of life after death.

79. *100*: plot

For example:

The Edinburgh Festival Fringe is the world's biggest festival of arts and takes place every August in Edinburgh, the Scottish capital. Thousands of performers take part in hundreds of arts events, all aiming to attract big audiences. As large numbers of events take place at the same time, many performances are staged in spaces that are not specific arts venues – such as community halls and function rooms in pubs. This kind of venue will not have full technical equipment or support. Therefore, when *100* was first performed at the festival in 2002, it would have been important to consider how to stage the play with minimum lighting, sound and props. In addition, many venues at the festival host a number of productions, one after the other. As a result, the production of *100* would have needed to be very quick to set up and strike. The minimalist performance style would have helped in this environment, as it means that the production can take place anywhere and be transferred quickly.

80. *Government Inspector*: overview

Examples may include (in addition to those listed on page 80):

- **Corruption** – As the different officials meet Khlestakov, they each bribe him (between 65 roubles and 500 roubles) in the hope that he will leave them alone rather than punishing them for not carrying out their duties.
- **Greed** – The Mayor warns the other officials not to 'fall short' (take bribes) until the Inspector has left. The bribes clearly show that those who have the power are taking advantage of the townspeople for their own financial gain.
- **Deception** – The Mayor does everything he can to pretend the town is clean and functioning properly. However, it is clear from the way he speaks with the other officials that the town is run on corruption and none of the officials are doing their jobs correctly (for example, the judge uses the courtroom to store all his hunting equipment and the Clerk of the Court is constantly drunk on vodka).
- **Mistaken identity** – Maria believes she is engaged to a Government Inspector. However, Khlestakov is not a Government Inspector and Khlestakov has no intention or marrying Maria.
- **Status and power** – The officials' treatment of the shopkeepers (taking money from them and punishing them severely for minor crimes) prevents the shopkeepers from improving their status and power.
- **Reform** – The town officials fall for Khlestakov's deception – believing he is an Inspector – because they assume that all political figures operate in the same corrupt way as they do. This highlights the need for reform.
- **Bureaucracy** – Because the administrative and legal systems of the town are so complex, expensive to access and run by corrupt officials who mistreat the shopkeepers, it is impossible for the shopkeepers to get justice. For example, the Mayor sends the locksmith to war because he does not have enough money or gifts with which to bribe him, even though it is illegal to send a married man to war.

81. *Government Inspector*: plot

For example:

In the 1830s, Russia was a vast empire. However, economically it was not very strong and there was a huge social class divide. This meant that those who had power were able to take advantage of those who did not.

When *Government Inspector* was first performed in St Petersburg in 1836, many people from the ruling classes were angry at the way in which Gogol poked fun at them. Not only had their corrupt ways been noticed, but the play also displayed this corruption to the wider population. They realised this could have dangerous consequences: people would begin to revolt and protest (in a similar way to the shopkeepers in the play) and the ruling classes would be less able to take advantage of them financially. The first performance of *Government Inspector* caused a great outcry from the audience, which was made up mainly of those who were being ridiculed, and they tried to shut the play down. However, Tsar Nicholas I loved the play and his influence meant that it continued to be performed.

82. *Twelfth Night*: overview

Examples may include (in addition to those listed on page 82):

- **Love** – Orsino opens the play by referring to his love for Olivia.
- **Deception** – Viola pretends to be a man and deceives Orsino and Olivia.
- **Social status** – Sir Toby breaks social convention and marries Maria, Olivia's maid.
- **Gender confusion** – Olivia falls in love with Viola, thinking she is a man.
- **Ambition** – Viola thinks the only way she will be able to progress in the duke's household is by pretending to be a man, as there were limited opportunities for women at that time.
- **Madness** – Olivia claims her own madness ('a most extracting frenzy of mine own') caused her to forget Malvolio's state of mind (which is a temporary madness caused by the cruel trick played on him).
- **Honour** – Sir Toby marries Maria to make up for the trouble he has caused her.

83. *Twelfth Night*: plot

For example:

At the start of the 17th century, there were significant changes to traditional religious beliefs in England. A split in the Christian Church led to strict Puritans (as represented by Malvolio). England was still coming to terms with a new religion – Protestantism – and both Anglicans and Catholics were persecuted. Shakespeare highlights this issue of religion by poking fun at Malvolio (and therefore at Puritans). The audience at the first performance of the play would have enjoyed seeing his downfall.

At this time, Elizabeth I's reign was nearly over (she died in 1603) and there was confusion about who would reign next (Elizabeth had not named an heir). This confusion is reflected in the way different characters in *Twelfth Night* have different amounts of power at different times in the play.

It was also still traditional for all the performers to be male. Therefore, the first audiences would have found it very funny to see a man, playing a woman, pretending to be a man.

Additionally, strict class laws governed Elizabethan society. These laws even stated what clothes could be worn by people from different classes. The costumes worn by characters of different social status reflected these laws, but Shakespeare also poked fun at this system by making the Duke marry Viola and Sir Toby marry Maria. In the first performance of the play, the audience (often made up of people from the lower classes) would have enjoyed the fact that someone of their own social class was able to marry 'up'.

SECTION A: BRINGING TEXTS TO LIFE

84. About Section A

For example:

Key words in the question are shown underlined:

Choose <u>one character</u> from your performance text, and choose <u>one scene</u> in which that character appears. <u>Explain two ways</u> you could use <u>vocal skills</u> to play the character in this scene. (4 marks)

In this question, you are asked to select only **one** character from **one** scene. The question asks you to **explain**. This means you need to demonstrate your understanding of the ways you can use the vocal skills and you need to justify any answer you give. The question asks you to give **two** examples and you must only focus on **vocal** skills.

85. Section A questions

Use of the correct technical vocabulary will help make your answers clearer and more focused. You should try to use technical vocabulary wherever it is appropriate.

- For Question (b), technical terms may include: materials, colour, proscenium arch, traverse, gel, focus, levels, shadow.
- For Question (c), technical terms may include: space, levels, cyclorama, shadow, traverse, barn doors.

86. Approaching the extract

The amount of time you spend on each question will depend on the marks available. You have 105 minutes in total, so you need to:

- be clear about how many marks are available for each question
- break down the amount of time you will need to complete each question, making sure you have enough time to answer the whole paper.

If the exam started at 12.30pm, the plan would look like this:

12.30 Find the correct extract and read it carefully. Open the question paper and read the questions relating to your extract. **8 minutes.**

12.38 Answer Question (a) (i) – 4 marks. **4 minutes.**

12.42 Answer Question (a) (ii) – 6 marks. **6 minutes.**

12.48 Answer Question (b) (i) – 9 marks. **14 minutes.**

1.02 Answer Question (b) (ii) – 12 marks. **20 minutes.**

1.22 Answer Question (c) – 14 marks. **23 minutes.**

1.45 Answer Section B: live theatre evaluation. Question 9 (a) – 6 marks. **10 minutes.**

1.55 Answer Question 9 (b) – 9 marks. **15 minutes.**

2.10 Check all answers. **5 minutes.**

2.15 End of exam.

If the exam started at 1.00pm, the plan would look like this:

1.00 Find the correct extract and read it carefully. Open the question paper and read the questions relating to your extract. **8 minutes.**

1.08 Answer Question (a) (i) – 4 marks. **4 minutes.**

1.12 Answer Question (a) (ii) – 6 marks. **6 minutes.**

1.18 Answer Question (b) (i) – 9 marks. **14 minutes.**

1.32 Answer Question (b) (ii) – 12 marks. **20 minutes.**

1.52 Answer Question (c) – 14 marks. **23 minutes.**

2.15 Answer Section B: live theatre evaluation. Question 9 (a) – 6 marks. **10 minutes.**

2.25 Answer Question 9 (b) – 9 marks. **15 minutes.**

2.40 Check all answers. **5 minutes.**

2.45 End of exam.

87. Question (a) (i): vocal skills

For example, for the character Alex from *100;* the final scene:

1. I would make each line louder, until I am shouting at the Guide. This would show my growing anger and frustration that I cannot focus on a suitable memory.

2. I would also start by speaking through clenched teeth, showing I am trying to control my anger.

88. Question (a) (i): physical skills

For example, for the character of Elizabeth from *The Crucible;* Act 3:

1. I would stand facing Danforth, but I would keep turning my face away, showing that I am nervous and also scared of him.

2. As I am being led out of the courtroom, I would let my legs collapse from underneath me, indicating my shock and distress at the realisation that I have missed the chance to end the situation.

89. Question (a) (ii)

For example, for Mrs Birling from *An Inspector Calls;* the final 90 lines of Act 2:

1. When Sheila interrupts Mrs Birling to comment that she and Mr Birling were responsible for Eva losing her jobs, I would shoot an angry look directly at Sheila. This would show I am annoyed about being interrupted and act as a warning to Sheila not to undermine me.

2. When the Inspector keeps challenging, I would raise the volume of my voice, indicating that I am angry and that I dislike him, and that I am trying to show my superiority over him.

3. When I realise the Inspector is referring to Eric, I would suddenly freeze, raising my hand slowly towards my heart, and shoot a sudden, wide-eyed look towards Mr Birling. This would not only show how shocked and afraid I am, but also that I am looking to my husband for support.

90. Question (b) (i): costume

The following notes are for an answer that uses the character of Adam from Act 3 in *DNA*. Points to consider include:

- There is a difference in status between Adam, who has been living wild for weeks, and the other characters, who are clean and cared for.
- Adam is terrified of the others, as they are the ones who bullied him in the first place. Also, his state of mind is very fragile.
- The text indicates clearly that Adam has been seriously injured after a fall into a deep pit. How could these injuries be represented through the costume?
- The text was created for performance as part of the National Theatre Connections programme, designed to be performed by student performers from schools and youth groups.
- Are there any other points you would want to communicate to an audience?

Remember to include evidence from the extract and wider text to support and justify your answers. You must also refer to the context in which the text was created and performed.

91. Question (b) (i): staging

The following notes are for an answer based on the beginning of Act 2 of *The Crucible*. Points to consider include:

- Take as much information as possible from the stage directions: there are two entrances and exits, a door leading outside and a staircase going upstairs.
- The fireplace is needed for cooking and the audience needs to see Proctor adding salt to the pot. Where should this be placed?
- Proctor is washing his hands and face in a basin when Elizabeth enters. Where could the basin be positioned to help emphasize their strained relationship?
- Are there any other points you would want to communicate to an audience?

Remember to include evidence from the extract and wider text to support and justify your answers. You must also refer to the context in which the text was created and performed.

92. Question (b) (i): props

The following notes are for an answer based on Act 2, Scene 5 of *Twelfth Night* (lines 15–105 of the prescribed edition). Points to consider include:

- In this extract, it is important to ensure the social status of both Sir Andrew and Sir Toby is clear to the audience. Additionally, Sir Andrew and Sir Toby are both comedic characters, and in this scene, Fabian, although lower in status, is poking fun at them.
- The letter could be extravagantly prepared with ribbon, to highlight the Sir Andrew's wealth.
- Sir Andrew and Sir Toby could carry expensive, elaborately carved walking sticks, to emphasise their status and wealth.
- Sir Andrew could carry a handkerchief, which he waves at key moments during the scene, to increase the dramatic impact of his letter. For example, Sir Andrew could do this when Malvolio first picks up the letter and again when he exclaims that he believes the letter to be from Olivia.
- Are there any other points you would want to communicate to an audience?

Remember to include evidence from the extract and wider text to support and justify your answers. You must also refer to the context in which the text was created and performed.

93. Question (b) (i): set

The following notes are for an answer based on *100*, on Sophie's memory from when she starts her new job in the office, aged 21.

- The main setting of *100* is the Void, which is 'an otherworldly place, perhaps outside time and space'. However, this scene takes place in a contemporary office setting, so the set should be modern with an airy, open-plan feel. The four boxes could be used to help define the office space as well as doubling as desks for other members of the cast, playing office staff, to sit at.
- The style of this play is abstract so the set should generally be non-naturalistic. The set may include flats, which in this scene could be used as dividers between the office desks, representing the formal atmosphere that Sophie finds 'daunting'.
- The set would need to be both simple and flexible. This scene is set in an office but there are several locations during Sophie's memory at this point in the play, and the time spent in each location is brief. For example, portable flats could be used in this scene to provide office furniture, and some could have sections which fold down to give the impression of workstations. The same flats could be used when the location switches to Christmas party, for example to provide the bar.
- The boxes could be used together with signs to indicate different locations. For example, a neon 'Bar' sign could appear on one of the boxes for the 'party' scene.'.
- When Sophie accepts her 'Manager Of The Year award', she could stand on one of the boxes. Her position on a higher level at this moment in the play would help to reinforce her success, creating a strong contrast with her next memory.
- How would the use of space and type of staging affect the set design and the audience's experience?
- Are there any other points you would want to communicate to an audience?

Remember to include evidence from the extract and wider text to support and justify your answers. You must also refer to the context in which the text was created and performed.

94. Question (b) (i): lighting

The following notes are for an answer based on Act 4, Scene 2 of *Government Inspector*. Points to consider include:

- Act 4, Scene 2 of *Government Inspector* is set in the Mayor's house, so it should be well lit, to indicate the comfort of the luxurious surroundings. The lights should give a warm feeling and enhance the rich colours used in the set.
- All of the characters that enter come from the room next door, which could remain lit throughout the scene. This would illuminate the characters, who could be trembling and shaking with fear to show how nervous they feel about meeting the Inspector.
- The scene is set indoors in the late afternoon/early evening. The sun will be setting and will be quite low in the sky. This could be indicated with a deep orange/red glow in the sky, coming through the windows of the set.
- The play is a comedy and this scene is filled with humour. The lighting should be relatively bright and warm to reflect the comic perspective of the audience and to ensure no tension is created.
- In this scene, the Judge passes Khlestakov a bribe. By narrowing the pool of light, this would focus the attention of the audience on the money, as well as providing a feeling of uncomfortable closeness between the characters.
- In this scene, a gobo could provide the shadows required for the windows, or barn doors.
- Are there any other points you would want to communicate to an audience?

Remember to include evidence from the extract and wider text to support and justify your answers. You must also refer to the context in which the text was created and performed.

95. Question (b) (i): sound

The following notes are for an answer based on *Blue Stockings*, Act 2, Scenes 11 and 12. Points to consider include:

- In this extract, there is initial excitement while the vote is taking place. However, the mood changes as the approaching protest becomes violent. Increasing the volume can also help to increase the tension.
- You could use sound effects to indicate the protest getting louder as the crowd gets closer. Specific techniques, such as a fade and crossfade, could help to achieve this.
- *Blue Stockings* is set in 1896, so the use of a steam train sound effect would be appropriate, whereas the use of a modern electric train would not. The sound of a steam train would be an excellent way to transition from the end of Scene 11 into Scene 12.
- A birdsong sound effect could be used to signal that it is daytime.
- Are there any other points you would want to communicate to an audience?

Remember to include evidence from the extract and wider text to support and justify your answers. You must also refer to the context in which the text was created and performed.

96. Question (b) (ii)

When answering Question (b) (ii), you will need to consider three aspects of performance in your answer:

- **Voice**. Consider what the character is trying to communicate and think carefully about how you want the performer to deliver the lines. You will need to refer to tone, pitch, pause and pace in your answer. Give specific lines as examples in your response.

- **Physicality**. The physicality must reflect the character's intentions. You will need to comment on facial expression, gesture, and body language, as well as posture and levels. Remember to consider any subtext that needs to be conveyed.
- **Stage directions and stage space**. Where is the character in relation to other characters on stage and the set? What might suggest about status and relationships? Consider whether the performer can use the space and set effectively – do any parts of the set make movement difficult? Remember to make refer to their stage directions and to think about the impact on the audience.

The following notes are for an answer based on the character of Mr Birling from Act 1 of *An Inspector Calls*. Points to consider include:

- Just after the Inspector has entered the house and has insulted Mr Birling with his direct manner and questions, Mr Birling wants to demonstrate his anger and establish his authority. He could speak with a rising volume, emphasising key words, to indicate what he thinks of the Inspector.
- As Mr Birling delivers his lines and prepares to leave the room, he would be standing, trying to dominate the space and intimidate the Inspector. His facial expression would be angry, making direct eye contact with the Inspector to demonstrate he is not afraid of him.
- As Mr Birling tells Gerald not to go after Sheila, as he is intending to go himself, he could raise his hand towards Gerald in a 'stop' motion, to highlight his desire to regain control over the situation. As Mr Birling tries to establish his status, he could move towards the Inspector, entering his personal space and trying to demonstrate that he is not willing to be intimidated by the Inspector in his own house.
- As the play progresses, Mr Birling continues to argue with the Inspector. However, it is only when the Inspector leaves that Mr Birling can try to re-establish his authority over the rest of the family. He does this by taking up dominant positions and challenging Eric and Sheila when they question his opinions and actions.

Remember to refer to the extract and the play as a whole.

97. Question (c): costume

When answering Question (c) about costume, you will need to refer to a range of aspects relating to costume. These include the following:

- How can costume help to indicate time period? Are there any specific styles or fashions that help to clarify the time?
- How can costume be used to reflect the status of different characters?
- How can the use of symbolic or representational costume aid the audience?

Throughout your answer, remember to:

- provide examples from the text to justify your ideas
- give clear reasons for each of your ideas
- indicate how your ideas would enhance the production for the audience.

The following notes are for an answer based on the torture scene in *1984* (found on pages 71–73 of the prescribed edition). Points to consider include:

- Winston could be dressed in a bland, colourless shirt and tie, representing and reflecting life in the Soviet Union during the 1970s and 1980s. Making Winston's clothes the same as those of the other workers would indicate the uniformity required by the Party.

- In contrast to Winston, O'Brien could be dressed in a high-quality, more colourful suit, hinting at his higher status and privileged position. Additionally, O'Brien's suit could be accessorised with cufflinks or a tiepin.
- In this scene, the torturers could each wear white coveralls with a large, disposable plastic apron. Together with a surgical mask, this would make the torture feel cold and efficient as well as making the torturers anonymous.

98. Question (c): staging

When answering Question (c) about staging you will need to refer to a range of aspects relating to staging. These include the following:

- Consider use of entrances and exits – how can they be used to support the plot?
- Think about the perspective of the audience. This will be different to the perspective of the characters on stage and the audience needs to understand what is going on and why. It is also vital to ensure any subtle elements of the performance are clear enough for the audience, to avoid confusion.
- Create an appropriate space for performers to move around in, ensuring there are clear sightlines and no health and safety issues. The space also needs to allow the performers to work with the agreed proxemics, so that they can tell the story effectively.

Throughout your answer:

- provide examples from the text to justify your ideas
- give clear reasons for each of your ideas
- indicate how your ideas would enhance the production for the audience.

The following notes are for an answer based on an extract from *Twelfth Night,* Act 3, Scene 4 (lines 385–400 in the prescribed edition) and Act 4, Scene 1 (lines 1–44 in the prescribed edition). Points to consider include:

- *Twelfth Night* is a comedy of errors and relies on mistaken identity and confusion for much of the comedy. In this extract, having multiple entrances and exits will help to create this confusion as Viola leaves and Sebastian then enters.
- Sir Andrew could use a different entrance to Sebastian, indicating he has come from another location. This will help to highlight Sir Andrew's sense of confusion as to why Sebastian is there (he thinks that Sebastian is actually Viola/Cesario, who moments earlier had apparently run away).
- A bench or plant pot positioned near the entrance used by Sir Andrew could help to create slapstick comedy for the audience: Sir Andrew could fall over it when Sebastian hits him, then Sir Toby and Fabian could trip over Sir Andrew as they hurry through the same entrance.

99. Question (c): props

When answering Question (c) about props and stage furniture, you will need to refer to a range of aspects relating to props and stage furniture. These include how props and stage furniture:

- help to establish character
- can be used to represent the appropriate time period
- represent the location of the play
- might have symbolic meaning, such as indicating status or corruption.

Throughout your answer:

- provide examples from the text to justify your ideas
- give clear reasons for each of your ideas
- indicate how your ideas would enhance the production for the audience.

The following notes are for an answer based on *Government Inspector,* Act 3, Scene 2 (the complete scene) and Scene 3 (from the beginning to Zemlyanika's line: 'That was the hospital, sir'). Points to consider include:

- The town in which *Government Inspector* is set is a rural, isolated place in significant need of repair – because the Mayor and other officials are using the money for their personal benefit. To show this, there could be an expensive vase on a plinth on either side of the doors to the room in the Mayor's house. This image would provide a strong contrast to the litter the policemen race to pick up from the floor.
- At the beginning of Scene 2, Osip could be carrying two old and battered suitcases that were once high-quality items. This would suggest they have been used a lot, but not looked after, so they have lost much of their value.
- The play is set in the 1830s, so the props must reflect this. For example, during Scene 3, Khlestakov (pretending to be the Inspector) could produce a notebook and pen, taking notes of the things he is being shown. Here, he should use a fountain pen rather than a biro. Comedy could then be produced as he makes one of the important town officials hold a pot of ink while he writes.

100. Question (c): set

When answering Question (c) about set, you will need to refer to a range of aspects relating to set. These include the following:

- If several locations are used for the production, you will need to ensure that the set you create is flexible and also representational. You could create a range of naturalistic locations in one large space; here, the performers would move from location to location. Alternatively, you could choose a more abstract, minimalistic style, in which one space is adapted to represent a range of different locations; here, you might use only key ideas for each location.
- Using levels will help to make each location clear and different, as well as communicating aspects such as the status and power of the characters.
- The style of the performance must be reflected in the style of the set, so that the production is consistent for the audience.

Throughout your answer:

- provide examples from the text to justify your ideas
- give clear reasons for each of your ideas
- indicate how your ideas would enhance the production for the audience.

The following notes are for an answer based on *Blue Stockings*, Act 1 (from the end of Scene 1: '*MR BANKS lets go of the bike and TESS cycles alone'* to Scene 3: 'MISS BLAKE I've heard you can ride a bicycle. What's stopping you?'). Points to consider include:

- Several locations are used in this extract, which crosses over three different scenes. Therefore, the stage needs to be flexible and locations could be represented symbolically, rather than naturalistically.

- In Scene 1, the characters could stand outside Girton College, indicated by a large wooden exterior door. The door should look old, to indicate it has been there for a long time, reflecting the age of the college.
- Scene 2, in which the men discuss seeing Tess on a bicycle, is short. Here, a simple set, such as a wooden park bench placed on the side of the stage and facing out towards the audience, would suggest an outdoor location some distance away from the location of the previous scene.
- For Scene 3, the classroom could be indicated by the women passing through the heavy door used in Scene 1 and sitting at the opposite side of the stage to the men in Scene 2. Each character could have a simple wooden chair, which should reflect the late Victorian setting. This would also be consistent with the symbolic, minimalist style. The large door could be on castors and swung around to reveal a chalkboard on the back, making the set work efficiently.

101. Question (c): lighting

When answering Question (c) about lighting, you will need to refer to a range of aspects relating to lighting. These include the following:

- Colour can be used to represent a range of different emotions and ideas. It is important to consider how different colours communicate different emotions and feelings to an audience.
- Lighting can also suggest location. You need to consider if the scene is taking place indoors or outdoors. Is the scene a comedic, positive scene, or does it build tension and lead to a distressing conclusion?
- Lighting is key in creating mood and atmosphere. It can communicate a wide range of feelings to an audience and help to enhance the mood.

Throughout your answer:

- provide examples from the text to justify your ideas
- give clear reasons for each of your ideas
- indicate how your ideas would enhance the production for the audience.

The following notes are for an answer based on the torture scene from *1984* (found on pages 71–73 of the prescribed edition). Points to consider include:

- Harsh bright, cold and functional white lighting could indicate to the audience the clinical and efficient way in which the Party tortures people who rebel against it.
- Before this scene, O'Brien and Winston say that they will meet again in 'the place where there is no darkness'. While Winston may have taken this comment to be positive, the use of the stark, bright light would reflect the brutal location that O'Brien meant – a place of cruel torture from which there is no escape.
- The brutal, harsh light would create an oppressive mood and an atmosphere filled with tension, especially as it would give the audience a clear view of the tools used for torture.

102. Question (c): sound

When answering Question (c) about sound, you will need to refer to a range of aspects relating to sound. These include the following:

- Consider how sound can help create both mood and atmosphere and then communicate these to an audience.

- Specific sound effects could make the time of day clear – for example an owl hooting to indicate night-time.
- Sound could be used to help make the location clear for example, the sound of the wind rustling through the trees to represent a wood.
- You could use music or sound effects to mark specific moments in the action. This may also build tension.

Throughout your answer:
- provide examples from the text to justify your ideas
- give clear reasons for each of your ideas
- indicate how your ideas would enhance the production for the audience.

The following notes are for an answer based on an extract from Act 3 of *DNA* – from the scene in the wood, from the point when Phil puts a plastic bag over Brian's head (page 59 of the prescribed edition), to Jan's last line in Section 4 (page 63 of the prescribed edition). This covers a total of three locations (a wood, a field and a street).

- *DNA* is a dark comedy, so although there are comic moments, the text feels serious throughout. This could be reflected in the music and sound effects used. For example, as the scene changes location, low-volume, slow, unharmonious piano music would reflect the tense atmosphere.
- In an urban environment, such as the street, background noises might include vehicles or the sounds of children playing a short distance away.
- For scenes set in the wood, the sound effects might be more nature-based, such as birdsong and the sound of leaves rustling in the wind.
- In the wood, after finding Adam, there is a choice of when in the day or night to set the scene. In a daytime scene, it would be possible to use birdsong; in a scene set late at night, the sound of owls hooting would be more appropriate.
- When the group discusses what they should do, they could be interrupted by the sound of an emergency vehicle siren. This would cause instant fear and build tension, indicating how terrified the characters are feeling.

SECTION B: LIVE THEATRE EVALUATION

103. About Section B

Answers will be based on the live performance text you have seen.

The following example answer uses the opening scene of the National Theatre's 2011 production of *Frankenstein* as a key moment.

Analysis of this key moment could focus on:
- the minimalist staging with the focus on the wood and fabric womb-like structure from which the performer emerges
- the use of physical theatre skills to show The Creature's birth
- the use of colour in the lighting with a red wash; the golden/amber spotlight on the womb-like structure
- The Creature's lack of costume and the make-up that creates a scar on the performer's face.

Evaluation of this key moment could focus on:
- the quality of the movement, including judgements on the performer's use of body language and strong physical skills to create animal-like movements

- how effectively the performer/designer/director staged the opening, with reference to the impact on the audience and the audience's response.

104. Section B questions

Answers will be based on the live performance text you have seen.

For the question, 'Analyse how stage space was used to engage the audience during the closing moments of the performance (6 marks)', the following is a suggested plan for an answer, based on the National Theatre's 2011 production of *Frankenstein*.

- Use of wide proxemics in the relationship between both characters: to show how different and separated The Creature and Frankenstein are at this moment in the play.
- Movement within the space: physical, focused, stylised movement and acting style of performer playing The Creature to show his animal-like characteristics, in contrast to the naturalistic acting style of the performer playing Frankenstein. Both took large steps and used the depth and breadth of the stage to give a sense of 'travelling' and 'movement' within the stage space.
- Staging: centre stage, upstage, with a sense of The Creature walking into the distance and Frankenstein chasing after him. Use of movement to upstage, effectively created perspective and indicated to the audience that the chase/journey would continue beyond the end of the play.
- Use of levels: Frankenstein fairly upright in terms of posture and walking with confidence, while The Creature was low to the floor, showing the difference in their status, even this late in the play.

For the question, 'Evaluate how lighting was used at different moments of the performance to create impact for the audience (9 marks)', the following is a suggested plan for an answer, based on the National Theatre's 2011 production of *Frankenstein*.

- Use of colour: red lighting in opening scene worked well, creating an effective atmosphere.
- Use of a focused profile spotlight to highlight The Creature was effective, as it allowed the audience to focus on the action as well as highlighting the beautiful and graceful develop of life.
- Incredible light bulb structure above the stage, created a sense of magic and wonder as well as suggesting the science behind Frankenstein's creation of life. This was present throughout but worked particularly well when the bulbs flashed alongside a sound effect of an electrical 'buzz' or 'pulse' – this was extremely effective when The Creature was born or experienced strong emotions.
- The use of a golden spotlight and gobo created a rising sun in the 'Creature discovers nature' scene. This worked superbly as it was easy to believe that this was the actual sun. On stage, the beauty of this moment means that The Creature was was spellbound; the audience was equally engaged.

105. Question 9 (a): performance

Answers will be based on the live performance text you have seen.

When answering Question 9 (a) – performance with a focus on physical skills – key points to consider are as follows.
- If it is not specified in the question, choose an appropriate key moment to focus on in your answer. Make it clear which moment of the performance you are analysing.

- Keep your analysis focused on physical skills. Make sure you comment on a range of the skills and techniques used at that point in the performance, such as the performer's use of body language, facial expressions, gait or posture.
- Comment on how the physical skills were used to engage the audience.
- Use technical vocabulary to demonstrate your knowledge. This might include talking about how relationships, characterisation and objectives were shown physically. Your answer might also draw on moments where physical ensemble performance skills created impact.

The following example answer uses the opening scene of the National Theatre's 2011 production of *Frankenstein* as the key moment:

In the opening scene of the National Theatre's 2011 production of *Frankenstein*, Jonny Lee Miller, as The Creature, used a striking range of physical skills to engage the audience. The performer's physicality was particularly impressive as The Creature's twisted body broke through the 'womb-like' structure at the centre of the stage. Miller's use of facial expression and exaggerated gestures created an uncomfortable atmosphere in the audience as they witnessed this birth. Miller moved awkwardly, crawling along the stage and tapping his arms and hands on the wooden floor. The movement was uncontrolled and suggested pain. The fact that The Creature was alone on stage held the audience's attention and also meant that Miller could use the stage space fully. This was an engaging use of physical skills, particularly as The Creature did not use language, only grunts.

106. Question 9 (a): design

Answers will be based on the live performance text you have seen.

When answering Question 9 (a) – design with a focus on sound – key points to consider are as follows.

- If it is not specified in the question, choose an appropriate key moment to focus on in your answer. Make it clear which moment of the performance you are analysing.
- Keep your analysis focused on sound. Make sure you comment on a range of the sound effects and techniques used at that point in the performance. This might include commenting on the levels of the sound, recorded sound effects, the use of delay or echo to create an effect, or the use of radio or static microphones.
- Comment on how the sound helped to engage the audience.
- Use technical vocabulary to demonstrate your knowledge. This may include commenting on the acoustics of the space, how sound created mood or atmosphere, and whether sound was used to underscore the action on stage.

The following example answer uses a key moment from the National Theatre's 2011 production of *Frankenstein*:

A key moment in the National Theatre's 2011 production of *Frankenstein,* was when The Creature discovered nature. Here, a wide range of recorded and live sounds, human and electronic, was used to engage the audience. Birdsong was quickly joined by uplifting recorded electronic music and choral song. The music was quite repetitive and built up to a crescendo that reflected The Creature's joy. The music gave way to the pitter-patter sound of rain as it bounced off The Creature's skin and the wooden stage. We then heard the sweet strumming of guitars and wonderful choral voices, mixed to create a surround of sound around the theatre. Constant birdsong, signified dawn as the sun rose and shades of light came through from upstage. All the time, The Creature made

sounds of joy as he lay in the grass, feeling nature against his naked skin. Towards the end of the scene, the recorded music died down, leaving only the sounds of The Creature. These were now more animal-like, perhaps symbolising his animalside as he discovered nature.

107. Question 9 (b): performance

Answers will be based on the live performance text you have seen.

When answering Question 9 (b) – performance with a focus on style – key points to consider are as follows.

- You need to make personal judgements about the performance that focus on style.
- Choose the moments from the performance you feel are most relevant to answering the question.
- Analyse how and where style has been used to create impact for the audience, and then evaluate how well this was done. Make your evaluation detailed. You could reflect on the response of the audience during these moments.
- Use technical vocabulary to demonstrate your knowledge.
- Try to show a real engagement with the live performance and offer a personal view on it. You can reflect negatively or positively, as long as your points are well justified and supported with specific examples.

The following sample answer uses the National Theatre's 2011 production of *Frankenstein* as the live performance:

The National Theatre's 2011 production of *Frankenstein* combined a naturalistic style with elements of physical theatre.

On Frankenstein and Elizabeth's wedding night, Frankenstein, played by Benedict Cumberbatch, portrayed a strong sense of panic as he paced up and down and shouted aggressively at Elizabeth, played by Naomie Harris. Cumberbatch's facial expressions were very effective, creating emotional impact for the audience, as you could see that Frankenstein was very concerned for their safety. This naturalistic style was supported by Cumberbatch's gait and posture, which suggested a character with a high class and status. Towards the end of the scene, when The Creature, played by Jonny Lee Miller, attacked Elizabeth, Naomie Harris's reaction was naturalistic and convincing: her cries and facial expression showed her terror. The audience was in complete silence as they watched the tragedy unfold. The scene with Elizabeth and The Creature was superbly acted and the audience was fully engaged.

This scene also included moments of physical theatre, particularly in Miller's effective use of body language and physicality as The Creature. He moved across the stage in a way that seemed both human and animal in places, particularly when he said, 'He broke his word, so I break mine' (Scene 29) with an expressive and exaggerated use of gesture. This balance of styles worked well in this moment, as it symbolised Frankenstein's two worlds: the safe, romantic world that he shares with Elizabeth, represented by the naturalistic style, and the monstrous world he has created with The Creature, represented by physical theatre. This is a good example of how the performers used their skills to communicate two very different theatrical styles in one scene.

108. Question 9 (b): design

Answers will be based on the live performance text you have seen.

When answering Question 9 (b) – design with a focus on sound – key points to consider are as follows.

- You need to make personal judgements about the performance that focus on sound. It is important that you draw on a variety of sources of sound. This might include the use of live and/or recorded music. You might focus on the use of sound effects (live and/or recorded) as well as how sound is created by the performers, including how the performers use their voices.

- Choose the moments from the performance you feel are most relevant to answering the question.

- Think about the contribution of the sound designer in how sound was created and used within the performance.

- Analyse how and where sound has been used to create impact for the audience, and then evaluate how well this was done. Make your evaluation detailed. You might reflect on the response of the audience during these moments.

- Use technical vocabulary to demonstrate your knowledge. You could talk about the levels of the sound, or whether there were any special effects used, such as reverb or echo.

- Try to show a real engagement with the live performance and offer a personal view on it. You can reflect negatively or positively, as long as your points are well justified and supported with specific examples.

The following example answer uses the National Theatre's 2011 production of *Frankenstein* as the live performance:

A scene that was particularly successful in the National Theatre's 2011 production of *Frankenstein* was the moment in which The Creature experienced early 19th-century society for the first time. This moment was especially memorable as it used sound, imagery, movement and voice together, creating a spectacular scene which put the audience in The Creature's shoes. Sounds of a train, of steam and machines, as well of hot sparks flying, created a powerful sense of an industrial setting. This reflected the Industrial Revolution experienced in Britain at the time and was accompanied by haunting voices, produced using echo. This was effective as it made the approaching humans even scarier to The Creature, who was experiencing these sights and sounds for the first time. A rhythmic drum in the background was used to suggest the sound of the train, and the noisy ensemble seemed to move as one as they crossed the stage to The Creature, who lay on the floor hiding from the crowd. The performers also spoke passages from the Bible and sang religious songs, to reflect the Christianity of the time. This worked on many levels – symbolising the first time that The Creature had heard religious words but also representing the idea that Frankenstein was 'playing God' by creating life. The use of sound in this scene effectively engaged the audience in the industrial society of the period, reflecting The Creature's own intense experiences.

109. Preparing for Section B

You could start with the following terms when developing a technical vocabulary bank.

Performance:	physicality, eye contact, diction, gesture, gait, facial expression, accent, ensemble
Design:	mood, symbolic, levels, echo (sound), wash (lighting), *mise-en-scène*, LEDs (lighting), texture

110. Preparing useful evaluation notes

Evaluation notes would normally be split equally between performance and design, with 250 words for each.

The following 100 words provide an example of notes for one key moment from the National Theatre's 2011 production of *Frankenstein* as the live performance. This would therefore allow for five key moments to be covered within the word count, each covering a number of elements of the performance. (Your own notes must be based on the live performance text you have seen.)

Key moment 1: William asks Frankenstein about creating life

- Design: flash of light, blue wash, sudden change, dramatic music, light bulb flashing to symbolise stars, sense of god and religious ideas of creating life. Naturalistic but also moments (with lights and dramatic music) where style more visual and expressive. Costume and hairstyles set historical context of play.

- Performance: curiosity of William (Jared Richard), facial expression, body language and movement in direction of Frankenstein, Frankenstein's anxiety and losing temper with William, doesn't want him to know, tension in scene, strong relationship between both, believable and committed performance from Cumberbatch as Frankenstein.

Notes

Notes

Published by Pearson Education Limited, 80 Strand, London, WC2R 0RL.

www.pearsonschoolsandfecolleges.co.uk

Copies of official specifications for all Pearson qualifications may be found on the website: qualifications.pearson.com

Text and illustrations © Pearson Education Ltd 2021
Typeset and illustrated by Tech-Set
Produced by Out of House Publishing
Cover design by Kamae Design Ltd
Cover illustration by Justin Hoffmann

The rights of William Reed and John Johnson to be identified as authors of this work have been asserted by them in accordance with the Copyright, Designs and Patents Act 1988.

First published 2021

24 23 22 21
10 9 8 7 6 5 4 3 2 1

British Library Cataloguing in Publication Data
A catalogue record for this book is available from the British Library

ISBN 978 1 292 32578 1

Printed in Slovakia by Neografia

Acknowledgements

Text credits
P11 (2), 14, 23, 64, 89 (2), 92, 113 (3), 128: Extract from Blue Stockings by Jessica Swale; 978-1-84842-329-9; Nick Hern Books, London, 2013; **P14, 112, 113, 126:** Extract from 100 by Diene Petterle, Neil Monaghan and Christopher Heimann; 978-1-85459-737-3; Nick Hern Books, London, 2003; **P21, 27, 88, 90, 93, 112, 113, 128:** Extract from 'Government Inspector' by Nikolai Gogol, version by David Harrower; 978-0-571-28049-0; Faber and Faber Ltd, London. 2011; **P87, P101:** Extract from The Crucible by Arthur Miller; 978-1-4081-0839-0; Bloomsbury Methuen Drama,; Bloomsbury Publisher Plc, 2010; First published 1952; **P87, 128:** Extract from 1984 by George Orwell, adaptation by Robert Icke and Duncan Macmillan; 978-1-78319-061-4; Oberon Books, London, 2013; **P130:** Extract from Frankenstein by Mary Shelley, adaptation by Nick Dear; 978-0-57127-721-6; Faber & Faber; Main edition 2011.

Photographs
The author and publisher would like to thank the following individuals and organisations for permission to reproduce photographs:

(Key: b-bottom; c-centre; l-left; r-right; t-top)

Alamy Images: A Astes 61b; **ArenaPAL:** Nobby Clark/ArenaPAL 1cl; **Getty Images:** Paul Zimmerman 33r, China Photos 35l, Dougal Waters 40tr, Marc Romanelli 40bl; **Photostage Limited:** Donald Cooper/photostage.co.uk 1br, 3, 4, 16, 18, 20, 24, 27, 30, 32, 33l, 36t, 42, 45b, 45t, 46, 49l, 50l, 51b, 52bl, 53br, 54, 56bl, 56br, 56tl, 56tr, 57t, 58l, 59, 60b, 61l, 61r, 62bl, 62br, 62t, 64, 65l, 65t, 66, 103, 104; **Shutterstock:** GlebStock 1t, YanLev 12, Leah-Anne Thompson 14, Emir Simsek 50r, Jarno Gonzalez Zarraonandia 52tr, Zhiltsov Alexandr 53tl; Simon **Annand:** 35r, 37t; **Tom Hurley:** 58r; **TopFoto:** Nigel Norrington/ArenaPAL 9, 47; Johann Persson/ArenaPAL 28, 52l; Francis Loney/ArenaPAL 36b. 38, 52br; Sheila Burnett/ArenaPAL 37b; Joan Marcus/ArenaPAL 48; Clive Barda/ArenaPAL 49r, 57b, 60t, Ivan Kydcl/ArenaPAL 51t; Simon Annand/ArenaPAL 53b

All other images © Pearson Education

Notes from the publisher
1. While the publishers have made every attempt to ensure that advice on the qualification and its assessment is accurate, the official specification and associated assessment guidance materials are the only authoritative source of information and should always be referred to for definitive guidance.

Pearson examiners have not contributed to any sections in this resource relevant to examination papers for which they have responsibility.

2. Pearson has robust editorial processes, including answer and fact checks, to ensure the accuracy of the content in this publication, and every effort is made to ensure this publication is free of errors. We are, however, only human, and occasionally errors do occur. Pearson is not liable for any misunderstandings that arise as a result of errors in this publication, but it is our priority to ensure that the content is accurate. If you spot an error please do contact us at resourcescorrections@pearson.com so we can make sure it is corrected.